Reprints of Economic Classics

A REPLY TO THE

ESSAY ON POPULATION

A

REPLY

TO THE

'ESSAY ON POPULATION'

BY THE REV. T. R. MALTHUS

In A Series Of Letters

TO WHICH ARE ADDED

EXTRACTS FROM THE 'ESSAY'

With Notes

[William Hazlitt]

[*1807*]

REPRINTS OF ECONOMIC CLASSICS

AUGUSTUS M. KELLEY · PUBLISHERS
NEW YORK · 1967

FIRST EDITION 1807

(London: Longman, Hurst, Rees & Orme,
Paternoster Row, 1807)

Reprinted 1967 by

Augustus M. Kelley · Publishers

Library of Congress Catalogue Card Number
66-21678

PRINTED IN THE UNITED STATES OF AMERICA
by SENTRY PRESS, NEW YORK, N. Y. 10019

A

REPLY

TO THE

ESSAY ON POPULATION,

BY THE REV. T. R. MALTHUS.

IN A SERIES OF LETTERS.

TO WHICH ARE ADDED,

EXTRACTS FROM THE ESSAY;

WITH NOTES.

LONDON:

PRINTED FOR LONGMAN, HURST, REES, AND ORME,
PATERNOSTER-ROW.

———

1807.

ADVERTISEMENT.

THE *three first of the following letters appeared originally in Cobbett's Weekly Political Register. There are several things, in which they may seem to require some apology. First, some persons, who were convinced by the arguments, have objected to the style as too flowery, and full of attempts at description. If I have erred in this respect, it has been from design. I have indeed endeavoured to make my book as amusing as the costiveness of my genius would permit. If however these critics persist in their objection, I will undertake to produce a work as dry and formal as they please, if they will undertake to find readers. Secondly, some of the observations may be thought too severe and personal. In the first place, I shall answer that the abuse, of which there is to be sure a plentiful sprinkling, is not I think unmerited or unsupported; and in the second place, that if I could have attacked* the work successfully, without attacking the author, I should have preferred doing so. But the thing was impossible. Whoever troubles himself about abstract reasonings, or calm, dispassionate inquiries after truth? The public ought not to blame me for consulting their taste. As to the diffuseness, the repetitions, and want of method to be found in these letters, I have no good defence to make. I may however make the same excuse for the great length to which they have run, as the Frenchman did, who apologised for writing a long letter by saying, that he had not time to write a shorter.

LETTERS

IN

ANSWER TO MALTHUS, &c.

LETTER I.

INTRODUCTORY.

Sir,

As the proposed alteration in the system of the Poor Laws must naturally engage your attention, as well as that of the public ; and, as the authority of Mr. Malthus has often been referred to, and has great weight with many people on this subject, it may not be amiss to inquire, how far the reputation which that gentleman has gained, as a moral and political philosopher, can be safely reposed on as the foundation of any part of a system which is directed to objects of national utility, and requires close, comprehensive, and accurate reasoning. You, Sir, are not ignorant, that a name will do more towards softening down prejudices, and bolster-

ing up a crude and tottering system, than any
arguments whatever. It is always easier to
quote an authority than to carry on a chain of
reasoning. Mr. Malthus's reputation may, I
fear, prove fatal to the poor of this country. His
name hangs suspended over their heads, *in ter-
rorem*, like some baleful meteor. It is the
shield behind which the archers may take their
stand, and gall them at their leisure. He has
set them up as a defenceless mark, on which
both friends and foes may exercise their malice,
or their wantonness, as they think proper. He
has fairly hunted them down, he has driven
them into his toils, he has thrown his net over
them, and they remain as a prey to the first in-
vader, either to be sacrificed without mercy at
the shrine of cold unfeeling avarice, or to linger
out a miserable existence under the hands of
ingenious and scientific tormentors.—There is a
vulgar saying, " Give a dog a bad name, and
hang him." The poor seem to me to be pretty
much in this situation at present. The poor, Sir,
labour under a natural stigma ; they are *naturally* despised. Their interests are at best but
coldly and remotely felt by the other classes of
society. Mr. Malthus's book has done all that
was wanting to increase this indifference and
apathy. But it is neither generous nor just, to
come in aid of the narrow prejudices and hard-

heartedness of mankind, with metaphysical distinctions and the cobwebs of philosophy. The
balance inclines too much on that side already,
without the addition of false weights. I confess
I do feel some degree of disgust and indignation
rising within me, when I see a man of Mr. Malthus's character and calling standing forward as
the accuser of those " who have none to help
them," as the high-priest of " pride and covetousness," forming selfishness into a regular code,
with its codicils, institutes and glosses annexed,
trying to muffle up the hand of charity in the
fetters of the law, to suppress " the compunc-
tious visitings of nature," to make men ashamed
of compassion and good-nature as folly and
weakness, " laying the flattering unction" of religion to the conscience of the riotous and luxurious liver, and " grinding the faces of the
poor" with texts of scripture. Formerly the
feelings of compassion, and the dictates of justice were found to operate as correctives on the
habitual meanness and selfishness of our nature:
at present this order is reversed ; and it is
discovered that justice and humanity are not
obstacles in the way of, but that they are the
most effectual strengtheners and supporters of
our prevailing passions. Mr. Malthus has " admirably reconciled the old quarrel between
speculation and practice," by shewing (I sup-

pose in humble imitation of Mandeville) that
our duty and our vices both lean the same
way, and that the ends of public virtue and benevolence are best answered by the meanness,
pride, extravagance, and insensibility of individuals. This is certainly a very convenient
doctrine; and it is not to be wondered at, that
it should have become so fashionable as it has.*

While the prejudice infused into the public
mind by this gentleman's writings subsists in its
full force, I am almost convinced that any serious attempt at bettering the condition of the
poor will be ineffectual. The only object at
present is to gain time. The less it is meddled
with either with good or bad intentions, the better. Tampering with the disease " will but skin
and film the ulcerous part, while foul corruption,
mining all within, infects unseen." I have not
confidence enough either in the integrity, the
abilities, or the power of our state-doctors to be
willing to trust it entirely in their hands. They
risk nothing, if they fail. The patient is in too

* The late Sir W. Pulteney, whose character for liberality is
well known, was firmly persuaded that the author of the Essay
on Population was the greatest man that ever lived, and really
wished to have bestowed some personal remuneration on Mr. M.
as his political confessor, for having absolved him from all
doubts and scruples in the exercise of his favourite virtue.

desperate a state to bring any imputation on
their skill ; and after all, it is only trying experiments *in corpore vili.* The only thing they
need be afraid of is in reality doing *too much*
good. This is the only error which would
never be forgiven by those whose resentment
they have most reason to dread. This however
there will be no danger of. The state of public
feeling, the dispositions of individuals, the narrow jealousy of parties, and the interests of the
most powerful members of the community will, I
suspect, suffer little effectually to be done for
bettering the condition, exalting the character,
enlightening the understandings, or securing the
comforts, the independence, the virtue and happiness of the lower classes of the people. But,
I am not equally sure that the means employed
for this very purpose may not be made a handle
for stifling every principle of liberty and honour
in the hearts of a free people. It will be no
difficult matter, as things are circumstanced,
under pretence of propriety and economy, to
smuggle in the worst of tyrannies, a principle of
unrelenting, incessant, vexatious, over-ruling
influence, extending to each individual, and to
all the petty concerns of life.

This is what strikes me on the first view of
the subject. I would ask, Is Mr. Whitbread

sure of the instruments he is to employ in the execution of his scheme ? Is he sure that his managing partners in this new political firm of opulent patronage will not play the game into the hands of those whose views of government and civilization are very different from his own? But it seems, that whether practicable, or no, Mr. Whitbread must bring in a Poor Bill. The effect of it appears to me to be putting the poor into the wardship of the rich, to be doing away the little remains of independence we have left, and making them once more what they were formerly, the vassals of a wealthy aristocracy. For my own part, who do not pretend to see far into things, and do not expect miracles from human nature, I should wish to trust as little as possible to the liberality and enlightened views of country squires, or to the *tender mercies* of justices of the peace.

The example of Scotland is held out to us as a proof of the beneficial effects of popular education, and we are promised all the same advantages from the adoption of the same plan. The education of the poor is the grand specific which is to cure all our disorders, and make the leper whole again ; and, like other specifics, it is to operate equally on all constitutions and in all cases. But I may ask, Is the education of the

poor the only circumstance in which Scotland
differs from England ?   Are there no other circumstances in the situation of this country that
may render such a scheme impracticable, or
counteract its good effects, or render it even
worse than nugatory ?   Is knowledge in itself a
principle of such universal and indisputable
excellence that it can never be misapplied, that
it can never be made the instrument and incen-
tive to mischief, or that it can never be mixed
and contaminated with "baser matter?" Do
not the peculiar principles and discipline of the
church of Scotland, does not the traditional and
habitual faith in the doctrines of religion, do
not the general manners not of the poor only,
but of the other classes of society, does not the
state of cultivation, do not the employments of
the people, the absence of luxury, and temptation, the small number of great towns, and the
remains of ancient customs, tend to strengthen,
to forward, to give consistency to, and secure
the good effects of education ?   Or will Mr.
Whitbread say that he can supply the place of
these with a beadle, a white wand, a spelling
book, and a primmer ?   Supposing it practicable, will the adoption of a general plan of education have the same effect in our great manufacturing towns, in our sea-ports, in the metro-
polis, that it has in the heart of Scotland, or in

the mountains of Cumberland? Will it not have the contrary effect?

It is not reading in the abstract, but the kind of reading they are likely to meet with, and the examples about them leading them to emulate the patterns of sobriety and industry, or of vice and profligacy held out to them in books, that will do either good or harm to the morals of a people. In the country the people read moral or religious, or, at least, innocent books, and therefore, they are benefited by them; in towns, they as often meet with licentious and idle publications, which must do them harm. It is in vain to say that you will give them *good* books, they will get *bad ones.* Will those hot-beds of vice, the factories of Manchester, &c. be less fruitful for having the *farina* of knowledge sprinkled over them? Will not corruption quicken faster, and spread wider for having this new channel opened to it? Will a smattering in books, and the current pamphlets of the day tend to quench and smother the flame of the passions, or will it add fuel to them? I do not scruple to assert, that religion itself, when it comes in contact with certain situations, may be highly dangerous. It is the soil in which the greatest virtues and the greatest vices take root, Where it has not strength to stop the

torrent of dissolute manners, it gives it additional force by checking it ; as the bow that has
been bent the contrary way, recoils back
with tenfold violence. It is for this reason
that the morals of the people in the trading
towns in the north of England are, I believe,
worse than they are farther south, because they
are brought up more religiously. The common
people there are almost all of them originally
dissenters. Again, it may be asked, will the poor
people in the trading towns send their children
to school instead of sending them to work at a
factory ? Or will their employers, forgetting
their own interests, compel them to do it ? Or
will they give up their profits and their wealth
for the sake of informing the minds, and pre-
serving the morals of the poor ? Oh ! no. It
may be replied, that it is chiefly for the peasantry and country people, who compose the lar-
gest part of the community, that this plan of
education is intended. But they are the very
people who do not stand in need of it, and to
whom, if it does no harm, it will do little good.
If working hard, and living sparingly are the
chief lessons meant to be inculcated in their
minds, they are already tolerably perfect in their
parts. As for the rest, it is in vain to attempt
to make men any thing else but what their

situation makes them. We are the creatures
not of knowledge, but of circumstances.

For all these reasons I cannot help looking at
this general parallel between the benefits derived
from education in Scotland, and those expected
from it in this country as little better than a
leurre de dupe. The advantages of education in
the abstract are, I fear, like other abstractions,
not to be found in nature. I thought that the
rage for blind reform, for abstract utility, and
general reasoning, had been exploded long since.
If ever it was proper, it was proper on general
subjects, on the nature of man and his prospects
in general. But the spirit of abstraction driven
out of the minds of philosophers has passed into the heads of members of parliament : banished from the closets of the studious, it has
taken up its favourite abode in the House of
Commons. It has only shifted its ground and
its objects according to the character of those in
whom it is found. It has dwindled down into
petty projects, speculative details, and dreams
of practical, positive matter-of-fact improvement. These new candidates for fame come in
awkwardly holding up the train of philosophy ;
and, like the squires of political romance, in-
vite you to sit down with them to the spoon-

fuls of whipt syllabub, the broken scraps of
logic, and the same banquet of windy promises
which had been so much more handsomely
served up, and to satiety, by their masters.

I know nothing of Mr. Whitbread personally.
His character stands fair with the public, for
consistency and good intention. But I cannot
recognise in his plodding, mechanical, but ill-
directed and unsuccessful endeavours to bring
to justice a great public delinquent, in his flowery common-place harangues, or in the cold,
philosophic indifference of the sentiments he
has expressed upon the present occasion, either
the genius, penetration, or generous enthusiasm,
(regulated, not damped by the dictates of reason)
which shall be equally proof against the artifices
of designing men, against the sanguine delusions
of personal vanity, or the difficulties, the delays,
the disgust, and probable odium to be encoun-
tered in the determined prosecution of such a
task. The celebrated Howard fell a martyr to
the great cause of humanity in which he em-
barked. He plunged into the depth of dungeons,
into the loathsome cells of disease, ignominy,
and despair; he sacrificed health and life itself
as a pledge of the sincerity of his motives. But
what proof has Mr. Whitbread ever given of his
true and undissembled attachment to the same

cause? What sacrifices has he made, what fatigues has he suffered, what pain has he felt, what privation has he undergone in the pursuit of his object, that he should be depended on as the friend and guardian of the poor, as the dispenser of good or ill to millions of his fellow-beings? The "champion" should be the " child" of poverty. The author of our religion, when he came to save the world, took our nature upon him, and became as one of us : it is not likely that any one should ever prove the *saviour* of the poor, who has not common feelings with them, and who does not know their weaknesses and wants. To the officious inquiries of all others, What then are we to do for them? The best answer would perhaps be, Let them alone.—

I return to the subject from which I set out, and from which I have wandered without intending it ; I mean the system of Mr. Malthus, under the auspices of whose discoveries it seems the present plan is undertaken, though it differs in many of its features from the expedients recommended by that author. I am afraid that the parent discovery may, however, in spite of any efforts to prevent it, overlay the ricketty offspring. Besides, the original design and principle gives a bias to all our subsequent proceedings, and warps our views without our perceiving it. Mr. Malthus's system must, I am sure, ever remain a stumbling block in the way of true political economy, as innate ideas for a long time confused and perplexed all attempts at philosophy. It is an *ignis fatuus*, which can only beguile the thoughtless gazer, and lead him into bogs and quicksands, before he knows where he is. The details of his system are, I believe, as confused, contradictory, and uncertain, as the system itself. I shall, however, confine my remarks to the outlines of his plan, and his general principles of reasoning. In these respects, I have no hesitation in saying that his work is the most complete specimen of *illogical*, crude and contradictory reasoning, that perhaps was ever offered to the notice of the public. A clear and comprehensive mind is, I conceive, shewn, not in the extensiveness of the plan which an author has chalked out for himself, but in the order and connection observed in the arrangement of the subject, and the consistency of the several parts. This praise is so far from being applicable to the reasoning of our author, that nothing was ever more loose and incoherent. " The latter end of his commonwealth always forgets the beginning." Argument threatens argument, conclusion stands opposed to conclusion. This page is an answer to

the following one, and that to the next. There
is hardly a single statement in the whole work,
in which he seems to have had a distinct idea of
his own meaning. The principle itself is neither new, nor does it prove any thing new ; least
of all does it prove what he meant it to prove.
His whole theory is a continued contradiction ;
it is a nullity in the science of political philosophy.

I must, however, defer the proof of these assertions to another letter, when, if you should
deem what I have already said worthy the notice of your readers, I hope to make them out
to their and your satisfaction.

LETTER II.

ON THE ORIGINALITY OF Mr. MALTHUS'S PRINCIPAL ARGUMENT.

Sir,

THE English have been called a nation of philosophers ; as I conceive, on very slender foundations. They are indeed somewhat slow and dull, and would be wise, if they could. They are fond of deep questions without understanding them ; and have that perplexed and plodding kind of intellect, which takes delight in difficulties, and contradictions, without ever coming to a conclusion. They feel most interest in things which promise to be the least interesting. What is confused and unintelligible they take to be profound : whatever is remote and uncertain, they conceive must be of vast weight and importance. They are always in want of some new and mighty project in science, in politics, or in morality for the morbid sensibility of their minds to brood over and exercise itself upon : and by the time they are tired of puzzling themselves to no purpose about one absurdity, another is generally ready to start up.

and take its place. Thus there is a perpetual restless succession of philosophers and systems of philosophy : and the proof they give you of their wisdom to-day, is by convincing you what fools they were six months before. Their pretensions to solidity of understanding rest on the foundation of their own shallowness and levity ; and their gravest demonstrations rise out of the ruins of others.

Mr. Malthus has for some time past been lord of the ascendant. But I will venture to predict that his reign will not be of long duration. His hour is almost come ; and this mighty luminary, " who so lately scorched us in the meridian, will sink temperately to the west, and be hardly felt as he descends." It is not difficult to account for the very favourable reception his work has met with in certain classes of society : it must be a source of continual satisfaction to their minds by relieving them from the troublesome feelings so frequently occasioned by the remains of certain silly prejudices, and by enabling them to set so completely at defiance the claims of " worthless importunity in rags." But it is not easy to account for the attention which our author's reasonings have excited among thinking men, except from a habit of extreme abstraction and over-refined speculation, unsupported by actual observation or a general knowledge of practical subjects, in consequence of which the mind is dazzled and confounded by any striking fact which thwarts its previous conclusions. There is also in some minds a low and narrow jealousy, which makes them glad of any opportunity to escape from the contemplation of magnificent scenes of visionary excellence, to hug themselves in their own indifference and apathy, and to return once more to their natural level. Mr. Malthus's essay was in this respect a nice *let-down* from the too sanguine expectations and overstrained enthusiasm which preceded it. Else, how a work of so base tendency, and so poorly glossed over, which strikes at the root of every humane principle, and all the while cants about sensibility and morality, in which the little, low, rankling malice of a parish-beadle, or the overseer of a workhouse is disguised in the garb of philosophy, and recommended as a dress for every English gentleman to wear, in which false logic is buried under a heap of garbled calculations, such as a bad player might make at cribbage to puzzle those with, who knew less of the game than himself, where every argument is a *felo de se*, and defeats its own purpose, containing both " its bane and antidote" within itself, how otherwise such a miserable reptile performance should ever have crawled to that height of reputation which it has reached, I am utterly unable to comprehend. But it seems Mr. Malthus's essay was a *discovery*. There are those whom I have heard place him by the side of Sir Isaac Newton, as both equally great, the one in natural, the other in political philosophy. But waving this comparison, I must confess, that were I really persuaded that Mr. Malthus had made any discovery at all, there is so little originality, and so much ill-nature and illiberality in the world, that I should be tempted to overlook the large share of the latter which Mr. Malthus possesses in common with the rest of mankind (and which in him may probably be owing to ill-digestion, to a sickly constitution, or some former distaste conceived against poverty) and to consider him merely in the light of a man of genius. *Multum abludit imago.* Indeed I do not much see what there is to discover on the subject, after reading the genealogical table of Noah's descendants, and knowing that the world is round. But even allowing that there was something in the nature of the subject which threw over it a veil of almost impenetrable obscurity, Mr. Malthus was not the first who found out the secret. Whatever some of his ignorant admirers may pretend, Mr. Malthus will not say that this was the case. He has himself given us a list of authors, some of whom he had read before, and some since the first publication of his Essay,* who fully understood and clearly stated this principle. Among these Wallace is the chief. He has not only stated the general principle with the utmost force and precision, by pointing out the necessary disproportion between the tendency in population and the tendency in the means of subsistence to increase after a certain period, (and till this period, namely till the world became *full*, I must contend in opposition to Mr. Malthus that the disproportion would not be *necessary*, but artificial); but what is most remarkable, he has brought this very argument forward as an answer to the same schemes of imaginary improvement, which the author of the Essay on population first employed it to overturn.† For it is to be remembered that the use which our author has since made of this principle to shut up the workhouse, to *snub* the poor, to stint them in their wages, to deny them any relief from the parish, and preach lectures to them

* Among the former are Hume, Wallace, Smith, and Price; among the latter are the Economists, Montesquieu, Franklin, Sir James Steuart, Arthur Young, Mr. Townshend, Plato, and Aristotle.

† I beg leave to refer the reader to some letters which appeared on this subject, in the Monthly Magazine, written by a well informed and ingenious man, who had too much good sense and firmness to be carried away by the tide of vulgar prejudice.

on the new-invented crime of matrimony, was an after-thought. His first, his grand, his most memorable effort was directed against the modern philosophy. It was the service his borrowed weapons did in that cause, that sanctified them at all other purposes. I shall have occasion by and by to examine how far the argument was a solid one; at present I am only inquiring into the originality of the idea. And here I might content myself with referring your readers to Wallace's work; or it might be sufficient to inform them that after indulging in the former part of it in all the schemes of fancied excellence and Utopian government, which Sir Thomas More and so many other philosophers and speculators have endeavoured to establish, he then enters into an elaborate refutation of them, by describing the evils, " the universal confusion " and perplexity in which all such perfect forms " of society must soon terminate, the sooner on " account of their perfection," from the principle of population, and as he expresses it, " from these primary determinations in nature, " a limited earth, a limited degree of fertility, " and the continual increase of mankind." However, as it is probable that most of your readers may not have the book within their reach, and as people do not like to take these things upon trust, or from a mere general representation of them, I must beg your insertion of the following extract from the work itself; and though it is pretty long, yet as you, Sir, seem to be of opinion with me that the subject of Mr. Malthus's reputation is a matter of no mean interest to the public, I am in hopes that you will not think your pages misemployed in dissipating the illusion. As to Mr. Malthus himself, if he is a vain man, he ought to be satisfied with this acknowledgement of his importance.

" But without entering furthei into these ab-
" stracted and uncertain speculations, it de-
" serves our particular attention, that as no go-
" vernment which hath hitherto been esta-
" blished, is free from all seeds of corruption, or
" can be expected to be eternal ; so if we sup-
" pose a government to be perfect in its original
" frame, and to be administered in the most
" perfect manner, after whatever model we sup-
" pose it to have been framed, such a perfect
" form would be so far from lasting for ever,
" that it must come to an end so much the
" sooner on account of its perfection. For,
" though happily such governments should be
" firmly established, though they should be
" found consistent with the reigning passions of
" human nature, though they should spread far
" and wide ; nay, though they should prevail

" universally, they must at last involve man-
" kind in the deepest perplexity, and in univer-
" sal confusion. For how excellent soever they
" may be in their own nature, they are altoge-
" ther inconsistent with the present frame of
" nature, and with a limited extent of earth.

" Under a perfect government, the inconve-
" niences of having a family would be so in-
" tirely removed, children would be so well
" taken care of, and every thing become so fa-
" vourable to populousness, that though some
" sickly seasons or dreadful plagues in particu-
" lar climates might cut off multitudes, yet in
" general, mankind would encrease so prodigi-
" ously, that the earth would at last be over-
" stocked, and become unable to support its
" numerous inhabitants.

" How long the earth, with the best culture
" of which it is capable from human genius and
" industry, might be able to nourish its perpe-
" tually encreasing inhabitants, is as impossible
" as it is unnecessary to be determined. It is
" not probable that it could have supported
" them during so long a period as since the
" creation of Adam. But whatever may be
" supposed of the length of this period, of ne-
" cessity it must be granted, that the earth

" could not nourish them for ever, unless ei-
" ther its fertility could be continually augment-
" ed, or by some secret in nature, like what
" certain enthusiasts have expected from the
" philosopher's stone, some wise adept in the
" occult sciences, should invent a method of
" supporting mankind quite different from any
" thing known at present. Nay, though some
" extraordinary method of supporting them
" might possibly be found out, yet if there was
" no bound to the increase of mankind, which
" would be the case under a perfect government,
" there would not even be sufficient room for
" containing their bodies upon the surface of
" the earth, or upon any limited surface what-
" soever. It would be necessary, therefore, in
" order to find room for such multitudes of men,
" that the earth should be continually enlarging
" in bulk, as an animal or vegetable body.

" Now since philosophers may as soon at-
" tempt to make mankind immortal, as to sup-
" port the animal frame without food ; it is
" equally certain, that limits are set to the fer-
" tility of the earth, and that its bulk, so far as
" is hitherto known, hath continued always the
" same, and probably could not be much altered
" without making considerable changes in the
" solar system. It would be impossible, there-

" fore, to support the great numbers of men who
" would be raised up under a perfect govern-
" ment ; the earth would be overstocked at last,
" and the greatest admirers of such fanciful
" schemes must foresee the fatal period when
" they would come to an end, as they are alto-
" gether inconsistent with the limits of that
" earth in which they must exist.

" What a miserable catastrophe of the most
" generous of all human systems of government !
" How dreadfully would the magistrates of such
" commonwealths find themselves disconcerted
" at that fatal period, when there was no longer
" any room for new colonies, and when the earth
" could produce no further supplies ! During
" all the preceding ages, while there was room
" for increase, mankind must have been happy ;
" the earth must have been a paradise in the li-
" teral sense, as the greatest part of it must have
" been turned into delightful and fruitful gar-
" dens. But when the dreadful time should at
" last come, when our globe, by the most dili-
" gent culture, could not produce what was
" sufficient to nourish its numerous inhabitants,
" what happy expedient could then be found
" out to remedy so great an evil ?

" In such a cruel necessity, must there be a

" law to restrain marriage ? Must multitudes
" of women be shut up in cloisters like the an-
" cient vestals or modern nuns ? To keep a
" ballance between the two sexes, must a pro-
" portionable number of men be debarred from
" marriage ? Shall the Utopians, following the
" wicked policy of superstition, forbid their
" priests to marry ; or shall they rather sacrifice
" men of some other profession for the good of
" the state ? Or, shall they appoint the sons of
" certain families to be maimed at their birth,
" and give a sanction to the unnatural institu-
" tion of eunuchs ? If none of these expe-
" dients can be thought proper, shall they ap-
" point a certain number of infants to be ex-
" posed to death as soon as they are born, deter-
" mining the proportion according to the exigen-
" cies of the state ; and pointing out the parti-
" cular victims by lot, or according to some es-
" tablished rule ? Or, must they shorten the
" period of human life by a law, and condemn
" all to die after they had compleated a certain
" age, which might be shorter or longer, as pro-
" visions were either more scanty or plentiful ?
" Or what other method should they devise (for
" an expedient would be absolutely necessary)
" to restrain the number of citizens within rea-
" sonable bounds ?

" Alas ! how unnatural and inhuman must
" every such expedient be accounted ! The na-
" tural passions and appetites of mankind are
" planted in our frame, to answer the best ends
" for the happiness both of the individuals and
" of the species. Shall we be obliged to contra-
" dict such a wise order ? Shall we be laid un-
" der the necessity of acting barbarously and in-
" humanly ? Sad and fatal necessity! And
" which, after all, could never answer the end,
" but would give rise to violence and war. For
" mankind would never agree about such regu-
" lations. Force, and arms, must at last decide
" their quarrels, and the deaths of such as fall in
" battle, leave sufficient provisions for the survi-
" vors, and make room for others to be born.

" Thus the tranquillity and numerous bles-
" sings of the Utopian governments would come
" to an end ; war, or cruel and unnatural cus-
" toms, be introduced, and a stop put to the
" increase of mankind, to the advancement of
" knowledge, and to the culture of the earth, in
" spite of the most excellent laws and wisest
" precautions. The more excellent the laws
" had been, and the more strictly they had been
" observed, mankind must have sooner become
" miserable. The remembrance of former times,
" the greatness of their wisdom and virtue, would

" conspire to heighten their distress ;* and the
" world, instead of remaining the mansion of
" wisdom and happiness, become the scene of
" vice and confusion. Force and fraud must
" prevail, and mankind be reduced to the same
" calamitous condition as at present.

" Such a melancholy situation in consequence
" merely of the want of provisions, is in truth
" more unnatural than all their present cala-
" mities. Supposing men to have abused their
" liberty, by which abuse, vice has once been
" introduced into the world; and that wrong
" notions, a bad taste, and vicious habits, have
" been strengthened by the defects of education
" and government, our present distresses may be
" easily explained. They may even be called
" natural, being the natural consequences of our
" depravity. They may be supposed to be
" the means by which providence punishes vice;
" and by setting bounds to the increase of man-
" kind, prevents the earth's being overstocked,
" and men being laid under the cruel necessity
" of killing one another. But to suppose that
" in the course of a favourable providence, a
" perfect government had been established,

* Yet it is extraordinary that with all their wisdom and virtue
they would not be able to take any steps to prevent this distress.
This is a species of fascination, of which it is difficult to form
any conception.

" under which the disorders of human passions
" had been powerfully corrected and restrained ;
" poverty, idleness, and war banished ; the
" earth made a paradise ; universal friend-
" ship and concord established, and human so-
" ciety rendered flourishing in all respects ; and
" that such a lovely constitution should be over-
" turned, not by the vices of men, or their abuse
" of liberty, but by the order of nature itself,
" seems wholly unnatural, and altogether disa-
" greeable to the methods of providence.

" By reasoning in this manner, it is not pre-
" tended that 'tis unnatural to set bounds to
" human knowledge and happiness, or to the
" grandeur of society, and to confine what is
" finite to proper limits. It is certainly fit to
" set just bounds to every thing according to its
" nature, and to adjust all things in due pro-
" portion to one another. Undoubtedly, such
" an excellent order, is actually established
" throughout all the works of God, in his wide
" dominions. But there are certain primary de-
" terminations in nature, to which all other
" things of a subordinate kind must be adjusted.
" A limited earth, a limited degree of fertility
" and the continual increase of mankind are
" three of these original constitutions. To these
" determinations, human affairs, and the circum-

" stances of all other animals, must be adapted.
" In which view, it is unsuitable to our ideas of
" order, that while the earth is only capable of
" maintaining a determined number, the human
" race should increase without end. This would
" be the necessary consequence of a perfect go-
" vernment and education. On which account
" it is more contrary to just proportion, to sup-
" pose that such a perfect government should be
" established in such circumstances, than that
" by permitting vice, or the abuse of liberty in
" the wisdom of providence, mankind should
" never be able to multiply so as to be able to
" overstock the earth.

" From this view of the circumstances of the
" world, notwithstanding the high opinion we
" have of the merits of Sir Thomas More, and
" other admired projectors of perfect govern-
" ments in ancient or modern times, we may
" discern how little can be expected from their
" most perfect systems.

" As for these worthy philosophers, patriots,
" and law-givers, who have employed their
" talents in framing such excellent models, we
" ought to do justice to their characters, and
" gratefully to acknowledge their generous
" efforts to rescue the world out of that distress

" into which it has fallen, through the imperfec-
" tion of government. Sincere, and ardent in
" their love of virtue, enamoured of its lovely
" form, deeply interested for the happiness of
" mankind, to the best of their skill, and with
" hearts full of zeal, they have strenuously en-
" deavoured to advance human society to per-
" fection. For this, their memory ought to be
" sacred to posterity. But if they expected
" their beautiful systems actually to take place,
" their hopes were ill founded, and they were
" not sufficiently aware of the consequences.

" The speculations of such ingenious authors
" enlarge our views, and amuse our fancies.
" They are useful for directing us to correct
" certain errors at particular times. Able legis-
" lators ought to consider them as models, and
" honest patriots ought never to lose sight of
" them, or any proper opportunity of trans-
" planting the wisest of their maxims into their
" own governments, as far as they are adapted to
" their particular circumstances, and will give
" no occasion to dangerous convulsions. But
" this is all that can be expected. Though
" such ingenious romances should chance to be
" read and admired, jealous and selfish politi-
" cians need not be alarmed. Such statesmen
" need not fear that ever such airy systems

" shall be able to destroy their craft, or disap-
" point them of their intention to sacrifice the
" interests of mankind to their own avarice or
" ambition. There is too powerful a charm
" which works secretly in favor of such poli-
" ticians, which will for ever defeat all attempts
" to establish a perfect government. There is
" no need of miracles for this purpose. The
" vices of mankind are sufficient. And we
" need not doubt but providence will make use
" of them, for preventing the establishment of
" governments which are by no means suitable
" to the present circumstances of the earth."
See Various Prospects of mankind, nature and
providence. Chap. iv. p. 113.

Here then we have not only the same argument stated ; but stated in the same connection
and brought to bear on the very same subject to
which it is applied by the author of the Essay.
The principle and the consequences deduced
from it are exactly the same. It often happens
that one man is the first to make a particular discovery or observation, and that another draws
from it an important inference of which the former was not at all aware. But this is not the
case in the present instance. As far as general
reasoning will go, it is impossible that any thing
should be stated more clearly, more fully and

explicitly than Wallace has here stated the argument against the progressive amelioration of human affairs, from the sole principle of population.
" So will his anticipation prevent Mr. Malthus's
" discovery ;" for it happens that Wallace's book
was published so long ago as the year 1761. As
to the details of the Essay, I shall leave them to
the *connoisseurs*, not pretending to know much
about the matter ; but as to the general principle
or ground-work, I must contend that it was completely pre-occupied: Mr. Malthus has no more
pretentions to originality on that score, than I or
any one else would have, who after having read
Mr. Malthus's work undertook to retail the arguments contained in it and did it in words a little
different from his own.—" Oh ! but," I hear some
one exclaim, " the geometrical and arithmetical
" series ! Has Wallace said any thing of them !
" did he find· them out, or was not this dis-
" covery reserved entirely for the genius and
" penetration of Mr. Malthus ?" Why really
I do not know : whether after having brought
his principle to light, he christened it himself, is
more than I can pretend to determine. It
seems to me sufficient for Wallace to have said
that let the one ratio increase as fast as it would,
the other would increase much faster, as this is
all that is practically meant by a geometrical
and arithmetical series. I should have no ob-

jection to let Mr. Malthus have the honour of
standing godfather to another's bantling (and
Mr. Shandy was of opinion that it was a matter
of as great importance to hit upon a lucky name
for a child as to beget it) but that the technical
phrase he has employed as a convenient short-
hand method of explaining the subject, in reality applies only to one half of it. The gradual
increase applies only to the degree of cultivation
of the earth, not to the quantity. These two
things are palpably distinct. It does not begin
to take place till the whole surface of the earth
has been cultivated to a certain degree, or only
with respect to those parts of it which have
been cultivated. It is evident that while most
of the soil remained wholly unoccupied and
uncultivated, (which must have been the case
for many ages after these two principles began
to operate, and is still the case in many countries) the power of increase in the productions
of the earth, and consequently, in the support
of population would be exactly in proportion to
the population itself, for there would be nothing
more necessary in order to the earth's maintaining its inhabitants, than that there should
be inhabitants enough to till it. In this case,
the cultivation of the earth would be limited by
the population, not the population by the state
of the cultivation. Where there was no want

of room, and a power of transporting themselves from place to place, which there would
naturally be in great continents, and in gradually increasing colonies, there could be no
want of subsistence. All that would be wanted
would be power to raise or gather the fruits
which the earth had in store, which as long as
men were born with hands they would be always
able to do. If a certain extent of ground easily
maintained a certain number of inhabitants, they
would only have to spread themselves over
double the surface to maintain double the number. The difficulty is not in making more land
maintain more men, but in making the same
spot of ground maintain a greater number than
it did before. Thus Noah might have taken
possession of the three contiguous quarters of
the globe for himself and his three sons ; and,
if instead of having three sons, he had had three
hundred, there would, I believe, have been no
danger of their starving, but the contrary, from
the rapid increase of population. What I mean
to shew is, that it is not true as a general principle that the increase of population and the increase in the means of subsistence are necessarily disproportionate to each other, that the one
is in a geometrical, the other is in an arithmetical ratio ; but, that in a particular and very
important view of the subject, the extent of

population is only limited by the extent of the earth, and that the increase of the means. of subsistence will be in proportion to the greater extent of surface occupied, which may be enlarged as fast as there are numbers to occupy it. I have been thus particular, because mathematical terms carry with them an imposing air of accuracy and profundity, and ought, therefore, to be applied strictly, and with the greatest caution, or not at all. I should say, then, that looking at the subject in a general and philosophical point of view, I do not think that the expression of an arithmetical and geometrical series applies : for, with respect to the extent of ground occupied, which is one thing on which population depends, and in the first instance always, this might evidently be increased in any ratio whatever, that the increase of population would admit, until the earth was entirely occupied ; and after that there would be no room either for a geometrical or arithmetical progression ; it would be at an absolute stand. The distinction is therefore confined to the degree of art and diligence used in the cultivation of those parts which have been already occupied. This has no doubt gone on at a very slow kind of snail's pace from the very first, and will I dare say continue to do so. Or to adopt Wallace's distinction, the increase of population is either not restricted at all by the " limited nature of

" the earth," or it is limited absolutely by it:
it is only kept back indefinitely by the "limited
fertility" of the earth ; and it cannot be said to
be kept back necessarily by this, while there are
vast tracts of habitable land left untouched. Till
there is no more room, and no more food to be
procured without extreme exertion and contrivance, the arithmetical and geometrical ratios do
not naturally begin to operate ; and the gradual
increase that might take place after that period,
is not in my opinion (who am no great speculator) of sufficient importance to deserve a pompous appellation. I would, therefore, rather
stop there, because it will simplify the question.
Till the world is full, or at least till every country
is full, that is, maintains as many inhabitants as
the soil will admit, namely, till it can be proved
satisfactorily that it might not by taking proper
methods be made to maintain double the number
that it does, the increase of mankind is not necessarily checked by the " limited extent of the
earth," nor by its " limited fertility," but by
other causes. Till then population must be said
to be kept down, not by the original constitution
of nature, but by the will of man. Till then, Mr.
Malthus has no right to set up his arithmetical
and geometrical ratios upon the face of the earth,
and say they are the work of nature. You, Sir,
will not be at a loss to perceive the fallacy which
lurks under the gloss which Mr. Malthus has

here added to Wallace's text. His readers looking at his mathematical scale will be apt to suppose, that population is a naturally growing and
necessary evil; that it is always encroaching on
and straitening the means of existence, and doing more harm than good : that its pernicious
effects are at all times and in all places equally
necessary and unavoidable ; that it is at all times
an evil, but that the evil increases in proportion
to the increase of population ; and that, therefore, there is nothing so necessary as to keep
population down at all events. This is the imperious dictate of nature, the grinding law of
necessity, the end and the fulfilling of the com-
mandment. I do not mean to say, that Mr.
Malthus does not often shift his ground on this
subject, or that he is not himself aware of the
deception. It is sufficient for him that he has
it to resort to, whenever he is in want of it ,
that he has been able to throw dust in his readers'
eyes, and dazzle them by a specious shew of accuracy ; that he has made out a bill of indict-
ment against the principle of population as a
common nuisance in society, and has obtained a
general warrant against it, and may have it
brought into court as a felon whenever he thinks
proper. He has alarmed men's minds with confused apprehensions on the subject, by setting
before their eyes, in an orderly series, the malignant nature and terrible effects of population,

which are perpetually increasing as it goes on :
and they are ready to assent to every scheme
that promises to keep these dreadful evils at
a distance from them. " *Sacro tremuere timore.*
Every coward is planet-struck," But nothing
of all this is the truth, Population is only an
evil, as Mr. Malthus has himself shewn, in proportion as it is excessive : it is not a necessary
evil, till the supply of food can, from natural
causes, no longer keep pace with it : till this is
the case, no restraints are necessary, and when
this is the case, the same wholesome degree of
restraint, the same quantity of vice and misery,
will operate equally to prevent any tremendous
consequences, whether the actual population is
great or small ; that is, whether it is stopped
only from having reached the utmost limits prescribed by nature, or whether it has been starved
and crushed down long before that period by positive, arbitrary institutions, and the perverse
nature of man. But this is entering upon a matter which I intended to reserve for another letter
in which I shall examine the force of the arguments, which Mr. Malthus has built upon this
principle. At present, I have done all that was
necessary to the performance of the first part of
my engagement, which was to shew that Mr.
Malthus had little claim to the praise of originality.

LETTER III.

ON THE PRINCIPLE OF POPULATION AS AFFECTING THE SCHEMES OF UTOPIAN IMPROVEMENT.

―――――

" A swaggering paradox, when once explained, soon sinks
into an unmeaning common-place."

BURKE.

―――――

SIR,

THIS excellent saying of a great man was never
more strictly applicable to any system than it is
to Mr. Malthus's paradox, and his explanation
of it. It seemed, on the first publication of the
Essay on Population, as if the whole world was
going to be turned topsy-turvy, all our ideas of
moral good, and evil were in a manner confounded, we scarcely knew whether we stood
on our head or our heels : but after exciting
considerable expectation, giving us a good shake,
and making us a little dizzy, Mr. Malthus, does as
we do when we shew the children *London,*—sets
us on our feet again, and every thing goes on as be-

fore. The common notions that prevailed on this subject, till our author's first population-scheme tended to weaken them, were that life is a blessing, and that the more people could be maintained in any state in a tolerable degree of health, comfort and decency, the better : that want and misery are not desirable in themselves, that famine is not to be courted for its own sake, that wars, disease and pestilence are not what every friend of his country or his species should pray for in the first place : that vice in its different shapes is a thing, that the world could do very well without, and that if it could be got rid of altogether, it would be a great gain. In short, that the object both of the moralist and politician was to diminish as much as possible the quantity of vice and misery existing in the world : without apprehending that by thus effectually introducing more virtue and happiness, more reason and good sense, that by improving the manners of a people, removing pernicious habits and principles of acting, or securing greater plenty, and a greater number of mouths to partake of it, they were doing a disservice to humanity. Then comes Mr. Malthus with his octavo book, and tells us there is another great evil, which had never been found out, or at least not sufficiently attended to till his time, namely excessive population : that this evil was infinitely greater and more to be dreaded than all others put together ; and that its approach could only be checked by vice and misery : that any increase of virtue or happiness, was the direct way to hasten it on ; and that in proportion as we attempted to improve the condition of mankind, and lessened the restraints of vice and misery, we threw down the only barriers that could protect us from this most formidable scourge of the species, population. Vice, and misery were indeed evils, but they were absolutely necessary evils; necessary to prevent the introduction of others of an incalculably, and inconceivably greater magnitude ; and that every proposal to lessen their actual quantity, on which the measure of our safety depended, might be attended with the most ruinous consequences, and ought to be looked upon with horror. I think, Sir, this description of the tendency and complexion of Mr. Malthus's first essay is not in the least exaggerated, but an exact and faithful picture of the impression, which it made on every one's mind.

After taking some time to recover from the surprise and hurry into which so great a discovery would naturally throw him, he comes forward again with a large quarto, in which he is at great pains both to say and unsay all that he had said in his former volume, and upon the whole concludes, that population is in itself a good thing, that it is never likely to do much harm, that virtue and happiness ought to be promoted by every practicable means, and that the most effectual as well as desirable check to excessive population is *moral restraint.* The mighty discovery, thus reduced to, and pieced out by common sense, the wonder vanishes, and we breathe a little freely again. Mr. Malthus is however, by no means willing to give up his old doctrine, or *eat his own words :* he stickles stoutly for it at times. He has his fits of reason and his fits of extravagance, his yielding and his obstinate moments, fluctuating between the two, and vibrating backwards and forwards with a dexterity of self-contradiction which it is wonderful to behold. The following passage is so curious in this respect that I cannot help quoting it in this place. Speaking of the reply of the author of the Political Justice to his former work, he observes, " But Mr. Godwin says, " that if he looks into the past history of the " world, he does not see that increasing population has been controlled and confined by vice " and misery *alone. In this observation I can-* " *not agree with him.* I will thank Mr. Godwin " to name to me any check, that in past ages has " contributed to keep down the population to the

" level of the means of subsistence, that does not
" fairly come under some form of vice or misery;
" except indeed the check of *moral restraint,*
" *which I have mentioned in the course of this*
" *work;* and which to say the truth, whatever
" hopes we may entertain of its prevalence
" in future, has undoubtedly in past ages ope-
" rated with very inconsiderable force."* When
I assure the reader that I give him this passage
fairly and fully, I think he will be of opinion
with me, that it would be difficult to produce
an instance of a more miserable attempt to reconcile a contradiction by childish evasion, to
insist upon an argument, and give it up in the
same breath. Does Mr. Malthus really think that
he has such an absolute right and authority over
this subject of population, that provided he
mentions a principle, or shews that he is not
ignorant of it, and cannot be caught *napping* by
the critics, he is at liberty to say that it has or
has not had any operation, just as he pleases, and
that the state of the fact is a matter of perfect indifference. He contradicts the opinion of Mr. Godwin that vice and misery are not the only checks
to population, and gives as a proof of his asser-

* The prevalence of this check may be estimated *by the general proportion* of virtue and happiness in the world, for if
there had been no such check there could have been nothing
but vice and misery.

tion, that he himself truly has mentioned another check. Thus after flatly denying that moral restraint has any effect at all, he modestly concludes by saying that it has had some, no doubt, but promises that it will never have a great deal. Yet in the very next page, he says, "On " this sentiment, whether virtue, prudence or " pride, which I have already noticed under " the name of moral restraint, or of the more " comprehensive title, the *preventive* check, it " will appear, that in the sequel of this work, I " shall lay considerable stress." p. 385. This kind of reasoning is enough to give one the head-ache. But to take things in their order.

The most singular thing in this singular performance of our author is, that it should have been originally ushered into the world as the most complete and only satisfactory answer to the speculations of Godwin, Condorcet and others, or to what has been called the modern philosophy. A more complete piece of wrong-headedness, a more strange perversion of reason could hardly be devised by the wit of man. Whatever we may think of the doctrine of the progressive improvement of the human mind, or of a state of society in which every thing will be subject to the absolute control of reason, however absurd, unnatural, or impracti-

cable we may conceive such a system to be, certainly it cannot without the grossest inconsistency be objected to it, that such a system
would necessarily be rendered abortive, because
if reason should ever get this mastery over all
our actions, we shall then be governed entirely
by our physical appetites and passions, without
the least regard to consequences. This appears
to me a refinement on absurdity. Several philosophers and speculatists had supposed that a
certain state of society very different from any
that has hitherto existed was in itself practicable ; and that if it were realised, it would be
productive of a far greater degree of human
happiness than is compatible with the present
institutions of society. I have nothing to do
with either of these points. I will allow to any
one who pleases that all such schemes are
" false, sophistical, unfounded in the extreme."
But I cannot agree with Mr. Malthus that they
would be *bad*, in proportion as they were *good*;
that their excellence would be their ruin ; or
that the true and only unanswerable objection
against all such schemes is that very degree of
happiness, virtue and improvement to which
they are supposed to give rise. And I cannot
agree with him in this because it is contrary to
common sense, and leads to the subversion of
every principle of moral reasoning. Without

perplexing himself with the subtle arguments of his opponents, Mr. Malthus comes boldly forward, and says, " Gentlemen, I am willing to make " you large concessions, I am ready to allow the " practicability and the desirableness of your " schemes, the more happiness, the more virtue, " the more refinement they are productive of the " better, all these will only add to the ' exu- " berant strength of my argument ;' I have a " short answer to all objections, to be sure I " found it in an old political receipt-book, called " Prospects, &c. by one Wallace, a man not " much known, but no matter for that, *finding* " *is keeping*, you know :' and with one smart stroke of his wand, on which are inscribed certain mystical characters, and algebraic propor- tions, he levels the fairy enchantment with the ground. For, says Mr. Malthus, though this improved state of society were actually rea- lised, it could not possibly continue, but must soon terminate in a state of things preg- nant with evils far more insupportable than any we at present endure, in consequence of the excessive population which would follow, and the impossibility of providing for its support.

This is what I do not understand. It is, in other words, to assert that the doubling the po- pulation of a country, for example, after a cer-

tain period, will be attended with the most pernicious effects, by want, famine, bloodshed,
and a state of general violence and confusion,
this will afterwards lead to vices and practices
still worse than the physical evils they are de-
signed to prevent, &c. and yet that at this period
those who will be the most interested in preventing these consequences, and the best ac_
quainted with the circumstances that lead to
them will neither have the understanding to
foresee, nor the heart to feel, nor the will to prevent the sure evils to which they expose themselves and others, though this advanced state of
population, which does not admit of any addition without danger is supposed to be the immediate result of a more general diffusion of
the comforts and conveniencies of life, of more
enlarged and liberal views, of a more refined and
comprehensive regard to our own permanent interests, as well as those of others, of correspondent habits and manners, and of a state of
things, in which our gross animal appetites will
be subjected to the practical control of reason.
The influence of rational motives, of refined and
long-sighted views of things is supposed to have
taken place of narrow, selfish and merely sensual motives : this is implied in the very statement of the question. " What conjuration and
what mighty magic" should thus blind our phi-

losophical descendants on this single subject in which they are more interested than in all the rest, so that they should stand with their eyes open on the edge of a precipice, and instead of retreating from it, should throw themselves down headlong, I cannot comprehend; unless indeed we suppose that the impulse to propagate the species is so strong and uncontrolable that reason has no power over it. This is what Mr. Malthus was at one time strongly disposed to assert, and what he is at present half inclined to retract. Without this foundation to rest on, the whole of his reasoning is unintelligible. It seems to me a most childish way of answering any one, who chooses to assert that mankind are capable of being governed entirely by their reason, and that it would be better for them if they were, to say, No, for if they were governed entirely by it, they would be much less able to attend to its dictates than they are at present: and the evils, which would thus follow from the unrestrained increase of population, would be excessive.—Almost every little Miss, who has had the advantage of a boarding-school education, or been properly tutored by her mamma, whose hair is not of an absolute flame-colour, and who has hopes in time, if she behaves prettily, of getting a good husband, waits patiently year after year, looks about her,

rejects or trifles with half a dozen lovers, favour‚
ing one, laughing at another, chusing among
them " as one picks pears, saying, this I like,
" that I loathe," with the greatest indifference,
as if it were no such very pressing affair, and
all the while behaves very prettily ; till she is at
last smitten with a handsome house, a couple of
footmen in livery, or a black-servant, or a coach
with two sleek geldings, with which she is more
taken than with her man :—why, what an idea
does Mr. Malthus give us of the grave, mascu-
line genius of our Utopian philosophers, their
sublime attainments and gigantic energy, that
they will not be able to manage these matters as
decently and cleverly as the silliest women can
do at present ! Mr. Malthus indeed endeavours
to soften the absurdity by saying that moral
restraint at present owes its strength to selfish
motives : what is this to the purpose ?   If Mr.
Malthus chooses to say, that men will always be
governed by the same gross mechanical motives
that they are at present, I have no objection to
make to it ; but it is shifting the question : it is
not arguing against the state of society we are
considering from the consequences to which it
would give rise, but against the possibility of its
ever existing.   It is absurd to object to a system on account of the consequences which
would follow if we were to suppose men to be

actuated by entirely different motives and principles from what they are at present, and then
to say, that those consequences would necessarily follow, because men would never be what we
suppose them. It is *very* idle to alarm the imagination by deprecating the evils that must follow
from the practical adoption of a particular
scheme, yet to allow that we have no reason to
dread those consequences, but because the
scheme itself is impracticable.—But I am
ashamed of wasting your reader's time and my
own in thus beating the air. It is not however my
fault that Mr. Malthus has written nonsense, or
that others have admired it. It is not Mr. Malthus's nonsense, but the opinion of the world
respecting it, that I would be thought to compliment by this serious refutation of what in itself neither deserves nor admits of any reasoning
upon it. If however we recollect the source
from whence Mr. Malthus borrowed his principle and the application of it to improvements in
political philosophy, we must allow that he is
merely *passive* in error. The principle itself
would not have been worth a farthing to him
without the application, and accordingly he took
them as he found them lying snug together; and
as Trim having converted the old jack-boots into
a pair of new mortars immediately planted them
against whichever of my uncle Toby's garrisons

the allies were then busy in besieging, so the
public-spirited gallantry of our modern engineer
directed him to bend the whole force of his
clumsy discovery against that system of philosophy which was the most talked of at the
time, but to which it was the least applicable of
all others. Wallace, I have no doubt, took up
his idea either as a paradox, or a *jeu d'esprit*, or
because any thing, he thought, was of weight
enough to overturn what had never existed any
where but in the imagination, or he was led
into a piece of false logic by an error we are
very apt to fall into, of supposing because he had
never been struck himself by the difficulty of
population in such a state of society, that therefore the people themselves would not find it out,
nor make any provision against it. But though
I can in some measure excuse a lively paradox,
I do not think the same favour is to be shewn to
the dull, dogged, voluminous repetition of an
absurdity.

I cannot help thinking that our author has
been too much influenced in his different feelings on this subject, by the particular purpose he had in view at the time. Mr. Malthus
might not improperly have taken for the motto
of his first edition. " These three bear record on
" earth, vice, misery, and population." In his

answer to Mr. Godwin, this principle was represented as an evil, for which no remedy could
be found but in evil ;—that its operation was
mechanical, unceasing, necessary ; that it went
strait forward to its end, unchecked by fear, or
reason, or remorse; that the evils, which it drew
after it, could only be avoided by other evils, by
actual vice and misery. Population was in
fact the great devil, the untamed Beelzebub that
was only kept chained down by vice and misery,
and that if it were once let loose from these restraints, it would go forth, and ravage the earth.
That they were therefore the two main props
and pillars of society, and that the lower and
weaker they kept this principle, the better able
they were to contend with it : that therefore
any diminution of that degree of them, which
at present prevails, and is found sufficient to
keep the world in order, was of all things chiefly
to be dreaded.—Mr. Malthus seems fully aware
of the importance of the stage-maxim, To ele-
vate and surprise. Having once heated the
imaginations of his readers, he knows that he
can afterwards mould them into whatever shape
he pleases. All this bustle and terror, and
stage-effect, and theatrical-mummery, was only
to serve a temporary purpose, for all of a sudden the scene is shifted, and the storm subsides.
Having frighted away the boldest champions of

modern philosophy, this monstrous appearance, full of strange and inexplicable horrors, is
suffered quietly to shrink back to its natural
dimensions, and we find it to be nothing more
than a common-sized tame looking animal,
which however requires a chain and the whip
of its keeper to prevent it from becoming mischievous. Mr. Malthus then steps forward
and says, " the evil we were all in danger of
" was not population,—but philosophy. No-
" thing is to be done with the latter by mere
" reasoning. I therefore thought it right to make
" use of a little terror to accomplish the end.
" As to the principle of population you need be
" under no alarm, only leave it to me and I
" shall be able to manage it very well. All its
" dreadful consequences may be easily pre-
" vented by a proper application of the motives of
" common prudence and common decency." If
however any one should be at a loss to know
how it is possible to reconcile such contradictions, I would suggest to Mr. Malthus the answer
which Hamlet makes to his friend Guilderstern,
" 'Tis as easy as lying: govern these ventiges (the
" poor-rates and private charity) with your
" fingers and thumb, and this same instrument
" will discourse most excellent music ; look
" you, here are the stops," (namely, Mr. Malthus's Essay and Mr. Whitbread's Poor Bill).

To sum up the whole of this argument in one word. Let us suppose with Mr. Malthus that population can only be kept down by a certain degree of vice and misery. Let us also suppose that these checks are for a time removed, and that mankind become perfectly virtuous and happy. Well, then, according to the former supposition, this would necessarily lead to an excessive increase of population. Now the question is, to what degree of excess it would lead, and where it would naturally stop. Mr. Malthus, to make good his reasoning, must suppose a miracle to take place; that after population has begun to increase excessively, no inconvenience is felt from it, that in the midst of the " imminent and immediate" evils which follow from it, people continue virtuous and happy and unconscious of the dangers with which they are surrounded; till of a sudden Mr. Malthus opens the flood-gates of vice and misery, and they are overwhelmed by them, all at once. In short he must suppose either that this extraordinary race of men, in proportion as population increases, are gradually reduced in size, " and less than smallest dwarfs, in narrow room, " throng numberless, like that pygmean race " beyond the Indian mount, or fairy elves;" or that they have some new world assigned them as a breeding-place, from which attempting to return they are immediately squeezed to death, like people rushing into a crowded theatre. On the other hand, I contend that in the natural course of things, that is, if we suppose people to retain their usual dimensions, to eat, and drink, and beget children, and bring them up in the usual way, all this could never happen : for it is impossible but they must see and feel that there was only room for a certain number. The moment population became excessive from the *excess* of virtue and happiness, its inconveniences would return, and people would no longer be *perfectly virtuous and happy* : that is, the old checks of a certain degree of vice and misery would come into play again, and a less degree of them (I suppose about as much as we enjoy the advantage of at present) would be sufficient to deter men from plunging into greater, would put a stop to the further increase of population, and anticipate those tremendous evils which Mr. Malthus apprehends from it, which could never happen unless we suppose people to have come to a previous, deliberate resolution mutually to starve one another to death. There is therefore no foundation for the alarm given by Mr. Malthus, for vice and misery are such ready and sure resources that we can be at a loss for them at no time ; and farther with respect to the state of society supposed by Mr. Malthus, that is if we could once drive vice and misery out of the world, I really do not see what occasion we should have for them afterwards.

The most important question yet remains, which is not how Mr. Malthus came by his discovery, nor whether he was right in endeavouring to exemplify it in the first instance by shewing its effects on an imaginary state of society where it would be naturally disarmed of its malignity, but whether the practical conclusions he has drawn from it are not of weight and moment in themselves, and whether they are not established so clearly and fully as to make it necessary for us to reverse almost entirely all our old reasonings on the principles of political economy. I confess, I have some difficulty in determining, whether Mr. Malthus's principles do or do not materially affect the commonly received notions on this subject, because I really do not know what those principles are, and till Mr. Malthus himself tells us, whether he would have us believe in the new revelation or the old, it is impossible that any one should. If we are to consider those as Mr. Malthus's real and chastized opinions which are the least like himself, which most flatly contradict his former assertions, which being forced from him may be looked upon as confessions of the truth, I see nothing in these that in any manner interferes with the common sense of mankind. And though Mr. Malthus still perseveres in almost all his extreme conclusions, yet as those conclusions are for the most part unwarrantable assumptions, disproved even by his own concessions, and shew nothing more than Mr. Malthus's qualifications for the delicate office of conscience-keeper to the rich and great, I am so far from considering them as new and important discoveries, that I must be excused if I consider them as in the highest degree false and dangerous, and treat them accordingly.

LETTER IV,

————

Sir,

Mr. Malthus's argument against a state of *un-limited* improvement, of perfect wisdom, virtue and happiness, from the vice, misery, and madness inseparable from such a state would, if admitted, be an effectual bar to all limited improvement whatever. It is for this reason, that I have dwelt so long on the subject. If out of timidity, or complaisance, or prejudice against an unpopular system, we suffer ourselves to be wheedled into a silly persuasion, that the worst thing that could happen for the human race would be their being able to realise not in words only, but in deed all the fine things, that have been said of them, we then fairly throw ourselves upon the mercy of our adversaries. For what is there in this case, to hinder Mr.

Malthus, or any one else, from representing
every degree of practical improvement as an ap-
proximation to this deplorable crisis, from bind-
ing up the slips and scyons of human happiness
with this great trunk of evil, and root of all our
woe, from marking with his slider and graduated
scale all our advances towards this ideal perfection, however partial or necessary, as so many
deviations from the strict line of our duty, and
only sphere of our permanent happiness ? It is
evident, that the only danger of all imaginary
schemes of improvement arises from their being
exaggerations of the real capacities of our nature, from supposing that we can pick out all the
dross, and leave nothing but the gold ; that is,
from their being carried to excess, and aiming
at more than is practicable. But if we allow
that improvement is an evil in the abstract, and
that the greater the improvement, the greater
the mischief, that the actual and complete success of all such schemes would be infinitely
worse even than their failure, for that the most
complete and extensive improvement would
only prepare the way for the most deplorable
wretchedness, and that the very next step after
reaching the summit of human glory would
plunge us into the lowest abyss of vice and
misery,—why truly there will be little encouragement to set out on a journey that promises so

very disagreeable a conclusion ; such a repre‐ sentation of the matter will not add wings to our zeal for practical reform, but will rather make us stop short in our career, and refuse to ad‐ vance one step farther in a road, that is beset with danger and destruction. People will begin to look with a jaundiced eye at the most obvious advantages, to resist every useful regulation, and dread every change for the better. Our feelings are governed very much by common-place asso‐ ciations, and are most influenced by that sort of logic which is the shortest. Thus, " that the " parts are contained in the whole," is a general rule which is found to hold good in most of the concerns of life ; and it is not therefore easy to drive it out of people's heads. For this reason, it will always be difficult to persuade the generality of mankind that a less degree of improvement is a good thing, though a greater would be a bad thing, or that the subordinate parts of a system, that would in reality embody all the ills of life, can be very desirable in themselves. Mr. Mal‐ thus has however by no means left this conclu‐ sion to the mere mechanical operation of our feelings. He endeavours formally to establish it. The following passage seems the connecting link in the chain, which unites the two worlds of theory and practice together; it cements the argument, gives solidity and roundness to it, and renders it complete against all improvement, real or imaginary, present or future, against all absolute perfection or imperfect attempts at it, and gradual approaches to it. It fairly blocks up the road.

" It cannot but be a matter of astonishment " that all the writers on the perfectibility of man, " and of society, who have noticed the argu- " ment of an overcharged population, treat it " always very slightly, and invariably represent " the difficulties arising from it, as at a great, and " almost immeasurable distance. Even Mr. " Wallace, who thought the argument itself of " so much weight as to destroy his whole sys- " tem of equality, did not seem to be aware " that any difficulty would occur from this " cause, till the whole earth had been cultivated " like a garden, and was incapable of any further " increase of produce. Were this really the " case, and were a beautiful system of equality " in other respects practicable, I cannot think " that our ardour in the pursuit of such a scheme " ought to be damped by the contemplation of so " remote a difficulty. An event at such a dis- " tance might fairly be left to providence ; but " the truth is, that if the view of the argument " given in this Essay be just, the difficulty so far " from being remote, would be imminent and

" immediate. *At every period during the pro-*
" *gress of cultivation,* from the present moment
" to the time when the whole earth was become
" like a garden, *the distress for want of food*
" *would be constantly pressing on all mankind,* if
" they were equa . Though the produce of
" the earth *might be increasing every year,* popu-
" lation *would be increasing much faster* ; and the
" redundancy must *necessarily* be repressed by
" the periodical or constant action of vice and
" misery."*

In answer to this statement (allowing however
that it is a fair inference from Wallace's reasoning, and from our author's own principle) I
would simply ask, whether *during this progress*
of cultivation, the distress for want of food would
be constantly pressing on all mankind more than
it does at present. Let us suppose that men
remain just as vicious, as imprudent, as regardless of their own interests and those of others
as they are at present, let us suppose them to

* In the second edition, it says, *moral restraint,* vice or
misery. What are we to think of a man who writes a book to
prove that vice and misery are the only security for the happiness of the human race, and then writes another to say, that vice
and folly are not the only security, but that our only resource
must be either in vice and folly, or in wisdom and virtue? This
is like making a white skin part of the definition of a man, and
defending it by saying that they are all *white,* except those
who are *black* or *tawny.*

continue just what they are, through all the stages of improved cultivation to the time when the whole earth was become like a garden, would this in the smallest degree detract from the benefit ? Would nothing indeed be gained by the earth's being cultivated like a garden, that is, by its producing ten times the quantity of food that it does at present, and being able to maintain ten times the quantity of inhabitants in the same degree of comfort and happiness that it does at present, because forsooth they would not at the same time be ten times better off than they are now ? Is it an argument against adding to the happiness of mankind ten-fold, by increasing their number, their condition remaining the same, that we cannot add to it a hundred-fold, by increasing their number and improving their condition proportionably ? Or is it any objection to increasing the means of subsistence by the improved cultivation of the earth, that the population would keep pace with it ? It appears to me that there must be a particular perversity, some egregious bias in the mind of any person who can either deny the inference to be drawn from these questions, or evade it as a matter of indifference, by equivocation and subterfuge. We might as well assert that because it is most likely that the inhabitants of the rest of Europe are not better, nor indeed quite so well off as the people of England, that it would therefore be no matter if the whole continent of Europe were sunk in the sea, as if human life was merely to be considered as a sample of what the thing is, and as if when we have a sample of a certain quality, all the rest might be very well spared, as of no value. As however I conceive that Mr. Malthus is not a man to be moved either by common feelings or familiar illustrations, I shall venture to lay down one dry maxim on the subject, which he will get over as well as he can, namely, that an improved cultivation of the earth, and a consequent increase of food must necessarily lead to one or other of these two consequences, either that a greater number of people will be maintained in the same degree of comfort and happiness, other things being the same, or that means will be afforded for maintaining an equal number in greater ease, plenty, and affluence. It is plain either that existence is upon the whole a blessing and that the means of existence are on that account desirable; that consequently an increased population is doubly a blessing, and an increase in the means of existence doubly desirable : or else life is an evil, and whatever tends to promote it is an evil, and in this case it would be well if all the inhabitants of the earth were to die of some easy death to-morrow !

For my own part, " who am no great clerk,"
I cannot by any efforts, of which I am capable,
separate these two propositions, that it is desirable either that population should have stood still
at first, or that it should go on increasing till the
earth is absolutely full ; or in other words, I see
no rational alternative between the principle of
extermination (as far as it is in our power) and
the principle of the utmost possible degree of populousness. It is, I conceive, an incontrovertible
axiom, that the proportion between the population and food being given (and Mr. Malthus tells
us that it holds nearly the same in all the stages
of society) the actual increase of population is to
be considered as so much clear gain, as so much
got into the purse, as so much addition to the sum
of human hapiness. Mr. Malthus says in another place, (second edition p. 357), " The only
" point in which I differ from M. Condorcet in
" this description" [of the evils arising from increased population,] " is with regard to the pe-
" riod, when it may be applied to the human
" race. M. Condorcet thinks that it cannot
" possibly be applicable, but at an æra extreme-
" ly distant. If the proportion between the
" natural increase of population and food, which
" was stated in the beginning of this essay, and
" which has received considerable confirmation

" *from the poverty that has been found to prevail*
" *in every stage and department of human society,*
" be in any degree near the truth, it will appear
" on the contrary, that the period, when the
" number of men surpass their means of sub-
" sistence, has long since arrived, &c." Mr. Malthus in different parts of his work makes a great
rout about the distinction between *actual* and
relative population, and lays it down that an
actual increase of population is an advantage, except when it exceeds the means of subsistence;
yet he here seems to treat the proportion between the increase of population, and food,
which he says has always continued pretty
much the same, as the only thing to be attended to, and to represent the progressive increase
of the actual population, unless we could at the
same time banish poverty entirely from the
world, as a matter of the most perfect indifference, or rather as the most dangerous experiment, that could be tried. Is not this being
wilfully blind to the consequences of his
own reasoning? Oh! but, says Mr. Malthus, you do not state the case fairly. If
men were to continue what they are at present; if there were the same proportionable
quantity of vice, and misery in the world, what
you say would be true. Every thing would
then go on as well, or indeed better than before.

But this is impossible, because this increased cultivation, and a more equal distribution of the produce of the earth could only take place, in consequence of the increased civilization, virtue, good sense, and happiness of mankind: and this would necessarily spoil all. For remove the present quantity of vice and misery existing in the world, and you remove the only checks, that can keep population down. " Though the produce of the earth " might be increasing every year, the popula- " tion would be increasing much faster; and the " redundancy must be repressed by the old re- " straints of vice and misery." That is to say, though (according to the second edition) vice, misery, and moral restraint, operate mutually as checks to population, and though the diminution of vice and misery could only be the consequence of the increased strength in the principle of moral restraint, yet this latter principle would in reality have no effect at all, and in proportion as the other checks to population, viz. vice and misery, were superseded, they would become more and more necessary. If there could be a gradual, and indefinite improvement in the cultivation of the soil, and every facility could be afforded for the supply of an increasing population, without supposing some change in the institutions of society,

which would render men better and wiser, than
they now are, Mr. Malthus will perhaps with
some reluctance, and uncertainty hanging
over his mind, allow that this would be a
considerable advantage ; the population might
in this case be kept within some bounds, and
not increase faster than the means of subsistence : but as this is a change that cannot be
looked for without supposing a correspondent
improvement in the morals and characters of men,
we must set off one thing against another, and
give up the chance of improvement, to prevent
the shocking alternative connected with it.
With our present *modicum* of wit and command
over our passions, we do contrive in some measure to make both ends meet, or to cut our
coat according to our cloth, or look before we
leap, and are not carried away, neck or nothing,
by this high-mettled courser, Population, over
all the fences and barriers of common sense.
But if we were to make any considerable improvements in horsemanship, or in our *knack* at
calculation, we should instantly, belying all reasonable expectation, throw the bridle on the
horse's neck, rush blindly forward in spite of all
obstacles, and freed from the shackles of necessity
without having acquired the discipline of reason,
though the one always instantly resumes its
sway, the moment the other ceases, plunge

into all the miseries of famine, without remorse, or apprehension.

This I conceive is an express contradiction in terms. Yet I grant that it is a logical inference from Mr. Malthus's original statement, that vice and misery are the only adequate checks to population. If this were indeed the case, all the consequences that Mr. Malthus describes, the utmost degree of vice and misery, would necessarily be the lot of man in all stages and departments of society, whether in his improved or unimproved state, because in all cases and at all times his reason would be of no use to him. However great or however small our attainments in arts or science, or in all other virtues might be, in this respect we should still be the same; that is, we should be exactly in the condition of the brutes, entirely governed by an impulse, over which we should have neither check nor control. Mr. Malthus, however, finding that this account is inconsistent with the state of human life, and with those checks which certainly do keep population back from going its natural lengths, now adds moral restraint as a convenient supplement to his theory, and as our chief security against vice and misery, though he still insists that where its effect must be greatest, it would have no effect at all. He gives up his principle, but retains his conclusion, to which he has no right. He is like a bad poet who to get rid of a false concord alters the ending of his first line, and forgets that he has spoiled his rhyme in the second. On the whole, then, it appears, that at no one period during the progress of cultivation from the present moment to the time when it should have reached its utmost limits, would the distress for want of food be greater than it is at present. In the mean time, the number of mankind, and consequently their happiness would go on increasing with the means of their happiness, or subsistence, till the whole earth had been cultivated like a garden, and was incapable of any further increase, and we should then be exactly where we are now with respect to the checks on population. That is, the earth would maintain ten times its present number of inhabitants in the same comfort as at present, without our having involved ourselves in any of those straits and difficulties, those pits and snares, against which we are so kindly warned by Mr. Malthus. The population, and the means of subsistence would indeed be stationary, but so they may be said to be at present. The only difference is that they are at present unnecessarily stationary from artificial causes, from moral and political circumstances ; in that case the line would be drawn by nature herself, in other words, by the limited extent of the earth, and by its limited fertility. *This being the case and were a beautiful system of equality in other respects practicable,* (or observe, reader, I leave the question as *to those other respects* exactly where I found it) *I cannot think that our ardour in pursuit of such a scheme can in any wise be damped by the contemplation of the difficulties attendant upon it from the principle of population.* All that could be gained, would be pure gain without any loss whatever. In short, the principle of population does not, as I conceive, affect the future improvement of society in any way whatever, whether on a larger or a smaller scale, theoretically or practically, generally, or particularly. I have thus, Sir, endeavoured to answer Mr. Malthus's argument against the improved cultivation of the earth, and an increase of population, from the increased difficulties (as he falsely represents them), that would all the way press upon society during its progress. He has rendered his paradox in some measure palatable to the reader, by introducing it as one branch of his answer to Condorcet, and others of the same school, herein imitating the policy of the house of commons, who sometimes prevail on the house of lords to pass a bill which they do not much like, by tacking a money-bill to it. However as the two subjects are entirely distinct, I beg that they may not be confounded.

The question is simply, whether we are to look upon the progress of agriculture, civilization, and the populousness which would follow, (no matter to what extent, nor by whom it is brought about, whether it is projected by a junto of philosophers, or decided upon in a committee of the house of commons, enlightened by the genius of Mr. Malthus and guided by Mr. Whitbread's wisdom), whether I say, as a general principle we are to look upon an addition to the inhabitants of a state, if there is enough to support them, as a good or an evil. Mr. Malthus has chosen to answer this question under the head, *modern philosophy*, so that he is secure of the protection of the court. I have been willing not to deprive him of this advantage, and have answered it under the same head. If however any of my readers should dislike the argument in this connection, they may easily take it out of the mould in which it is cast, without doing it the least hurt. To shew how lightly all schemes of improvement sit on Mr. Malthus's mind, how easily he thinks they may be puffed aside with the least breath of sophistry, it will be sufficient to quote the following passage. After allowing in general that even the best cultivated countries in Europe might be made to produce double what they do at present, he says, "We should not be too ready to make inferences

" against the internal economy of a country from
" the appearance of uncultivated heaths without
" other evidence." [It is wonderful with what
slowness and circumspection Mr. Malthus
always proceeds in his disapprobation of any
thing, that comes in the prepossessing garb of
an evil. He is only confident and severe in his
decisions against those hidden mischiefs, which
lie concealed under a delusive appearance, of
good. There is something in the prospect of
dearth and barrenness which is perfectly con-
genial to the disposition of Mr. Malthus. He
is unwilling to give up a subject which promises so much scope for his singular talents of
bringing good out of evil]. " But the fact is,
" that as no country has ever reached, or pro-
" bably will ever reach its highest possible acme
" of produce, it *appears always*, as if the want
" of industry, or the ill-direction of that in-
" dustry was the actual limit to a further in-
" crease of produce and population, and not
" the absolute refusal of nature to yield any
" more; but a man who is locked up in a room,
" may be fairly said to be confined by the walls
" of it, *though he may never touch* them; and
" with regard to the principle of population, it is
" never the question whether a country will
" produce *any more*, but whether it may be
" made to produce a sufficiency to keep pace

" with an unchecked increase of people." This
I confess is a singular passage for a practical
philosopher to write. Mr. Malthus here lays it
down that the question is not whether we
should do all the good we can, but whether we
should do what we cannot. As to his illustration of a man locked up in a room, though it is
smart and clever, it is not much to the purpose.
The case is really that of a man who has the
range of a suite of rooms and who in a fit of the
spleen, or from indolence, or stupidity, or from any
other cause you please, confines himself to one of
them, or of a man who having hired a large com-
modious apartment, says, I never make use of the
whole of this apartment, I never go within a foot
of the walls, I might as well have it partitioned
off, it would be snugger and warmer, and so still
finding that he does not run against his partition
any more than against the wall, should continue,
being determined to have no unnecessary spare-
room, to hemm himself in closer and closer till
at last he would be able to stir neither hand
nor foot. That any one, allowing as Mr. Malthus does, that with proper management and industry this country might be made to maintain
double its present number of inhabitants, or
twenty millions instead of ten, should at the same
time affect to represent this as a mere trifling
addition, that practically speaking cannot be

taken into the account, can I think only be explained by supposing in that person either an extreme callousness of feeling, or which amounts to pretty much the same thing, a habit of making his opinions entirely subservient to his convenience, or to any narrow purpose he may have in view at the moment.—Perhaps if the truth were known, I am as little sanguine in my expectations of any great improvement to be made in the condition of human life either by the visions of philosophy, or by downright, practical, parliamentary projects, as Mr. Malthus himself can be. But the matter appears to me thus. It requires some exertion and some freedom of will to keep even where we are. If we tie up our hands, shut our eyes to the partial advantages we possess, and cease to exert ourselves in that direction in which we can do it with the most effect, we shall very soon " go deep in the negative series." Take away the hope and the tendency to improvement, and there is nothing left to counteract the opposite never-failing tendency of human things " from bad to worse." There is therefore a serious practical reason against losing sight of the object, even when we cannot attain it. However, I am "free to confess" (to borrow the language of my betters) that there is as much selfishness as public spirit in my resistance to

Mr. Malthus's contradictions. It is a remote question whether the world will ever be much wiser than it is : but what I am certainly interested in, is not to submit to have all my ideas confounded by barren sophistry, nor to give up the little understanding which I may actually possess. Nor for my own part, were I confined to my room, should I think myself obliged to any one for blocking up my view of a pleasant prospect, because I could not move from the place, where I was.

The fundamental principle of Mr. Malthus's essay is that population has a constant tendency to become excessive, because it has a tendency to increase not only in a progressive, but in a geometrical ratio, whereas the means of subsistence are either positively limited, or at most can only be made to increase in an arithmetical ratio. But to be sure of avoiding any thing like misrepresentation in this part of the argument, where the least error or omission might be fatal to our author's whole scheme, let us take his own words.

" It may be safely affirmed that population " when unchecked goes on doubling itself every " twenty-five years, or increases in a geometrical " ratio.

" That we may be the better able to com-
" pare the increase of population and food, let
" us make a supposition, which without pro-
" tending to accuracy, is clearly more favourable
" to the power of production in the earth, than
" any experience that we have had of its quali-
" ties will warrant.

" Let us suppose that the yearly additions
" which might be made to the former average
" produce, instead of decreasing, which they
" certainly would do, were to remain the same;
" and that the produce of this island might be
" increased every twenty-five years by a quan-
" tity equal to what it at present produces ; the
" most enthusiastic speculator cannot suppose a
" greater increase than this. In a few centuries
" it would make every acre of land in the island
" like a garden.

" If this supposition be applied to the whole
" earth, and if it be allowed that the subsistence
" for man which the earth affords, might be in-
" creased every twenty-five years by a quantity
" equal to what it at present produces ; this will
" be supposing a rate of increase much greater
" than we can imagine that any possible exer-
" tions of mankind could make it.

" It may be fairly pronounced therefore that
" considering the present average state of the
" earth, the means of subsistence, under cir-
" cumstances the most favourable to human in-
" dustry, could not possibly be made to increase
" faster than in an arithmetical ratio.

" The necessary effects of these two different
" rates of increase, when brought together, will
" be very striking. Let us call the population
" of this island eleven millions ; and suppose
" the present produce equal to the easy sup-
" port of such a number. In the first twenty-
" five years the population would be twenty-
" two millions, and the food being also doubled,
" the means of subsistence would be equal to
" this increase. In the next twenty-five years,
" the population would be forty-four millions,
" and the means of subsistence only equal to
" the support of thirty-three millions. In the
" next period, the population would be eighty-
" eight millions, and the means of subsistence
" just equal to the support of half that number.
" And at the conclusion of the first century,
" the population would be a hundred and
" seventy-six millions, and the means of sub-
" sistence only equal to the support of fifty-
" five millions ; leaving a population of a hun-

" dred and twenty-one millions totally unpro-
" vided for.

" Taking the whole earth instead of this
" island, emigration would of course be ex-
" cluded : and supposing the present popula-
" tion equal to a thousand millions, the human
" species would increase as the numbers 1, 2,
" 4, 8, 16, 32, 64, 128, 256, and subsistence as
" 1, 2, 3, 4, 5, 6, 7, 8, 9.   In two centuries
" the population would be to the means of sub-
" sistence as 256 to 9 ; in three centuries as
" 4096 to 13, and in two thousand years, the
" diffcrence would be almost incalculable."

" In this supposition no limits whatever are
" placed to the produce of the earth.   It may
" increase for ever, and be greater than any
" assignable quantity ; yet still *the power of*
" *population being in every period* so much supe-
" rior, the increase of the human species can
" only be kept down to the level of the means
" of subsistence by the *constant operation of the*
" *strong law of necessity* acting as a check upon
" "the greater power ;" or as he elsewhere expresses
it " *by misery, or the fear of misery.*"

Oh ! my good Sir, spare your calculations.
We do not wish to be informed what would be the
exact proportion of the *imaginary* means of sub-

sistence to the *imaginary* population at a period, and at a rate of increase, at which, if it had been possible for it to have gone on only half so long as you suppose, the whole race would have been long ago *actually* extinct. Mr. Malthus here treats us as the fantastical landlord treated *Sancho Panza*, by giving him a magnificent list of a great variety of delicacies, which it appeared on examination were not to be had, but made no mention of an excellent dish of cow-heel, which was the only thing he had in the house, and which exactly suited the stomach of the squire. I am, like Sancho, disposed to be satisfied with what I can get; and therefore I must fairly tell Mr. Malthus that if he will only spare me that first ratio of his, of a doubled population with respect to this island, or to the whole earth (though there, begging his pardon, if all other things went right, his arithmetical and geometrical distinction would not as I have shewn come into play for some time) I say if he will allow, as far as the principle of population is concerned, that it is possible to double the number of inhabitants of this country or of the world without any injury, I shall be perfectly content with this concession: this first ratio shall be to me the golden number of Pythagoras, and he may do as he pleases with all the remaining links of an impossible series, which he has started only, I imagine, as we throw out a tub to a whale by way of diversion. As to any serious argument, it is perfectly immaterial, perfectly irrelevant to the question, *whether we should double our population*, that we cannot forsooth go on doubling it for ever ; unless indeed it could be shewn that by thus doubling it once, when we can do it without any inconvenience, we should be irresistibly impelled to go on doubling it afterwards when it would have become exceedingly inconvenient, and in fact till the consequence would be general famine and the most extensive misery. Without this addition to his argument, either expressed or implied, Mr. Malthus's double series is of no use or avail whatever : it looks very pretty upon paper, and reads very neat, but is of no practical importance. The evils which it describes so accurately as arising from the increased disproportion between the ratios at every step are mere imaginary things, existing no where but in the morbid enthusiasm of Mr. Malthus's mind, unless we suppose that every increase of the existing population, either with or without a proportionable increase in the means of subsistence, is a vicious habit, a species of phrensy, where one step only leads to another, till we are plunged into irretrievable ruin. But I would ask, supposing the inhabitants of a country to have increased gradually in consequence of an increase in the means of subsistence, from two millions to four, how that population of four millions would have a greater tendency to excess, than the present population of two millions? Would not the same sense of inconvenience, the same dread of poverty, the same regard to the comforts of life, operate in the same way and just as much upon every individual of the four millons, as upon every individual of the two millions? What then becomes of the increased tendency to excessive population in consequence of its actual increase? Yet without this, an increased population is not in itself an evil, or a good necessarily leading to evil, but a pure and unmixed good unconnected with any greate evil.

Even our author's own account will give us a new country and a new earth; it will double all the happiness and all the enjoyment that there is at present in the world. If he had been a man of sanguine or poetical feelings, methinks this single consideration would have been enough to have made his heart leap up with a lively joy—to see " fast by hanging in a golden chain this pendant world," &c. but he is a man whom you may call rather of a saturnine than of a sanguine disposition. He therefore had no leisure to behold this cheering object, but passes on " to nature's farthest verge," till he enters once more into " the confines of " Chaos, and the bosom of dim night." Mr. Malthus somewhere speaks familiarly of the association of ideas, as if he were acquainted with that doctrine. He has here at any rate very skilfully availed himself of that kind of reasoning, which owes all its weight to that mechanical principle. In all the stages of an unchecked population, except the first, it having appeared that there is a great disproportion between this principle and the progress of agriculture, our author concludes that his readers will forget that that, which is so often represented as an evil, can ever be a good, and therefore peremptorily adds, in defiance of his own statement, that in *every period* of the increase, the power of population is much superior to the other. Though it appears to me then that Mr. Malthus by his ratios has gained nothing in point of argument over his readers, he has gained much upon their imagination. By representing population so often as an evil, and by

magnifying its increase in certain cases as so
enormous an evil, he raises a general prejudice
against it. Whenever you talk of any
improvement or any increase of population
consequent upon it, he immediately plays off
his infinite series against you. He makes
the transition from a practicable to an
impracticable increase of population, from
that degree of it, which is desirable to that
which is excessive, by the assistance of his
mathematical scale, as easily as you pass
from the low notes of a harpsichord to the
high ones. There seems no division between
them. It is true that so long as we confine
ourselves to the real question before us and
distinguish between what is practicable, and
what can never possibly happen, the evil
consequences of the system we contend for
are merely chimerical. But as Hercules in
order to strangle the earth-born Antæus was
obliged to lift him from the ground, Mr.
Malthus, in order to complete his triumph over
common sense, is obliged to call to his aid
certain airy speculations and fanciful theories
of dangers, that, by his own confession, can
never possibly exist. Whenever you are for
setting out on the road of reform, Mr. Malthus
stops you on the threshold, and says, Do you
consider where you are going? Don't you

know where this road will lead you? and then, with a ' Come on, sir, here's the place ; look how fearful and dizzy 'tis to cast one's eye so low ;' he hurries you forward to his imaginary precipice, and shews you the danger you have so narrowly escaped. However, it is not Mr. Malthus's rhetoric, but our own wilful blindness, that must persuade us that we have escaped being dashed to pieces down any precipices, when he himself tells us that the road is nothing more than a long winding declivity.

I conceive there were two very capital errors in Mr. Malthus's first essay, which though he has abandoned or in a great measure softened them down in his subsequent edition, still adhere to all his reasonings, and give them a wrong bias. The first of these was, that vice and misery are the only checks to population : secondly, that if population were for any time freed from these restraints, it would in that case go on increasing with a force and rapidity, which nothing would be able to withstand, and which would bear down the feeble mounds that had before opposed its progress till the whole would end in one wide scene of universal uproar and confusion. As if, in the first place, mere misery of itself, without a sense of greater misery, and a

desire to avoid it, would do any thing to prevent
population ; and in the second place, as if though
the tax of vice and misery were taken off for a
time, yet the recurrence of the same evils
afterwards would not operate in the same way
to repress population, or as if population would
in the mean time have acquired any preternatu-
ral strength, with which its counteracting causes
would be unable to contend, or as if the mere
mechanical checks to population from the actual evils attendant upon it were not always
necessarily a match for, and proportioned to,
the strength of the principle itself, and its immediate tendency to excess. It is astonishing
to see how those men, who pique themselves
the most on the solidity of their understandings,
and on a kind of dull matter-of-fact plodding
accuracy, are perpetually led away by their
imaginations: the more so because they are the
dupes of their own vanity, and never suspect
that they are liable to any such deception.
In the present instance our author has been
hurried into an unfounded assumption by having
his imagination heated with a *personification*. He
has given to the principle of population a personal existence, conceiving of it as a sort of infant Hercules, as one of that terrific giant brood,
which you can only master by strangling it in its
cradle; forgetting that the antagonist principle

which he has made its direct counterpoise, still grows with its growth and strengthens with its strength, being in fact its own offspring: and that the sharper evils which excessive population brings along with it, more severe in proportion to its excess, naturally tend to repress and keep population down to the same level, other circumstances being supposed the same. Nothing can be clearer to my understanding than this; yet it is upon the misrepresentation or misconception of this principle that most of Mr. Malthus's sophisms and ambiguities hinge.

It is necessary to make a distinction between the tendency in population to increase, and its power to increase; otherwise we may fall into great errors. The power of population to increase is an abstract thing independent of circumstances, and which is therefore always the same. Its effects may therefore be very well described by a mathematical series. When we speak of the power of population to increase in a certain continued ratio, we do not mean to say that it will or will not do so, but merely that it is possible that it should do so from the nature of the principle itself. The power of population to increase is in fact the same both before and after it has become excessive. But

I conceive this is not the case with its *tendency* to increase, unless we mean its *unchecked tendency*, which is saying nothing ; for if we speak of its real tendency to increase, this certainly is not always the same, but depends exceedingly on circumstances, that is, is greater or less in proportion as the population is or is not excessive. The ratio in which Mr. Malthus has represented population as having a natural tendency to increase, can therefore only relate to its unchecked progress, or to its increase while the means of subsistence can be made to keep pace with it ; inasmuch as it has an actual tendency to increase in this ratio, only while it is free from checks; but the moment these checks begin to operate it is necessarily limited by them, or kept down within a certain point to the level of the means of subsistence. In short, as a practical guide, Mr. Malthus's table is extremely fallacious ; for the population has a tendency to go on as 1, 2, 4, 8, &c. only while the subsistence answers to it, or is as 1, 2, 4, 8, &c. and when the means of subsistence can only be made to increase as 1, 2, 3, 4, &c. then the population will, in the natural course of things, come down to it and increase only as 1, 2, 3, 4, &c. or supposing it to have generally a certain tendency to excess, it will then increase as $1\frac{1}{4}$, $2\frac{1}{2}$, $3\frac{3}{4}$, 5, &c. The actual, positive, practical tendency in population *to increase* is not therefore always the same, and for that very reason its tendency *to excess* is always the same, neither greater nor less, in consequence of the absolute increase in population. Mr. Malthus himself admits fully the distinction between the actual increase of population and its excessive increase, between the tendency of population to increase with the means of subsistence and its tendency to increase beyond those means. In fact, almost one half of his voluminous work is taken up by extensive historical researches to prove that the population is in all ages and countries, in every form of society, and stage of civilization kept down *nearly* to the means of subsistence: that population has not therefore at one time more than another, when it is strong than when it is weak, in an improved than in a neglected state of cultivation, a tendency to rush on beyond its necessary limits: yet if there is any one inference to be drawn from the general spirit and tenor of Mr. Malthus's reasonings, it is this, that we ought not to encourage population, nor be anxious about the increase of the means of subsistence, but ought rather to keep them back as much as possible, because every addition made to population by whatever means or in whatever circumstances, has a direct and unavoidable tendency to make it go on increasing with an accelerated force; or that the positive benefit of an enlarged population is always counterbalanced by the increased danger of the excess to which it naturally leads. Mr. Malthus by setting a certain degree of plenty against a certain degree of excessive population, has made it appear as if the two things were inseparably connected, as if supposing a certain progress made in the one ratio you may then by passing over to the opposite line see immediately what progress had been made at the same time in the other, that is, what quantity of actual and excessive population, proportioned to the increase in the means of subsistence and its immediate consequence, would require to be cut off by forcible and unnatural means, by vice and misery. It therefore looks very much as if plenty were the immediate fore-runner of famine, as if by sowing the seeds of virtue and happiness you were ensuring a larger harvest of vice and misery, the evil engrafted on any good being always greater than the real benefit itself, and as if by advancing population and increasing the means of its support, you were only opening a new Iliad of woes, and giving larger scope to the baneful operation of this principle. So that it is not the increase of good that we are to think of, but the introduction of evil that we are to guard against. The proportion by which we are to be guided is clear and demonstrable ; it is as 256 to 9, and so regularly through all the gradations upwards and downwards. At this rate it is pretty clear that our only object must be to confine human happiness within as narrow limits, and to keep the population down as low as possible, at least to suffer no addition to it. We are something in the condition of a man suspended on a balance with sharp-pointed spikes placed close to his body, and who must not stir for his life. Now the source of this fallacy (on which the whole turns, for without it it is null and abortive) lies here, namely, in supposing that of the two ratios here connected together, the one is the cause of, or has any thing to do with the other. For the ratio in the upper line being at number 256 does not depend on the other ratio being at number 9, but simply on its being so many removes from the root or first number. It only expresses a possible or imaginary series, or the independent, direct, physical power of increase, or abstract tendency to increase in population at each step, and what that increase would amount to in a given number of steps, being left entirely to itself. If it expresses any thing else, or the actual increase of population combined with and in reference to the means of subsistence, it is utterly false and delusive, and a contradiction in terms. For population as regulated by, and arising out of the means of subsistence cannot have got the start of it in so prodigious a manner, and as unconnected with the increase of the latter cannot depend upon it. In the one case, population instead of being to the means of subsistence as 256 to 9, will only be a little a head of it, or as 9½ to 9 : in the other case it will be as 256, whether the food has in a given time increased from 1 to 9, or only from 1 to 6, or whether it has stood still at 1. The number of inhabitants from the beginning of the world, proceeding by the geometrical ratio, would have been going on just the same whether they had ever had any thing to eat or not (they are a kind of enchanted people who live without food) whether the quantity of food had been more or less, whether there had ever been any improvements in agriculture or not. Though the improvements in agriculture had stood still at 1 in the arithmetical scale, this would not lessen or alter the height to which the geometrical scale would have mounted in the interval. " It keeps on its way unslacked of motion." By advancing in the arithmetical scale or increasing the means of subsistence, you do not advance the geometrical scale, much less by increasing the disproportion between the two, do you increase the *waste* population of the world, which must be greater in proportion as less of it had been provided for. On the other hand, you necessarily lessen this disproportion. For instead of supposing that if we had remained at 1 in the lower scale, we should then have been at 1 in the upper, or that if we had advanced no further than 3, the disproportion would then only have been 4 to 3, and so on, whereas by going on it is now as 256 to 9, the fact is that the disproportion instead of being as 256 to 9, would have been 256 to 1, or 2, or 3 ; and that the farther we go in the one scale, though we cannot keep up with, or overtake the other, yet we lose so much the less ground and are nearer it than we should otherwise be. To argue otherwise is to be like the children who when they cannot keep up with others, stand still and begin to cry, thinking this the likeliest way to make them slacken their pace. I shall therefore beg leave to look upon every increase in the means of subsistence or actual population, as so much gained upon the *infinite series* : by keeping back the *actual* means of subsistence, I do not lessen the *possible* or abstract tendency of population to increase, and I only add to its actual tendency to increase in proportion as I add to its actual means of support. We have therefore a clear addition to its actual quantity without any addition to its tendency to excess, or without strengthening the evil principle, the germ of in-calculable mischief, which population contains within it. Mr. Malthus has taken no pains to guard his readers against the conclusion, that by increasing the actual population, you increase its actual tendency to increase, as if either the disposition to propagate the species were stronger in proportion to the number of those who possess it, or as if in proportion as the power is spread over a larger surface, it were not counteracted by being accompanied in each individual with a proportionable share of com-mon sense and reason, so that he will not be a bit more likely to run upon famine because there will be twice as many to keep him com-pany as there used to be. The tendency to excessive population in any community does not depend upon the number of individuals in it, who have the power of abusing their liberty, or on the quantity of mischief they *might* do, but upon the moral character of the individuals composing it, upon the difference between the strength of moral restraint and the strength of physical appetite, or on the actual inconve-niences to which they *will* submit for the sake of gratifying their passions. In short the tendency to excess does not depend on the point in the scale where the *limit* is drawn, but upon the tendency to overleap that limit ; now this tendency or *impetus* is not increased by the distance which it has gone, like a stone rolling down a hill, or like a torrent of water accumulating, but is like a cart or waggon left on a declivity with a drag-chain fastened to one of the wheels, which is carried forward till the chain is pulled tight and then it stops of itself. This is a very clumsy comparison, but it has some resemblance to the thing. We are not to calculate the actual tendency to excess in population by the excess of the power itself over the means of subsistence, which is greater as we advance, but by the excess of the power restrained by other motives and principles over the means of subsistence. In algebraic language the tendency to excess is not equal to the power of population simply, but to the power, *minus* the difficulty of providing for its support, or the influence which that difficulty has on the conduct of rational beings.

If we suppose a barren island with half a dozen savages upon it, living upon roots, vermin, and crawfish, without any of the arts or any of the conveniences of life, ignorant of agriculture, neither knowing nor caring how to improve their condition, passing their time in stupid indolence, with as little pretensions to reason or refinement as can well be desired, in short a very unphilosophical, improgressive, viscious, miserable set of barbarians as need be; now what difference would it make in the condition of these poor uninformed wretches, or how would it add to their vices, their ignorance, or " squalid poverty," if we suppose another island at a few leagues distance, of about the same circumference, maintaining nearly the same number of inhabitants living in the same manner ? Yet as it is probable that even these poor lousy wretches* leading a life of sloth

---

* I here follow the text of Mr. Malthus, who takes great pains to give a striking description of the savage tribes, as a pleasing contrast, no doubt, to the elegancies and comforts of polished life. Mr. Malthus's extreme sensibility to the grossness and inconveniences of the savage state, may be construed into refinement and delicacy. But it does not strike me so. There is something in this mis-placed and selfish fastidiousness, that shocks me more than the objects of it. It does not lead to compassion but to hatred. We strive to get rid of our uneasiness, by hardening ourselves towards the objects which occasion it, and lose the passive feelings of disgust excited in us by others in the active desire to inflict pain upon them. Aversion too easily changes into malice. Mr. Malthus seems fond of indulging this feeling against all those who have not the same advantages as himself. With a pious gratitude he seems fond of repeating to himself, " I am not as this poor Hottentot." He then gives you his bill of fare, which is none of the most delicate, without omitting a

and hunger, may upon the whole have more enjoyment than misery (for even the life of a savage seems better than no life at all, nay some have gone so far as to say that it was better than any .other life) it would be desirable that there should be such another island so inhabited. But it is exactly the same thing whether we suppose twice the number of people inhabiting twice the extent of ground, or maintained on the same ground, being twice as much cultivated; popu-

---

single article, and by shrugging up his shoulders, making wry mouths at him, and fairly turning your stomach, excites in you the same loathing and abhorrence of this poor creature, that he takes delight in feeling himself. "Your very nice people have the nastiest imaginations." He triumphs over the calamities and degradation of his fellow-creatures. He lays open all the sores and blotches of humanity with the same calmness and alacrity as a hospital surgeon does those of a diseased body. He turns the world into a charnel-house. Through a dreary space of 300 " chill and comfortless" pages, he ransacks all quarters of the globe only " to present a speaking picture of " hunger and nakedness, in quest of objects best suited to his " feelings, in anxious search of calamities most akin to his " *invalid* imagination," and eagerly gropes into every hole and corner of wretchedness to collect evidence in support of his grand misery-scheme, as at the time of an election, you see the city-candidates sneaking into the dirty alleys, and putrid cellars of Shoreditch or Whitechapel, and the candidates for Westminster into those of St. Giles's, canvassing for votes, their patriotic zeal prevailing over their sense of dignity, and sense of smell.

lation would not press the more on the means of subsistence, nor would the misery be greater, nor the checks required to prevent it greater. That is to say, an advance made in the state of cultivation and in the arts of life so as to maintain double the population must always be the means of doubling the numbers and enjoyment of any people. The only possible difference would be that as this increased population would be the consequence of greater industry and knowledge, it would, one should think, denote of itself, that the people would be less liable to unforeseen accidents, and less likely to involve themselves in wilful distress than before. This is the first step in the progress of civilization and in the history of all nations. From this description of a barren island supporting a few wandering half-starved ignorant savages, such as England might have been once, let us turn our eyes to what England is now;—populous, enlightened, free, rich, powerful and happy; excelling equally in arts, and arms, the delight and terror of the rest of the world; the abode of science, the nurse of virtue, the darling seat of the muses; boasting her long line of heroes, and sages; her Bacon, her Newton, her Shakespear, her Milton, and

her Locke ;* blest with the most perfect government administered in the most perfect
manner ; having a king, lords, and commons,
each balancing the other, and each in their
several station and degree being security for
every kind of liberty and every kind of property, harmoniously conspiring together for
the good of the whole, taking care first of
their own rights and interests as the most
important, and then of those of others : subject to mild and equal laws, which afford
the same immediate protection to every one
in the enjoyment of his liberty and his property, whether that property is five thousand a year or no more than a shilling a
day : maintaining in different degrees of
comfort, and affluence, from the common necessaries to the highest luxuries of life, ten
millions of souls, all supported by their own
labour and industry or that of others ; all
plying close with cheerful and patient activity to some ingenious and useful handi-
craft, or some more severe but necessary
labour, or else reclining in ease and ele-
gance, and basking in the sunshine of life ;

* I mention these names because it is always customary to
mention them in speaking on this subject : and there are some
readers who are more impressed with a thing, the oftener it is
repeated.

her meanest beggar owing the rags which
cover his nakedness, and the crust of bread
which keeps his body and soul together to
some of the most useful inventions which
support, and to that humanity which is only
to be found in civilized society. Shall we
forget her schools, her colleges, her hospi-
tals, her churches, her crowded cities, her
streets lined with shops, enriched with the
produce and manufactures of her own soil,
or glittering with the spoils of a hundred
nations, her thronged assemblies, her thea-
tres, her balls, her operas, her " palaces, her
" ladies and her pomp ;" her villas, her parks,
her cottages, her hamlets, her rich cultivated
lands, teeming with plenty, her green valleys,
her " upland swells, echoing to the bleat of
" flocks," her brave contented peasantry, their
simple manners and honest integrity ; and shall
we wish to degrade this queen of nations, this
mistress of the world once more into a horde
of fierce barbarians, treading back our steps,
and resigning this splendid profusion of all that
can adorn and gladden human life, this gay
variety, this happy union of all that is useful
and all that is ornamental, the refinements of
taste and decorations of fashion, the beautiful
distinctions of artificial society, and the solid
advantages derived from our constitution in

church and state, for the groveling dispositions, the brutal ignorance, the disgusting poverty, the dried skins and miserable huts of
the inhabitants of Terra del Fuego, or New
Holland ? Yet this it seems from the doctrine
of Mr. Malthus is our only safe policy, since the
lower we are in the scale of existence, the
fewer and more miserable we are, the farther
removed we must be from the tremendous
evils of excessive population, which are the
necessary consequences of the progress of refinement and civilization. But as the fact *so far*
does not, as I suppose Mr. Malthus will himself
allow, square with his theory, (for at no time
during the progress of cultivation does the population appear to have been pressing with en-
creased force on the means of subsistence,
so that though the produce of the earth was
increasing every year, the inhabitants were increasing much faster, every addition to the
actual produce only occasioning some new addition to the swoln and bloated state of
population, and aggravating the already dreadful symptoms of the disease) as I say the
progress of cultivation and improvement of
different kinds has not produced any of those
fatal consequences we might be led to expect
from it, so neither do I apprehend any of these
fatal consequences in future from carrying it as

much farther as it can go. I should just re-verse the reasoning of Mr. Malthus, who taking the evil as at its greatest height when the world is supposed to be completely full and com-pletely enlightened, thence argues downwards against all attempts at improvement as dan-gerous innovations ; so I, finding that an im-proved cultivation and enlarged population are good things through the inferior gradations, am apt to think they would continue so, proceeding upwards to the topmost round of the ladder, as far as population is concerned, for I once more give full and fair warning that I engage in this question no farther, any loose, general or acci-dental expressions to the contrary notwith-standing. To make good Mr. Malthus's argu-ment against population, we must suppose, as I have said before, that the tendency in popula-tion to increase goes on increasing with the thing itself: this would be true, if as our author supposes in his first edition, the passion always re-quired the same vent, in all circumstances, that is if we suppose man to be a mere headstrong animal in this respect, his reason having no in-fluence whatever over his conduct, or which amounts to the same thing, that *actual* vice and misery (not foreseen, but felt) are the only checks to population. At this rate, it is evi-dent that the degree of misery attending the

gratification of the passion would have no effect
to restrain it, all degrees being alike indifferent
or that the quantity of actual misery incurred
would be in proportion to the increased power
of producing it. I shall examine these positions
more at large in another letter; I here wish to
shew in a few words that as applied to the
subject of increasing population, they lead to a
direct absurdity. If we suppose this passion
to be perfectly blind and insensible, to be deaf
to all remonstrance, and regardless of all consequences, then no matter in what depths of
misery it involves us, it will have its way, and
go its own lengths. Take away the preventive
check of *moral restraint* (which only comes in as
a snivelling interpolation in some places of the
second edition) and the population would no
doubt go on doubling as fast as it could, not as
fast as the means of subsistence would let it;
that is, the excess of population would be great
in proportion to the actual previous increase,
or the excessive multiplication of the species
would be the necessary consequence of, and
commensurate with the power of excessive
multiplication, which would depend on the
number of persons having that power. Now
this is contrary to all we know of facts and
human nature, since in this case there could be
no restraint to population at any time, but the

extreme of vice or the extreme of misery. The power of population to increase is (we will grant) unlimited, but the tendency to increase is necessarily limited by its tendency to excess, and limited by it in proportion to the excess. That is to say, it does not follow that though when there ought to be only two millions of in- habitants, there may be four, owing to the weak- ness of the above-mentioned principle of *moral restraint*, that therefore that four (by the ten- dency of population to increase in a geome- trical ratio or to double itself,) will in like manner become eight, and so on, namely because the checks to it will increase in proportion ; or though the prospect of the inconveniences arising from doubling the population in the first instance, the quantity of food remaining the same, might not be sufficient to deter people, or overcome this propensity, yet the prospect of famine consequent upon the second doubling undoubtedly would, because their regard to consequences is supposed to remain the same, and the evils they have to dread in the one case are greater, and unless we suppose them to have become more stupid and brutal, must operate upon them more forcibly than in the other. The strength of the passion itself may be con- sidered as always the same, or a given quantity: but the motives to resist it arising from the consequences of its indulgence are not always the same, but may be either none at all, or very slight, or considerable, or extreme, as the obstacles to its indulgence may be either none at all, or a trifling inconvenience, or poverty, or absolute famine. Now the degree of excess in population, or the inconveniences to which we expose ourselves by inconsiderate gratification will depend entirely on the difference, be it more or less, between the strength of the passion in each individual, and the strength of moral restraint. If the latter principle is weak, it will require to be stimulated by the immediate apprehension of some very great inconvenience, before it will become a match for the importunity of physical desire. If it is strong, a general conviction of the propriety or prudence of self-denial will be sufficient to incline the balance. But in no case unless we suppose man to be degraded to the condition of the brutes, will this principle be so low and weak as to have no effect at all, so that no apprehension of the last degree of wretchedness, as the consequence, would take off or abate the edge of appetite. There is therefore always a point at which the excess ceases, and we have seen what this point at all times is. Thus if the operation of rational motives is so much upon a level with the physical impulse, as to keep population exactly or nearly down to the means of subsistence, it will do so equally whether that population is actually greater or less, whether it is stationary or progressive, for it will increase only with the means by which it is supported. On the other hand if from the manners, the habits, and institutions of society, there is a considerable tendency in population to excess, this tendency to excess will not be greater or less in proportion to the actual number of inhabitants, or the actual quantity of food, nor will it depend on their being progressive or stationary, but on the morals of the people being retrograde, progressive, or stationary ; for the tendency of population itself to excess or to *increase* excessively (a dubious kind of expression) is not a perpetual, indefinite, invariable tendency to increase from 2 to 4, from 4 to 8, &c. (as I have just shewn) but a tendency to increase *beyond* the means of subsistence to a certain point or degree. This tendency to excess will consequently be the same wherever we fix the point of subsistence, because it is only a given tendency to outstrip that limit whether nearer or farther off, whether advancing or retreating.* It is true there is a

---

* I here leave out of the question, as not essential to it, the effect of sudden rises or falls, and other accidental variations in the produce of a country which cannot be foreseen or provided against, on the state of population.

tendency in population in this case to increase *faster* than the means of subsistence, but not to increase *faster and faster* or to get more and more a head of it. It is in fact only a disproportionate superiority in certain motives over others, which subjects the community or certain classes of it to a great degree of want and hardship : and as far as their imprudence and folly will carry them, they will go, but they will not go farther. They will submit to be *pinched*, but not to be *starved*, unless this con-sequence may sometimes be supposed to follow from the partial and unnatural debasement of certain classes of the community, by driving them to despair and rendering them callous to suffering. But the general tendency in popu-lation to become excessive can only be increased by the increased relaxation of moral restraint, or by gradually weakening the motives of pru-dence, reason, &c. I cannot make this matter plainer.

Mr. Malthus has not I conceive given this question of increasing population and practical improvement fair play. He has contrived to cover over its real face and genuine features with the terrible mask of modern philosophy. His readers having been prevailed upon to give up the fee-simple of their understandings into his

hands, that no undue advantages might be taken
of them by the *perfectibility* school, they find
it difficult to get it back out of his hands,
though they want it to go on again (the alarm
being over) in the old road of common sense,
practical improvement, and liberal discussion.
He had persuaded himself that population was
such an enormous evil in connection with a
scheme of unlimited improvement, that he can
hardly reconcile himself to it, or tell whether to
think it a good or an evil in any shape, or according to any scheme. By indulging his prejudices, he has so confounded his perceptions,
that he cannot judge rightly, even when he
wishes to do it. He found it most convenient,
when he had to confute Mr. Godwin, to describe
reason as a principle of no practical value whatever, as a mere negation. As therefore by the
removal of vice and misery the office of checking population would devolve upon this principle, which could do nothing, population would
in fact have no check left to it, and then certainly the most terrible consequences would ensue. The only question would be, how soon we
should begin cutting one another's throats, or
how many (whether a greater or a smaller number) had better be employed on this kind of
work. We perceive very plainly that this must
be the inevitable consequence of increased

population, if it can only be kept down by the positive checks of vice and misery. We apply the theory very clearly to a future stage of the progress ; but though, if the theory were true, exactly the same scenes ought to be acting before our eyes at present on a smaller scale, yet as we find that this is not the case, we leave this circumstance out of the question, and conclude that there must be some secret difference, some occult cause, something we cannot very well explain, which makes the present state of things preferable to all others : at least whatever might be the consequences of population, if certain alterations and improvements were to take place, we are sure that it produces no such consequences at present. With respect to the lower, or actual stages of population and improvement, Mr. Malthus supposes the *preventive* checks to operate as well as the *positive*, the fear of misery as well as the misery itself, because we know that it does : but whenever you suppose any alteration or improvement to take place in the world, so that you have not the fact to confront him with, he immediately assumes the positive checks, or actual vice and misery, as the only checks to population ; herein trusting to his theory. Whenever you are found to be advancing in the scale (which must be indeed from some of the restraints being taken off) he directly supposes that you are to be set free from all restraints whatever. He lets loose his ratios upon you, and away they go like a clock running down. This indeed would not be so well. Mr. Malthus thus artfully makes the question of progressive improvement to be, whether we are to be governed as now by mixed motives, or to be released from all moral restraint, for he supposes that if population once passes a certain bourne, which he points out to you, it will then become perfectly untractable, all its future excesses will be prevented only by actual vice and misery. Thus though all the good of our present situation, all wherein it differs from a state of brutal violence or lingering want, is in fact owing to the prevalence of a less degree of reason and foresight, yet that if that principle were strengthened, and the consequence were an increase of population, and a more general diffusion of the comforts of life, this principle would then be of no avail in preventing or correcting the excesses to which the unrestrained indulgence of our appetites would give rise. There is a degree of absurdity, which staggers belief and almost challenges our conviction, by making it incredible that if we ourselves do not labour under some strong deception, the human

understanding should be capable of such extreme folly.

I shall conclude this letter by laying down
two or three general maxims, which appear to
me to follow clearly from the view which has
been here taken of the subject.

First, while population goes on increasing at
that tremendous rate described by Mr. Malthus, it shews that there is nothing to restrain
it; that there is no need of any thing to restrain
it : that it is wanted, that its increase is a thing
to be desired, not to be dreaded, and that if it
were possible for it to increase ten times faster,
it would be so much the better.

Secondly, when it arrives at a certain point,
that is, where the population begins to press on
the means of subsistence, either from natural or
artificial causes, or when it threatens to become
an evil from excess, it naturally stops short of
its own accord, the checks to it from vice,
misery and moral restraint taken all together
becoming stronger as the excess becomes
greater. It therefore produces it's own antidote
and produces it in quantities exactly in proportion to it's own extent. It is not therefore (as
Mr. Malthus would, when he pleases, have us

believe) like a stone hanging suspended over a
precipice, which if it once loses its balance will
be hurled furiously down, rolling and bounding
from steep to steep with increased velocity till
it reaches the bottom, but like a balance suspended by a check-weight, where you cannot
increase the pressure on one side without increasing the resistance proportionably on the
other. It may therefore at worst be left very
safely to itself, instead of being considered as
an evil against whose unforeseen ravages no precautions are sufficient.

Thirdly, as the same quantity of vice and
misery co-operating with the same degree of
moral restraint, will always keep population at
the same (relative) point, so a less degree of
actual vice and misery operating on a greater
degree of moral restraint, that is, of reason,
prudence, virtue, &c. will produce the same
effect: and we may always judge of the happiness of a people, and of the beneficial effects of
population by the prevalence of moral restraint
over vice and misery, instead of supposing that
vice and misery are the best pledges of the happiness of a state, and the only possible security
against excessive population. Consequently,
the object of the philosopher must be to
increase the influence of rational motives, and

lessen the actual operation of vice and misery.
It is only in proportion as he does this, that he
does any thing ; for not only are vice and misery
such cheap commodities that they may be had
at any corner merely with asking for (any
bungler may contract for them in the gross) but
farther though they undoubtedly operate as
checks to population, I must be excused from
admitting that they *remedy* the evils of population, unless the disease can be considered as its
own remedy, for in the degree in which they
generally exist, they are the only evils, that are
ever likely to arise from it, and as to those
imaginary, unknown and unheard of evils, with
which Mr. Malthus is perpetually threatening
us in order to reconcile us to those we bear, I
deny the possibility of their existence upon any
known principles of human society, either in its
improved, or unimproved state.

I do not mean to say that there is any thing
in the general principles here stated that Mr.
Malthus is at present disposed to deny, or that
he has not himself expressly insisted on in some
part or other of his *various* work ; it is enough
for my purpose that there are other parts of his
work in which he has contradicted them and
himself, and that the uniform tenor of his first
work leans directly the opposite way ; and it is

not my business so much to inquire, how much Mr. Malthus retains of his old philosophy, as how many of their old feelings his readers retain on the subject, on which he will be able to build as many false conclusions as he pleases, and with more safety to himself, than if he still persevered in the direct and unqualified assertion of exploded error. Plain, downright consistent falsehood is not dangerous : it is only that spurious mixture of truth and falsehood, that perpetual oscillation between the two extremes, that wavering and uncertainty that baffles detection by rendering it difficult to know on what ground you are to meet your adversary, that makes the sophist so formidable as he is. In order therefore that Mr. Malthus may not avail himself of his inconsistencies, I shall assume a right to contradict him as often as he contradicts himself, and to consider the peculiar doctrines of his work as its essential and only important doctrines.

LETTER V.

WHETHER VICE AND MISERY ARE THE NECESSARY CON-
SEQUENCES OF, AND THE ONLY CHECKS TO, THE PRIN-
CIPLE OF POPULATION.

Sir,

I have in my last letter taken more pains than,
I believe, was necessary to shew that the tendency of population to increase is not a *dangerous* one; or at any rate that the actual increase of population does not increase the danger. The same proportionable quantity of vice
and misery would always be *sufficient* to keep
down the excess of population beyond the
means of subsistence, whether we suppose
those means to be great or small: there is another question, whether the same quantity of
vice and misery is always *necessary* for this
purpose; and further, whether all the vice and
misery in the world are not only necessary
checks to, but the immediate effects of, the
principle of population, and of nothing else.

Before I proceed, I must stop to observe that
I have just been perusing the corrections, additions, &c. to the third and *last* edition of the
Essay ; and I confess I have not much heart to
go on. The pen falls from my hand. For to
what purpose is it to answer a man, who has
answered himself, who has hardly advanced an
opinion that he has not retracted, who after
all your pains to overturn the extravagant assertions he had brought forward, comes and tells
you, Why I have given them up myself; so
that you hardly know whether to look upon
him in the light of an adversary or an ally. I
do not like this shadow-fighting, any more
than Sancho liked his master's fighting with
enchanters. When Don Quixote had to en-
counter the knight of the Prodigious Nose, his
valour was inflamed, and he rushed fiercely on
his antagonist, but when after having unhorsed
him, he found that it was his old friend and
neighbour the Batchelor Carrasco, the fury of
his arm was suspended, and he knew not what
to say or do.* Till Mr. Malthus lays aside his
harlequin's coat and sword, and ceases to chase
opinions through a rapid succession of varying
editions, it is not an easy matter to come up

* I find there is here some transposition of names and circumstances, but it does not much matter.

with him or give him fair battle. It was thought a work of no small labour and inge-nuity to make a harmony of the Evangelists. I would recommend it to some one (who thinks himself equal to the task) to make a harmony of Mr. Malthus's different performances. Till this is done, it seems impossible to collect the sense of his writings, and consequently to answer them. It should not therefore be the object of any one who would set himself to answer Mr. Malthus, so much to say that such and such are the real and settled opinions of that author, as that such opinions are floating in different parts of his writings, that they are floating or fixed in the minds of his readers, and that those opinions are not so correct as they might be. If Mr. Malthus had chosen to disclaim certain opinions with their conse-quences, advanced in the first edition, instead of denying that he ever held such opinions, though he may still be detected with the *maner*, he would have saved me the trouble of writing, and himself the disagreeable task of reading, this *rude* attack upon them.

Mr. Malthus lays down as the basis of all his reasonings the two following positions, viz. " First, that food is necessary to the existence " of man."

" Secondly, That the passion between the " sexes is necessary, and will remain nearly in " its present state."

" These two laws," he adds, " ever since we " have had any knowledge of mankind, appear " to have been fixed laws of our nature ; and " as we have not hitherto seen any alteration in " them, we have no right to conclude that they " will ever cease to be what they are now, " without an immediate act of power in that '' Being who first arranged the system of the " universe. The best arguments for the perfec- " tibility of man are drawn from a contemplation " of the great progress that he has already made " from the savage state, and the difficulty of " saying where he is to stop. But towards the " extinction of the passion between the sexes, " no progress whatever has hitherto been made. " It appears to exist in as much force at present " as it did two thousand, or four thousand " years ago. There are individual exceptions " now as there always have been. But, as these " exceptions do not appear to increase in num- " ber, it would surely be a very unphilosophical " mode of arguing to infer merely from the " existence of an exception, that the exception " would in time become the rule, and the rule " the exception."

As to the first position here laid down that food is necessary to the existence of man, I shall not certainly dispute it. As to the second kind of necessity, the gratification of the passion between the sexes, I must beg leave to deny that this necessity is " like unto the first" or to be compared with it. Does Mr. Malthus really mean to say that a man can no more abstain from the commerce of women, than he can live without food ? If so, he states what is not the fact. Does he mean to assert, that the impulse to propagate the species, call it lust, or love, is a principle as strong, as ungovernable, as importunate, as uniform in its effects, as incapable of being subjected to the control of reason, or circumstances, in short as much an affair of mere physical appetite, as hunger ? One would suppose so, for he makes no distinction between them, but speaks of them both in the same terms, as equally *necessary*, as equally fixed, and immutable laws of our nature, the operation of which nothing short of a miracle can suspend or alter. There are two circumstances, the mentioning of which will however be sufficient to shew that the two kinds of necessity here spoken of are not of the same order, or cogency, and cannot be reasoned upon in the same manner, namely, that there are many instances of persons who have lived all their lives without any intercouse with the other sex, whereas there is no instance of any person living without food; in the second place, what makes a most marked distinction between the two cases, is that the longer we have been accustomed to do without the indulgence of the one appetite, the more tractable we find it, whereas the craving occasioned by the want of food, the longer it continues, becomes more and more pressing, and at last utterly ungovernable, and if not satisfied in time, is sure in all cases whatever, without a single exception, to destroy the person's life. These two considerations are of themselves quite sufficient to overturn the analogy which is here pretended to be set up between love and hunger (a delicate comparison)—to shew that the first of these impulses is not an affair of mere physical necessity, that it does not operate always in the same way, and that it is not a thing, over which reason, or circumstances have no power. What can be a stronger instance of the power of reason, or imagination, or habit over this principle than the number of single women, who in every country, till the manners become quite corrupt, preserve either through their whole lives, or the best part of them the greatest purity and propriety of conduct ? One would think that female modesty had been a flower that blossomed only in other climes (instead of being the peculiar growth of our own time and country!) that Mr. Malthus in the heat of his argument, and urged on by the ardour of his own feelings, is blind to the example of so many of his fair countrywomen, in whom the influence of a virtuous education, of virtuous principles, and virtuous dispositions prevails over the warmth of the passions and force of temptation. Mr. Malthus's doctrine is a most severe satire against the modesty and self-denial of the other sex, and ruins in one sweeping clause the unblemished reputations of all those expecting or desponding virgins who had hitherto been supposed to live in the daily, hourly practice of this virtue. Trenched as he is behind history, philosophy, and a knowledge of human nature, he laughs at all their prudery and affectation, and tells them fairly that the thing is impossible ; and that unless a miracle could be worked in their favour, they might as well pretend to live without eating or drinking, or sleeping as without the men. He must be of opinion with Iago, that " their greatest merit is " not to leave it undone but keep it unknown." Surely, *no maid could live near such a man,*— Though this is what Mr. Malthus *might* say, it is not what he *does* say : on the other hand, when he comes to particulars, (as he is rather a candid man, and does not trouble himself much about consistency) instead of representing real chastity as a kind of miracle or monster in nature, he represents it as a very common thing and bears honourable testimony to the virtue of most women, particularly in the middle and higher ranks of life, in this respect. But then this virtue is confined entirely to the women ; the men neither do, nor ever will be able to practise it; and this again salves the objection to his argument. But this is of all others the strongest proof of the futility of Mr. Malthus's reasoning : for to what is this difference owing but to the opinion of the world respecting their conduct, that is, to moral causes ? It cannot be said I presume that the greater command which the other sex have over themselves is because their heads are stronger and their passions weaker, (this would, I am sure, be out of all anatomical proportion) : it is owing solely to the institutions of society, imposing this restraint upon them ; though these institutions, if we are to believe Mr. Malthus, can never in any circumstances whatever have any effect on this passion. It is impossible to add any thing to the force and conclusiveness of this argument by enlarging upon it : it speaks for itself. I can only say, that I am willing to rest the whole controversy on this single fact. If the passion is thus capable of being modified and influenced by circumstances, opinion, and manners, and not merely slightly modified, or for a short time, in one or two solitary instances, as an exception to the general rule (though even this would shew that the necessity is not absolute, invincible, fatal) but actually kept under (as far as it has any thing to do with population, or child-bearing) by one half the sex in every well-regulated community, I conceive Mr. Malthus can only be justified in saying, that no possible circumstances will ever render this passion entirely subject to the control of reason, by saying that no circumstances will ever arrive in which it would be the imperious and indispensable duty of every one to habituate himself to such restraint, in which that necessity would be generally felt and understood and enforced by the opinion of the whole community, and in which nothing but a general system of manners formed upon that opinion could save the community from ruin, or from the evils of excessive population, which is point-blank contrary to Mr. Malthus's whole doctrine. In short, Mr. Malthus's whole book rests on a malicious supposition, that all mankind (I hope the reader will pardon the grossness of the expression, the subject is a gross one) are like so many animals *in season*. " Were they as " prime as goats, as hot as monkeys, as salt as

" wolves in pride, and fools as gross as ignorance
" made drunk," matters could then be no worse
than he represents them. Population could then
only be checked by vice and misery and by nothing
else. But I hope things are not quite so bad.*
Mr. Malthus says, " that the passion between
" the sexes is necessary, or at least that it
" will remain nearly in its present state." To
this I might perhaps assent, if I knew what
" its present state" is. Does Mr. Malthus
mean by its present state its present state in
England or in Scotland, or in Italy, or in Asia,
or in Africa, or America, for in all or most of
these places is its present state a very different
thing from what it is in the rest of them ? One
would imagine from the easy complacency
with which Mr. Malthus treats the subject, that
the present state of this passion was a something really given, a fixed quantity, a general
rule like the relation between two and two and
four, or *between food and the human stomach*,†

* I am happy to find that a philosophical work, like Mr.
Malthus's, has got a good deal into the hands of young ladies
of a liberal education and an inquisitive turn of mind. The
question is no doubt highly interesting ; and the author has
thrown over it a warmth of colouring, that can hardly fail to
please. Even Miss Howe was fond of ardours.

† I have here purposely left an opening for Mr. Malthus's ingenuity. He will I hope take the hint and write another quarto
volume to prove by anatomical and medical inquiries into the
state of all countries, beginning at the north and ending at the

that it was indulged universally and equally in all countries, instead of being as various in itself and its effects as climate and all other causes, natural and artificial, can make it.— Thus to give an example as much in point as can be, is the present state of this passion, *i. e.* of the indulgence of it, the same in Lancashire, that it is in Westmoreland, the very next county to it? In the one you find the most profligate manners, and the most extreme licentiousness, in the other there is hardly any such thing. Mr. Malthus often says, he will never dispute any thing that is proved by experience and a real observation of human life. Now I conceive that the observation which I have just stated is a *fact*. Yet Mr. Malthus seems to have been quite insensible to this, and many other facts of the same kind. But the truth is, that your practical reasoners, your matter-of-fact men are the dullest of all mortals. They are like justices of the peace who are bound to receive no evidence unless it is given in upon oath, and who without descending from the bench and forfeiting the dignity of their pretensions cannot attend to any of those general

---

south pole, that there is the same variation in the quantity and kind of food required by the human stomach in different climates and countries, as there is in the quantity of sexual indulgence.

surmises, those obvious sources of information
or casual impressions, by which other people arrive at common sense, and human feelings.—
They shut their eyes to the general face of nature, and trying to grope their way by the help
of facts as they call them, wander like blind
men from *pillar to post*, without either guide or
object, and are lost in a labyrinth of dates,
names, capital letters, numeros, official docu-
ments, authenticated copies of lying affidavits,
curious records that are nothing to the purpose, registers of births, deaths, marriages, and
christenings, voyages and travels.—Mr. Malthus
may perhaps mean, when he says that " the
" sexual passion will remain nearly in its pre-
" sent state," that it will remain in the same
state in each country. To this I should also
assent, if I could agree with him, " that ever
" since we have had any knowledge of mankind,
" the passion of which we are speaking, ap-
" pears to have been a fixed law of our nature, and
" that as we have not hitherto seen any al-
" teration in it, we have no right to conclude
" that there will ever be any." If Mr. Malthus
in this passage meant to confine him to the
passion or impulse itself, I should not certainly
be at much pains to contradict him. But that
is not the question. The question relates solely
to the irregular indulgence of, or the degree of

restraint imposed on the passion ; and in this respect his assertion is evidently false. The difference in the state of manners in the same country at different periods is as striking and notorious as that between the manners of different countries. There is as much difference between what England was in this respect a hundred and sixty years ago, and what she is now, as there is between England and Italy at the present day. Was there no difference between the manners of ancient Rome in the early periods of her history, and towards the decline of the empire? May not the state of manners in Italy under the republic, under the emperors, and under the popes, be distinctly traced to the influence of religious or political institutions, or to other causes, besides the state of population, or the facility of gratifying the abstract instinctive propensity to sexual indulgence? Was there not a striking difference between the severity and restraint which was required and undoubtedly practised under Charles I. and in the time of the Puritans, and that torrent of dissipation and undisguised profligacy which burst upon the kingdom after the restoration of Charles II.? This sudden transition from demure and saint-like or hypocritical austerity to open shameless licentiousness cannot assuredly be accounted for from the increasing pressure of population. Nor can it be pretended to have been owing to this principle that the tide afterwards turned again at the Revolution with the habits and fashions of the court, and with the views and maxims of that party who had now got the ascendancy. A learned writer might easily fill a volume with instances to the same purpose. But the few which are here skimmed from the mere surface of history, and which must be familiar to every one, are sufficient to disprove Mr. Malthus's assertion, not as a metaphysical refinement, but as a practical rule, that the passion between the sexes and the effects of that passion have remained always the same. The indulgence of that passion is so far from being a law antecedent to all other laws, and paramount to all other considerations, that it is in a manner governed almost entirely by circumstances, and may be said to be the creature of the imagination. But Mr. Malthus says, that no regular or gradual progress has hitherto been made towards the extinction of this passion, and that it exists in as much force at present, as it did two thousand, or four thousand years ago. The question is whether this passion is fixed and stationary, always remaining at the same point, controuling circumstances, but not controuled by them, not whether the change of circumstances and lapse of time may not bring it back to the same point again. I think it probable that if Mr. Malthus had to preach a sermon on the truth and excellence of revealed religion, he would be inclined to take for one of his topics the benefit we have derived from it in the government of our passions, and general purity of our manners. He might launch out into a description shewing how the contemplation of heavenly things weans the affections from the things of the world, and mortifies our carnal desires, how a belief in future rewards and punishments strengthens our resolution, and is indeed the only thing that can render us proof against every species of temptation ; he might enlarge on the general purity and elevation which breathes through the sacred writings, on the law confining the institution of marriage to pairs ; he might dwell on the grossness and pernicious tendency of the Pagan mythology ; he might glance at the epistle to the Romans, or the preamble to the Jewish laws, and finding that the practices there described are not common among *us*, without travelling to Rome, or inquiring into the present state of Chaldæa, conclude by felicitating his hearers on the striking contrast between ancient and modern manners, and on the gradual improvement of morals and refinement of sentiment produced by the promulgation of christianity. Though we in general reason very incorrectly in comparing ancient and modern manners, (for we always confound the former with eastern, and the latter with our own manners) I am apt to think that some change has taken place in this passion in the course of time. It seems to be more modified by other feelings than it used to be ; it is less a boiling of the blood, an animal heat, a headlong, brutal impulse than it was in past ages. The principle is somewhat taken down and weakened, the appetite is not so strong, we can stay our stomachs better than we used to do, we do not gorge indiscriminately on every kind of food without taste or decency. The vices of the moderns are more artificial than constitutional. They do not arise so much from instinct as from a depraved will. The spirit is willing, but the flesh is weak. We stimulate ourselves into affected passion : we are laborious imitators of folly, and ape the vices of others in cold blood. But whatever may be the result of an inquiry into the comparative state of ancient and modern manners, I cannot allow that it has any thing to do with the present question. I will allow that the progress of refinement and knowledge has in ninety-nine instances out of a hundred tended to deprave instead of improving the morals of men, that at the same time that it has taken away the gross impulse, it has introduced an artificial and studied depravity, the operation of which is more subtle, dangerous and universal ; in short that nations as they grow older like individuals grow worse, not from constitution, but habit. Still this fact if granted (and I am afraid it is too near the truth) will not at all prove Mr. Malthus's theory, that this passion remains always the same, being influenced neither by time nor circumstances. Secondly, it will not overturn the speculations respecting the possibility of making an entire change in the passion " in a state of society altogether different from " any that has hitherto existed," but will on the contrary render such a change more desirable and necessary, as our only resource against the general contagion of vice and profligacy. If this vice is found to spread gradually wider and wider, clinging to the support of institutions, which in all other respects favour selfishness and sensuality, if it is not the only one among the vices, which, while all others spread and flourish and are fostered in the eye of the world, does not hide its diminished head, this is not to be wondered at. But it would be a singular way of defending the present institutions of society, that from all our past experience we find that their progress has been attended with the gradual corruption of manners, and has uniformly ended in an utter debasement of character and the relaxation of every moral tie ; and it would be a strange kind of inference to say that no alteration in the circumstances or institutions of society would ever make men different from what they are, because as long as those circumstances and institutions have been known to exist, mankind have remained always the same, or have been growing worse instead of better. Mr. Malthus denies that Mr. Godwin has any right to conclude that because population has not produced the dreadful effects he ascribes to it in any known state of society, it would not therefore produce them in a state of society quite different from any other ; and in the same manner I should deny that Mr. Malthus has any right to infer because the progress of the human mind has not in the past history of the world been productive of any very beneficial consequences, that it will never be productive of any such consequences under very different circumstances. Knowledge, as I have shewn in a former letter, is not a necessary, absolute good : neither is it a necessary evil. Its utility depends on the direction which is given to it by other things ; e. g. in Scotland, the case before alluded to, knowledge does not seem to be the enemy of sobriety and good manners, but a support to them. The decay in the purity and simplicity of Scotch manners, whenever it arrives, will not I dare say be owing to the increase of knowledge, but to the spread of luxury, or other external causes. When the whole mass is tainted, it cannot be expected that knowledge should escape the infection. All therefore that the advocates for the future progressive improvement of mankind have to prove in order to make out a consistent case, is that the state of the passion between the sexes depends not upon physical, but moral causes ; that where these latter causes have been favourable to severity of manners, and the elevation of the character, these effects have uniformly flowed from them, and may be seen not in one or two singular exceptions, but in large classes of people, in the prevailing manners of whole ages and nations. Thus we do not merely know that Scipio was chaste, and Nero profligate, but we know that there was nothing singular in the chastity of the one, or the profligacy of the other; it was little more than the emanation of the character and circumstances of the times in which they lived. The leaders of the republican party in the time of Cromwell, such men as Milton, Hampden, Pym, Marvel, Sydney, were not I believe in the command over their passions exactly on a level

with the young courtiers in the following reign :
but though the names of these men stand out
and ever will stand out in history, giving dignity
to our nature in all its parts, yet it is not to be
supposed that they alone drank of the pure
waters of faith and reason, which flowed freely
at that time ; but that the same lofty thoughts,
the same common exertions, and the same passions, growing out of the circumstances of the
times, must have imparted a sort of severe and
high-toned morality to men's minds in general,
influencing the national character in a very
different way from the foreign fopperies and
foreign vices, from the train of strumpets,
buffoons, fiddlers, and obscene rhymers let loose
upon the people in the succeeding reign. It is not
necessary to prove that manners have always
changed for the better, but that they have
always changed for the better, as far as those
general causes have operated in part, from the
complete success of which a total change is
predicted. This passion as it runs into licentiousness is certainly one great obstacle in the
way of improvement, and one of those passions
which we must conquer before we can hope to
become perfectly reasonable beings (if this is a
thing either desirable or possible). But to
say, that we may get a complete mastery
over our passions, and that we shall still

be in danger from the principle of population is to me a paradox. Population is only dangerous from the excess of this passion, and I see no reason why its excesses may not be restrained as well as those of any other passion. We find by uniform experience that it is, like other passions, influenced by example, institution, and circumstances, according to the degree of strength they have; and if there is reason to suppose it possible that any of the other passions should ever be totally eradicated, or subjected to moral restraint, there is no reason why this should not be so too. It does not form any anomaly to the other prevailing passions of men. It is not, like hunger, a necessary instinct. Its effects are more like those of drunkenness: and we might as well make this latter vice an insurmountable objection to the good order and happiness of society, by saying that there will always be as many drunken disputes, brawls and riots, as there are at present, because there are as many instances of people getting drunk now as there were two thousand years ago, as pretend to deduce the same consequence from the existence of such a passion as lust.—To judge from his book, I should suppose Mr. Malthus to be a man of a warm constitution, and amorous complexion. I should not hesitate in my own mind, to con-

clude that this is " the sin that most easily
" besets him." I can easily imagine that he
has a sufficient command over himself, in all
other respects. I can believe that he is quite
free from the passions of anger, pride, avarice,
sloth, drunkenness, envy, revenge, and all those
other passions which create so much disturbance
in the world. He seems never to have heard
of, or never to have felt them ; for he passes
them over as trifles beneath the notice of a
philosopher. But the women are *the devil*.—
The delights and torments of love no man, he
tells us, ever was proof against : there all our
philosophy is useless ; and reason but an empty
name. " The rich golden shaft hath killed the
" flock of all affections else," and here only he
is vulnerable. The smiles of a fair lady are to
him irresistible ; the glimpse of a petticoat
throws him into a flame ; and all his senses are
up in arms, and his heart fails within him, at
the very name of love. His gallantry and
devotion to the fair sex know no bounds ; and
he not only answers for himself, but undertakes to prove that all men are made of the
same combustible materials. His book reminds
one of the title of the old play, " All for love,
" or the world well lost." If Mr. M.'s passions
are too much for him, (though I should not
have the worse opinion of him on this account)

I would advise him to give vent to them in writing love-songs ; not in treatises of philosophy. I am aware, however, that it is dangerous to meddle in such matters. As long as Mr. Malthus gravely reduces the strength of the passion to a mathematical certainty, he is sure to have the women on his side ; while I, for having the presumption to contradict his amorous conclusions, shall be looked upon as a sour old batchelor, and convicted of rebellion against the omnipotence of love.

But to return. It is the direct object of Mr. Malthus's philosophy to draw our attention from the slight and superficial influence which human institutions have had on the happiness of man, to those " deeper-seated" causes of misery which arise out of the principle of population. These, he says, are by far the most important, and the only ones worth our attending to, because they are the only ones on which all our reasonings and all our exertions will have no effect. He very roundly taxes Mr. Godwin and others as men who talked about what they did not understand, because they did not perceive that social institutions, and the different forms of government, and all the other means in our power of affecting the condition of human life are " but as the dust

" in the balance," compared with a principle entirely out of our power, which renders the vices of those institutions necessary, and any essential improvement in them hopeless. He is also angry with Hume for saying something about " indolence." We are in no case to look beyond the principle of population, in accounting for the state of man in society, if we would not fall under Mr. Malthus's displeasure, but are to resolve every thing into that. In his hands, population is the Aaron's rod which swallowed up all the other rods. The piety of some of the old divines led them to see all things in God : Mr. Malthus's self-complacency leads him to see all things in the Essay. He would persuade us that his discovery supersedes all other discoveries ; that it is the category of political science ; that all other causes of human happiness and misery are merged and sunk in that one, to which alone they owe their influence, and their birth. So that we are in fact to consider all human institutions, good, bad, and indifferent, all folly, vice, wisdom, virtue, knowledge, ignorance, liberty and slavery, poverty and riches, monarchy, aristocracy, democracy, polygamy, celibacy, all forms and modes of life, all arts, manufactures, and science, as resulting mechanically from this one principle ; which though simple in itself, yet in its effects is a jumble, a chaos of contradictions, a mass of inconsistency and absurdity, which no human understanding can unravel, or explain. Over this crew and medley of opinions, Mr. Malthus " sits umpire, and by decision more embroils the fray by which he reigns :" for he is not quite undetermined in his choice between good and evil, but is always inclined to give the 'preference to vice and misery, not only as the most natural, but as the most safe and salutary effects of this principle, as we prescribe a low diet and blisters to persons of too full a temperament. " Our greatest good " is but plethoric ill."—Mr. Malthus may perhaps plead in his own defence that at the outset of his work (second edition) he professes to treat only of *one* of the causes which have hitherto impeded the progress of virtue and happiness, and that he was not therefore, by the terms of the agreement, bound to take cognizance of any of the other causes which have tended to produce the same effect. He is like a man who takes it into his head to make a huge map of Scotland, (larger than any that ever was made of the whole world besides) and gives you into the bargain as much or as little of Ireland or the rest of Great Britain as he pleases. Any one else who chuses, may make a map of England or Ireland on the same scale.

There is something fair and plausible in this. But the fact really is, that Mr. Malthus will let nobody make a map of the country but himself: he has put England, Wales, and Ireland in the three corners of his great map (for the title takes up one of the corners) and he insists upon it that this is quite sufficient.—What he aims at in all his plans and calcula‑ tions of existing grievances is to magnify the evils of population, to exonerate human insti‑ tutions, and to throw the whole blame on na‑ ture herself. I shall therefore try to give such a sketch, or bird's-eye view of the subject as may serve to shew the unfairness of our au‑ thor's statement. How little he has confined himself to his professed object, and how little he can be considered in the light of a joint‑ inquirer after truth, will be seen by quoting the following passages at large.

" The great error under which Mr. Godwin " labours throughout his whole work is, the " attributing of almost all the vices and misery " that prevail in civil society to human insti‑ " tutions. Political regulations, and the esta‑ " blished administration of property are with " him the fruitful sources of all evil, the hot‑ " beds of all the crimes that degrade mankind. " Were this really a true state of the case, it

" would not seem an absolutely hopeless task
" to remove evil completely from the world ;
" and reason seems the proper and adequate
" instrument for effecting so great a purpose.
" But the truth is, that though human institu-
" tions *appear* to be the obvious and obtrusive
" causes of much mischief to mankind, they
" are, in reality, light and superficial, in com-
" parison with those deeper-seated causes
" of evil which result from the laws of
" nature."

Now by " the laws of nature," of which
human institutions are here made only a sort
of *cat's-paw*, our author means neither more
nor less than the principle of population. For
after supposing, in compliment to Mr. Godwin,
a state of society in which the spirit of oppression, the spirit of servility, and the spirit
of fraud, in which envy, malice, and revenge,
in which every species of narrowness and selfishness are banished from the world, where
war and contention have ceased to exist, where
unwholesome trades and manufactures are no
longer encouraged, &c, he breaks out into his
usual cant of, " I cannot conceive a form of
" society so favourable upon the whole to po-
" pulation." He then proceeds gravely to shew,
by a train of reasoning which has been already

recapitulated, and which need not surely be refuted twice, how in such a state of happy
equality population would go on increasing
without limit, because all obstacles to it,
" all anxiety about the future support of
" children," would be entirely removed, though
it would at the same time be attended in every
stage of the progress with increasing and aggravated wretchedness, because those very obstacles, and the same difficulty of providing for
the support of children would still remain.

" Here then," he says, " no human institu-
" tions existed, to the perverseness of which
" Mr. Godwin ascribes the original sin of the
" worst men. No opposition had been pro-
" duced by them between public and private
" good. No monopoly had been created of
" those advantages which reason directs to be
" left in common. No man had been goaded to
" the breach of order by unjust laws. Benevo-
" lence had established her reign in all hearts.
" And yet in so short a period as fifty years,
" violence, oppression, falsehood, misery, every
" hateful vice, and every form of distress, which
" degrade and sadden the present state of so-
" ciety, seem to have been generated by the
" most imperious circumstances, by laws inhe-

" rent in the nature of man, and absolutely in-
" dependent of all human regulations."

" It is a perfectly just observation of Mr.
" Godwin, that *there is a principle in human so-*
" *ciety by which population is perpetually kept*
" *down to the level of the means of subsistence.*
" The sole question is, what is this principle ?
" Is it some obscure and occult cause ? Is it
" some mysterious interference of heaven, which
" at a certain period strikes the men with impo-
" tence, and the women with barrenness ? Or
" is it a cause open to our researches, within
" our view ; a cause which has constantly been
" observed to operate, though with varied force,
" in every state in which man has been placed ?
" Is it not misery, and the fear of misery,"
[certainly two very different things] " the ne-
" cessary and inevitable results of the laws of
" nature, which human institutions, so far from
" aggravating, have tended considerably to miti-
" gate, though they can never remove." He
then proceeds to shew how the distinctions of
property and the other regulations of society
would necessarily result from the principle of
population, and adds, that " certainly if the
" great principle of the Essay be admitted, it
" affects Mr. Godwin's whole work, and essen-
" tially alters the foundations of political jus-

" tice. A great part of his book consists of an
" *abuse* of human institutions" [very sad in-
deed] " as productive of all or most of the evils
" which afflict society. The acknowledgement
" of a new and totally unconsidered cause of
" misery must evidently alter the state of these
" arguments," [comfortable again] " and make
" it absolutely necessary that they should be
" either newly modified, or *entirely rejected.*" —
How fortunate to have discovered that the evils
in society are not owing to a cause which might
be remedied, but to one that renders their removal absolutely hopeless !

I might here, if I were to follow the impulse
of my own levity, say that the yellow fever has
I believe made its appearance since the first
edition of the Political Justice, though I do not
know that this circumstance would make it necessary entirely to new-model the arguments.
As to Mr. Malthus's " new and unconsidered
" cause of misery," I deny that the necessity of
providing a proportionable quantity of food for
an increase of people was new or unconsidered.
All that Mr. Malthus has discovered is that the
population would go on increasing, though
there was nothing to support it !—Our author
has chosen to justify or palliate the real disorders which prevail in society by supposing a

case of fictitious distress ; by which means he
proves incontestably that the present vices and
defects of political institutions, &c. are *comparative* blessings. He supposes that in a state of
society where the public good was the constant
guide of action, men would entirely lay aside
the use of their reason, and think of nothing
but begetting children, without considering in
the least how they were to be maintained.
Now I will also for a time take a license from
common sense, and make a supposition as wise
as Mr. Malthus's. I will suppose all the inhabitants of this town to come to a determination
to live without eating, and do nothing but drink
gin. What would be the consequence ? Perpetual intoxication, quarrels, the fierceness of
hunger, disease, idleness, filth, nakedness, maud-
lin misery, sallow faces, sights of famine and
despair, meagre skeletons, the dying, and the
dead. But why need I attempt to describe
what has been already so much better described
by Hogarth ? Here then, I might exclaim, no
human institutions existed, no unjust laws, no
excessive labour, no unwholesome trades, no inequality, no malice, envy, lust, or revenge, to
produce the dreadful catastrophe we have just
witnessed : yet in the short space of a single
month or fortnight we see that scenes of distress,
shocking beyond any thing of which we can at
present form even a conception, would arise out

of the most imperious circumstances, from laws inherent in the nature and constitution of man, and absolutely independent of all human regulations, namely, *from the unrestricted use of gin.* The inference is direct and unavoidable, that we ought to submit patiently and thankfully to all the abuses, vices, and evils that are to be found in this great city, and flatter, excuse, and encourage them by all the means in our power, *because* they all of them together do not amount to a tenth part of the mischief that would be the consequence of the unrestrained indulgence of a single pernicious habit. This is something the way in which Mr. Malthus reasons about the unrestricted increase of population. But the absurdity is too gross even for burlesque.

The following is, I conceive, a fair summary of Mr. Malthus's theory. First, that the principle of population is a necessary, mechanical thing, that it is the " grinding law of necessity," unavoidably leading to a certain degree of vice and misery, and in fact accounting for almost all the evils in human life. Secondly, that all the other sources of vice and misery which have been so much and idly insisted on, have no tendency to increase the necessary evils of population, but the contrary, or that the removal of those different sources of evil would instead of lessening the evils of population, which are much the most important, really aggravate them. —Here then three questions naturally present themselves.

First, how much of the vice and misery in society is actually owing to human institutions, or the passions, follies, imperfections, or perversities of human nature, independently of the principle of population.

Secondly, whether the removing or diminishing the evils produced by those causes would necessarily increase the evils of population, and open a door to the influx of more vice and misery than ever.

Thirdly, whether the tendency of population to excess is the effect of a simple principle operating mechanically, whether it is to be looked upon as one of the laws inherent in our very nature, or whether the state of morals in every country does not depend greatly and principally on the state of society, on the condition of the people, on public opinion, and on a variety of other causes which are more or less within our power ; that is, whether human institutions, laws, &c. instead of being the mere blind instruments of this principle, do not re-act very powerfully upon it, and give it its direction and limits.—If it can be shewn under this last head, that there is some connection between the form of government and the state of morals, and that the better the government, the better the morals, the evils of population instead of forming an excuse for bad governments will only aggravate their mischief, and increase the necessity of getting rid of them. Again, if it can be made to appear that there is no necessary, or general proportion between the degree of vice in in any country, and the pressure of population on the means of subsistence, that it is not al·ways the effect of want, but constantly outruns the occasion, being self-propagated, and often spreading like a contagion through those countries and those ranks in life, where the difficulty of providing for a family is least felt, this will shew that the mere existence of vice is no proof of its being necessary, or that it is to be considered as a test of the excessive increase of population.

Farther, if on the other hand, improving the condition of the lower classes of the people is generally found, instead of leading to an unrestrained increase of population, and thus adding to their misery, to give them a greater attachment to the decencies and comforts of life, to make them more cautious how they part with them, to open their ideas and prospects, to

strengthen the principle of moral restraint, and
so confine population within reasonable limits,
this will be an additional motive for improving
their condition (really and truly, not by taking
from them the comforts and privileges they already possess.) Again, if it should be found
that independently of the immediate acts of
tyranny exercised by particular governments,
and the poverty and wretchedness experienced
by certain classes of the community there is a
tendency in some governments to keep population down infinitely below the level to which it
might rise by a proper encouragement of agriculture, and the methods of industry by which
population is supported, it will be but a poor defence of the folly or tyranny of such governments to say, that they are a necessary expedient to prevent the excess of population.

Lastly, if those states or communities, where
the greatest equality prevails, are those which
maintain the greatest number of inhabitants, and
where the principle of moral restraint is likely to
operate with most effect, that is, where population is soonest able to reach its utmost limits,
and goes the least beyond them, certainly those
institutions which favour the greatest disparity
of conditions, the extremes of poverty and the
extremes of luxury, will receive no very strik-

ing support from the principle of population.
These are I think the chief points and inferences to which I wish to direct the reader's attention in the few slight remarks which I have
to make upon the subject.

It may be proper to observe, in the first place,
that Mr. Malthus by making vice and misery
the necessary consequences of his favourite
principle lays himself open to a very obvious
objection. For if he means to prove any thing
by his theory, the question immediately is, what
degree of vice and misery is rendered necessary
by this principle, or by the *physical constitution
of man* ? .Are we to suppose that only so much
evil is necessary as naturally grows out of the
British constitution ? Or does this principle also
prove that all the evils that are suffered under the
Turkish government, or that were suffered
under the old government of France, or that
may arise out of its present government are
equally necessary and salutary ? How far are we
to go ? Where are we to stop ? Are we to consider every evil and abuse as necessary, merely
because it exists, or only as much of the thing
as we cannot get rid of? But how much can we
really get rid of ? Are vice and misery uniformly
owing to the developement of this principle
in certain situations, or are they to be in part

ascribed to the intervention of other arbitrary, and gratuitous causes, the operation of which may be more easily set aside ? In what manner are we to distinguish between what is necessary, and what is not ? All these questions require to be asked before we can proceed to build any practical conclusions on Mr. Malthus's theory of the evils of population. The vague, general term, " vice and misery," gives us no clue. It is mere cant ; and applies equally to the best and worst of all possible governments. It proves either nothing, or it proves a great deal more than I conceive Mr. Malthus would in all cases wish to prove by it.

There is no species of vice or oppression that does not find a ready excuse in this kind of reasoning. And besides, by leaving the quantity of vice and misery always uncertain, we never subject ourselves to the necessity of following a general principle into any obnoxious conclusions ; and are always at liberty to regulate our opinions according to our convenience by saying—I would have no more vice and misery than at present prevails : but that degree of vice and misery which is inwoven with the present constitution of things, I would by no means have removed, it might endanger the whole fabric. This is a double advantage. We thus sacrifice to the powers that be, without violating decorum, or being driven off our guard by an inflexible and pedantic logic. I have so good an opinion of Mr. Malthus that I do not think he has any predilection for vice and misery in the abstract, or for their own sakes : I do not believe he would stand forward as the advocate of any abuses from which he himself does not reap some benefit, or which he may not get something by defending.

I do not know that I can go so far as with Mr. Godwin to ascribe the original sin of the worst men to social institutions, but of this I am very sure that that original sin and those institutions do not proceed entirely from the principle of population. There are other vices and mischievous propensities inherent in our nature, besides the love of pleasure. We are troubled with a complication of disorders, and it is bad advice to say, that we ought to direct all our attention to the one that is perhaps the most inveterate, or because we despair of doing any thing with that, make no attempts to counteract the progress of the others, either by palliatives or otherwise. If we are deceived with respect to the real extent, and sources of our disorders, it is impossible we should hit upon the right method of cure, whatever might be the case, if we were informed of our true situation.—The principle of population alone, according to the description Mr. Malthus gives of it as a principle of unbridled and insatiable lust, would indeed be sufficient to account for all the vice and misery in the world, and for a great deal more than there is in the world. It would soon overturn every thing. But we have seen that that account is not just. It is in fact only one of the principles or passions by which the conduct of mankind is influenced ; and he would be a bold man who should assert that neither ambition, nor avarice, nor sloth, nor ignorance, nor prejudice have had any share in producing the various evils that abound in civil society. The other passions are sturdy claimants and know how to bustle for themselves, and will not be so easily pushed out of the world. Let any one write the words, ambition, pride, cruelty, hatred, oppression, falsehood, selfishness, indolence, lust, and hunger in the same line, and let him see if there is any peculiar charm in the two last, which draws all their virtue and meaning out of the rest. Yet this is the impression which Mr. Malthus seems anxious to leave on the minds of his readers. Indeed all the others appear to owe their efficacy and their sting to lust alone. If it were not for this one principle, the world might go on very well.

Mr. Malthus charges it as a great error on Mr. Godwin's system that " political regulations " and the established administration of property " are with him the fruitful sources of all evil, " the hotbeds of all the crimes that degrade " mankind." Be it so, that this is an error. The next question is, as Mr. Malthus does not deny that these institutions are the immediate causes of many of the evils that exist, to what principle they really owe their rise. Mr. Malthus says, they are the necessary results of laws inherent in our nature, and that though all the other passions and vices of men could be got rid of altogether, the principle of population alone would still render those institutions with all the abuses belonging to them as necessary as ever. This I take upon me to dispute. Will he say, that (leaving the principle of population entirely out of the question) pride, avarice, and indolence have had no share in the establishment, or continuance of the inequality of property, in goading men on to the accumulation of immense riches by oppression, extortion, fraud, perjury, and every species of villainy, or in making them undergo every kind of distress, sooner than apply themselves to some regular

and useful occupation. If I were inclined to
maintain a paradox on the subject, I might take
up Hume's assertion, " that indolence is the
" source of all mischief in the world." For if
men had not been averse to labour, if there had
been no idlers to take advantage of, to offer
temptation to, and enlist upon any terms in any
lawless enterprize, that promised an easy booty,
the tyrant would have been without his slaves,
the robber without his gang, and the rich man
without his dependents. But these smart
points and pithy sayings are soon found to be
fallacious, if we attend a little closely to the
subject. For instance, it may be true that if
there had been no idle people, there would have
been no one to take advantage of, but if there
had been no pride, rapacity, or selfishness, there
would have been no one to take an undue advantage of them, or foment the mischief. The
fellows that generally compose a gang of
robbers only wish to gain a cheap livelihood by
acts of violence ; the captain of the gang is
also actuated by vanity, revenge, the spirit of
adventure, and the desire to keep the country
for twenty or thirty miles round in awe of him.
The common soldier is glad of sixpence a-day
to be shot at every now and then, and do nothing the rest of his time : the general is not
easy, unless he can lay waste provinces, over-

run kingdoms, and make the world ring with the terror of his name. The lazy and unthinking would not do half the mischief, of which they are capable, without the active, the enterprizing and turbulent : fools and knaves are as necessary to the body politic, as the head and limbs are to the human body. The Romans might have staid quietly within their own walls, but for the plotting heads at home that sent them out to victory; and his thirty thousand followers would no more have thought of setting out to India of their own accord, than Alexander would have thought of marching there by himself.

It is to me pretty clear that as long as there are such passions as sloth and rapacity, these will be sufficient to account for the unequal division of property, and will render the laws relating to it necessary : and it is equally clear to my mind that if these passions could be completely subdued, so that no one would refuse his share in the common labour, or endeavour to take an unfair advantage of others either by force or fraud, that the established administration of property would be no longer necessary.* If, as Mr. Malthus supposes, " Bene-

* Such a change would not require the perfect subjugation, or rather annihilation of these passions, or perfect virtue, in

" volence had so far established her reign in all
" hearts," that every one was ready to give up
the enjoyments of ease and luxury as far as re-
lated to himself, I do not think that in such a
state of unparalleled disinterestedness and heroic
virtue, any madman would be found to violate
the public happiness, and begin the work of con-

the literal sense, as Mr. Malthus seems to imply in a late publication—which I have not read. It might as well be pretended
that no man could ever keep his fingers off bank-notes, or pay
his debts, who was not perfectly honest. In neither case is there
required any thing more than such a superiority in one set for
motives over another, from pride, habit, example, opinion, &c.
as just to incline the balance. The gentlemen of the society of
Lloyd's fund would no doubt scorn to touch a shilling of the
money entrusted to their care : yet we should hardly conclude
from hence that they are all of them persons of perfectly disinterested characters, and altogether indifferent to money-matters.
The Turks, it is said, who are very far from the character of
perfection, leave their goods for sale on an open stall, and the
buyer comes and takes what he wants, and leaves the money on
the stall. Men are not governed by extreme motives. If perfect virtue were necessary to common honesty, fair dealing, and
propriety of conduct, there would be nothing but swindlers and
black-guards in the world. Men steer clear of the law not so
much through fear, as because it stamps the public opinion.
It is a positive thing. If men could make up their minds as
decidedly about the general characters and conduct of individuals without, as they do with, the rough rebuke of the law
to sharpen their moral sense (to which by the bye Mr. Godwin's
plan of plain speaking would contribute not a little) this would
go a great way towards rendering a system of equality practicable. But I meddle with these questions only as things of
idle speculation. *Jactet se in aulis, &c.*

tention anew, for the sake of transmitting **a**
contingent inheritance of vice and misery *to his
heirs!* If reason and virtue are at present no
match for the principle of population, neither
are they a match for the principle of selfishness,
or for any of our other passions. But truly, if
benevolence had once established her reign in
all hearts, we should see wonders, she would
perform the part of vice and misery to a miracle.—It is evident then that the seeds of
inequality, of vice and misery are not sown
entirely in the principle of population; that
the same untoward passions which first rendered
civil establishments necessary, have continued
to operate ever since, that they have produced
most of the disorders in the world, and are still
in as much force as ever; that they very well
deserve a chapter by themselves in the history
of human nature, and ought not to come in as
a note or parenthesis to Mr. Malthus's great
work.

But whatever account we may chuse to give
of the origin of the establishment of property or
government in general, this has nothing to do
with the real question, unless it could be shewn
that the same form of government, the same inequality of conditions, and the same degree of
vice and misery are to be found alike in every

country. Mr. Malthus's system goes to the support of all political regulations and existing evils, or it goes to the support of none. Let us cast our eyes over the map of Europe, and ask whether all that variety of governments and manners by which it is distinguished took their rise solely from the principle of population. A principle common to human nature, a law inherent in the physical constitution of man, may in its progress be necessarily attended with a certain degree of vice and misery; but it cannot be productive of different degrees of vice and misery in different countries; as the stern law of necessity, it must operate every where alike. If it does not do so, this of itself shews that it is not the sole moving spring in all human institutions, that it is not beyond the reach of all regulation and control, and that there are other circumstances, accidents, and principles on which the happiness of nations depends. Whatever difference there is, then, between one government and another, whether that government is despotic, or mixed, or free; whatever difference there is in the administration of that government, whether it is cruel, oppressive, and arbitrary in the extreme, or mild, just, and merciful; whatever difference there is between the manners of one nation and those of another, whether the most licentious that can be, or strict and exemplary; whatever difference there is in the arts and conveniences of life, in the improvements of trade and agriculture in various countries, whatever differences are produced by religion, by contrarieties of opinion, by the state of knowledge, by useful or mischievous regulations of all kinds, all these cannot be owing to one and the same cause.

Will Mr. Malthus say that all these differences are as nothing, that they are not worth insisting on, or contending about, that they are nominal, rather than real, or at any rate that what is gained in one way is lost in another, for that the principle of population still requires the same vent, and produces first or last the same quantity of vice and misery of one sort or other in every country? He must assert on the one hand that all other causes put together do not materially affect the happiness of a people, or on the other hand that the state of all those other causes depends on, and arises out of the state of population, though they do not in the least influence the principle of population itself. These absurdities, than which it would be difficult to advance greater, are however necessary to bear out the author's conclusion, that arts, knowledge, liberty and virtue, and the best institutions can do little for the hap-

piness of mankind. For instance, if it is true
that religion or opinion of any kind exerts a
direct influence over morals, then it is not true
that morals depend entirely on the state of
population. Or if it is true, that the invention
of a useful art, which is accident, or the public
encouragement of it, which is design, may
contribute to the support of a larger population
without multiplying its inconveniences, then it
is not true that all human happiness or misery
can be calculated according to a mechanical
ratio. But these matters are, I confess,
set in the clearest light by a reference to facts,
and I can quote no better authority than Mr.
Malthus himself.

He says, " It will not be difficult, from the
" accounts of travellers, to trace the checks to
" population, and the causes of its present de-
" cay [in Turkey] ; and as there is little dif-
" ference in the *manners* of the Turks, whether
" they inhabit Europe or Asia, it will not be
" worth while to make them the subject of dis-
" tinct consideration." [I shall presume that I
have so far reconciled the reader's mind to the
bug-bear, population, that he will not regard *depopulation* as one of the most beautiful features
in the economy of a state.]

Our author then proceeds, " The funda-
" mental cause of the low state of population
" in Turkey, compared with its extent of terri-
" tory, is undoubtedly the nature of its govern-
" ment. Its tyranny, its feebleness, its bad
" laws and worse administration of them, with
" the consequent insecurity of property, throw
" such obstacles in the way of agriculture, that
" the means of subsistence are necessarily de-
" creasing yearly, and with them, of course, the
" number of people. The *miri* or general land-
" tax, paid to the sultan, is in itself moderate ;
" but by abuses inherent in the Turkish govern-
" ment, the pachas, and their agents have found
" out the means of rendering it ruinous.
" Though they cannot absolutely alter the im-
" post which has been established by the sultan,
" they have introduced a number of changes,
" which, without the name, produce all the ef-
" fect of an augmentation. In Syria, according
" to Volney, having the greatest part of the land
" at their disposal, they clog their concessions
" with burthensome conditions, and exact the
" half, and sometimes even two-thirds of the crop.
" When the harvest is over, they cavil about
" losses, and, as they have the power in their
" hands, they carry off what they think pro-
" per." [What they leave behind them, is
what Mr. Malthus wnen he gets into his ab-

stractions calls " *the fund appropriated to the*
" *maintenance of labour,*" or, " *the aggregate*
" *quantity of food possessed by the owners of*
" *land beyond their own consumption.*"] " If the
" season fail, they still exact the same sum, and
" expose every thing that the poor peasant pos-
" sesses to sale. To these constant oppressions
" are added a thousand accidental extortions.
" Sometimes a whole village is laid under con-
" tribution for some real or imaginary offence.
" Arbitrary presents are exacted on the acces-
" sion of each governor ; grass, barley, and
" straw are demanded for his horses ;" [Mr.
Malthus thinks, farther on in his book, that
" the waste of the rich, and the horses kept for
" pleasure" in this country are no detriment to
the poor *here*, but rather a benefit, page 478.]
" and commissions are multiplied, that the sol-
" diers who carry the orders may live upon the
" starving peasants, whom they treat with the
" most brutal insolence and injustice. The
" consequence of these depredations is, that the
" poorer class of inhabitants, ruined, and unable
" any longer to pay the *miri*, become a burden
" to the village," [something I suppose in the
same way that the poor among us become a burden to the parish] " or fly into the cities ; but
" the *miri* is unalterable, and the sum to be
" levied must be found somewhere. The por-

" tion of those who are thus driven from their
" homes falls on the remaining inhabitants,
" whose burden, though at first light, now be-
" comes insupportable. If they should be
" visited by two years of drought and famine,
" the whole village is ruined and abandoned ;
" and the tax, which it should have paid, is
" levied on the neighbouring lands. The same
" mode of proceeding takes place with regard
" to the tax on Christians, which has been
" raised by these means," [by what means, by
the principle of population ?] " from three,
" five, and eleven piastres, at which it was first
" fixed, to thirty-five and forty, which absolutely
" impoverishes those on whom it is levied, and
" obliges them to leave the country. It has
" been remarked that these exactions have made
" a rapid progress during the last forty years,
" from which time are dated the decline of
" agriculture, the depopulation of the country,
" and the diminution in the quantity of the
" specie carried to Constantinople. The pea-
" sants are every where reduced to a little flat
" cake of barley, or *doura*, onions, lentils, and
" water. Not to lose any part of their corn
" they leave in it all sorts of wild grain, which
" often produces bad consequences. In the
" mountains of Lebanon and Nablous, in time
" of dearth, they gather the acorns from the oak

" which they eat after boiling or roasting them
" on the ashes. By a natural consequence of
" this misery, the art of cultivation is in the
" most deplorable state. The husbandman is
" almost without instruments, and those he has
" are very bad. His plough is frequently no
" more than the branch of a tree cut below a
" fork and used without wheels. The ground
" is tilled by asses and cows, rarely by oxen,
" which would bespeak too much riches. In
" the districts exposed to the Arabs, as in Pa-
" lestine, the countryman must sow with his
" musket in his hand, and scarcely does the
" corn turn yellow before it is reaped and con-
" cealed in subterraneous caverns. As little as
" possible is employed for seed corn, because
" the peasants sow no more than is barely
" necessary for their subsistence. Their whole
" industry is limited to the supply of their
" immediate wants, and to procure a little bread,
" a few onions, a blue shirt, and a bit of woollen,
" much labour is not necessary. The peasant
" lives therefore in distress, but at least he does
" not enrich his tyrants, and the avarice of
" despotism is its own punishment." [*Note.*—
These are the unhappy persons, as our
author expresses it in a passage, which may
hereafter be quoted at length, " who in
" the great lottery of life have drawn a

" blank ; and with whose exorbitant and un-
" reasonable demands the owners of the afore-
" said surplus produce neither think it just nor
" natural to comply." I confess, I cannot account for all the contention and distress which is
here implied, for the conflict between famine and
riches, when I seriously consider with Mr. Malthus, "that the quantity of food, which one man
" can consume, is necessarily limited by the nar-
" row capacity of the human stomach ; that it is
" not certainly probable that he should throw
" away the rest; or if he exchanged his surplus
" produce for the labour of others, that this
" would be better than that these others should
" absolutely *starve.*" But human life, as well as
our reasonings about it, is a mystery, a dream.]
" This picture which is drawn by Volney, in
" describing the state of the peasants in Syria,
" seems to be confirmed by all the other tra-
" vellers in these countries, and according to
" Eton, it represents very nearly the condition
" of the peasants in the greater part of the
" Turkish dominions. Universally the offices
" of every denomination are set up to public
" sale, and in the intrigues of the seraglio, by
" which the disposal of all places is regulated,
" every thing is done by means of bribes. The
" pachas in consequence, who are sent into the
" provinces, exert to the utmost their power of

" extortion, but are always outdone by the
" officers immediately below them, who, in their
" turn, leave room for their subordinate agents.
" The pacha must raise money to pay the tri-
" bute, and also to indemnify himself for the
" purchase of his office; support his dignity,
" and make a provision in case of accidents ;
" and as all power, both civil and military, cen-
" ters in his person, from his representing the
" sultan, the means are at his discretion, and the
" quickest are invariably considered as the best.
" Uncertain of to-morrow, he treats his pro-
" vince as a mere transient possession, and en-
" deavours to reap, if possible, in one day, the
" fruit of many years, without the smallest re-
" gard to his successor, or the injury that he
" may do to the permanent revenue.   The
" cultivator is necessarily more exposed to
" these extortions than the inhabitants of the
" towns.   From the nature of his employment,
" he is fixed to one spot, and the productions of
" agriculture do not admit of being easily con-
" cealed. *The tenure of the land and the right*
" *of succession are besides uncertain.*   When a
" father dies, the inheritance reverts to the sul-
" tan, and the children can only redeem the suc-
" cession by a considerable sum of money.
" These considerations naturally occasion an in-

" difference to landed estates. The country is
" deserted, and each person is desirous of flying
" to the towns, where he will not only in gene-
" ral meet with better treatment, but may hope
" to acquire a species of wealth, which he can
" more easily conceal from the eyes of his rapa-
" cious masters. To complete the ruin of agri-
" culture, a maximum is in many cases estab-
" lished, and the peasants are obliged to furnish
" the towns with corn at a fixed price. It is a
" maxim of Turkish policy, originating in the
" feebleness of the government, and the fear of
" popular tumults, to keep the price of corn
" low in all the considerable towns. In the
" case of a failure in the harvest, every person
" who possesses any corn is obliged to sell it at
" the price fixed, under pain of death : and if
" there be none in the neighbourhood, other dis-
" tricts are ransacked for it. When Constanti-
" nople is in want of provisions, ten provinces
" are perhaps famished for a supply. At Da-
" mascus, during a scarcity in 1784, the people
" paid only one penny farthing a pound for their
" bread, while the peasants in the villages were
" absolutely dying with hunger. *The effect of*
" *such a system of government* on agriculture,
" need not be insisted on. The causes of the
" decreasing means of subsistence are but too
" obvious ; and the checks which keep the po-

" pulation down to the level of these decreasing
" resources, may be traced with nearly equal
" certainty, and will appear to include almost
" every species of vice and misery." Happy
country, secured by the very nature of its
government from the terrors of increasing population, and where every species of vice and misery, wisely anticipated, on the principle that
the imagination of a thing is worse than the
reality, takes away all fear of any greater evils
than those they already endure !

In the same chapter, he says, that in Persia
" the lower classes of people are obliged to de-
" fer marriage till late ; and that it is only
" among the rich that this union takes place
" early. The dreadful convulsions to which
" this country has been subject for many hun-
" dred years, must have been fatal to her agri-
" culture. The periods of repose from exter-
" nal wars, and internal commotions have been
" short and few, and even during the times of
" profound peace, the frontier provinces have
" been constantly subject to the ravages of the
" Tartars.—The effect of this state of things is
" such as might be expected. The proportion
" of uncultivated to cultivated land, Sir John
" Chardin states to be, ten to one ; and the
" mode in which the officers of the state and

" private owners let out their lands to husband-
" men, is not that *which is best calculated to re-*
" *animate industry.* The other checks to popu-
" lation in Persia are nearly the same as those
" in Turkey. *The superior destruction of the*
" *plague in Turkey is perhaps nearly balanced*
" *by the greater frequency of internal commotions*
" *in Persia.*"

These extracts furnish, I think, a tolerably
clear idea of the manner in which it is possible
for human institutions to aggravate instead of
mitigating the *necessary* evils of population.
We have a sufficient specimen of the effects of
bad government, of bad laws, of the worse execution of them, of feeble and selfish policy, of
wars and commotions, or of diseases probably
occasioned for the most part by the numbers of
people who are huddled together in dirt and
poverty in the great towns in the manner we
have seen—in altering the natural proportion between the produce of the soil, and the maintenance of the inhabitants ; in wantonly diminishing the means of subsistence by a most unjust and unequal distribution of them ; in di-
verting the produce of industry from its proper
channels, in drying up its sources, in causing a
stagnation of all the motives and principles
which animate human life, in destroying all

confidence, independence, hope, cheerfulness,
and manly exertion, in thwarting the bounties
of nature by waste, rapacity, extortion and violence, and spreading want, misery, and desolation in their stead. How admirably does Mr.
Malthus balance his checks ! What the plague
does in Turkey, is in Persia happily effected by
means of civil commotions. Population is thus
kept down to the level of the means of subsistence. But it seems, that wars, and intestine
commotions, those blind drudges of Providence
in clearing away the filth, rubbish, and other
evils of a too crowded population, sometimes go
beyond their errand, or do their work the
wrong way, by striking at the root of population
instead of lopping off its superfluous branches.
According to our author's general system, the
killing ten, or twenty, or a hundred thousand
men is an evil of a very trifling magnitude, if it
is to be looked upon as an evil at all. Population will only go on with the greater alacrity,
marriage will be rendered more practicable, and
the deficiency will be soon supplied from the
sprightly and ever-teeming source of nature.
The dreadful convulsions, however, to which
Persia has been subject for so many hundred
years have not been merely vents to carry off
the excess of population beyond the means of
subsistence, but they have further been fatal to

agriculture itself, or to those very means of subsistence.   The proportion of *uncultivated* to *cultivated* land, we find, is ten to one ; so that the
population is not only reduced to a level with
the means of subsistence, but reduced ten times
lower than it need be.*

I beg leave to accompany this description of
the effects of political regulations and the es-
stablished administration of property in Turkey,
with the following critical commentary, taken
from another part of the same work, which will
throw considerable light on the *necessity* of those
institutions to prevent the evils of population.
Mr. Malthus's usual plea for " vice and misery,"
is that nothing else can put a stop to the excesses of population ; which *they* do in the most
effectual and eligible manner.   But he has here
deserted his idols.

" It has appeared, I think, clearly, in the
" review of different societies given in the for-
" mer part of this work, that those countries,
" the inhabitants of which were sunk in the
" most barbarous ignorance, or oppressed by the
" most cruel tyranny, however low they might

---

* See also other passages giving an account of the state of
population in Africa, &c. which will be found at the end.

" be in actual population, were very populous
" in proportion to their means of subsistence ;
" and upon the slightest failure of the seasons,
" generally suffered the severities of want."
[Yet it was the sole object of Mr. Malthus's
discovery to prove the converse proposition, that
the highest degree of knowledge, and a perfect
exemption from every species of tyranny would
only lead to the lowest state of human wretchedness.] " Ignorance and despotism seem to
" have no tendency to destroy the passion which
" prompts to increase ; *but they effectually de-*
" *stroy the checks to it from reason and foresight.*
" The improvident barbarian who thinks only
" of his present wants, or the miserable peasant,
" who from his political situation feels little
" security of reaping what he has sown, will
" seldom be deterred from gratifying his passions
" by the prospect of inconveniences which can-
" not be expected to press on him under three
" or four years. But though this want of
" foresight, which is fostered by ignorance and
" despotism, tend thus rather to encourage the
" procreation of children, it is absolutely fatal
" to the industry which is to support them. In-
" dustry cannot exist without foresight and
" security. The indolence of the savage is
" well known ; and the poor Egyptian or Abys-
" sinian farmer, without capital, who rents

" land, which is let out yearly to the highest
" bidder and who is constantly subject to the de-
" mands of his tyrannical masters, to the casual
" plunder of an enemy, and not unfrequently to
" the violation of his miserable contract, can
" have no heart to be industrious, and if he had,
" could not exercise that industry with suc-
" cess. Even poverty itself, which appears to
" be the great spur to industry, when it has
" once passed certain limits, almost ceases to
" operate. The indigence which is hopeless,
" destroys all vigorous exertion, and confines
" the efforts to what is sufficient for bare exis-
" tence. *It is the hope of bettering our condition*
" *and the fear of want, rather than want itself,*
" *that is the best stimulus to industry, and its*
" *most constant and best directed efforts will*
" *almost invariably be found among a class*
" *of people above the class of the wretchedly*
" *poor.*"

What a pity that a man, who writes so well
at times, should, for the sake of an hypothesis,
" involve himself in absurdities and contradic-
" tions that would disgrace the lips of an
" ideot." Mr. Malthus will excuse me, if I
make use of some of the hints contained in this
excellent passage, for the benefit of our English
poor, who I think should not have harder mea-

sure dealt them than others, and try to soften some of the harshest constructions of the grinding law of necessity in their favour. I do not see why they alone are to be the martyrs of an abstraction. But Mr. Malthus reserves the application of his theory *in its purity* for his own countrymen. He has some natural feelings, and a certain degree of tender weakness for the distresses of other countries, but he will not suffer his feelings for a moment to get the better of his reason, with regard to those to whom he is bound by stronger ties, and over whose interests he watches with a paternal anxiety. He will hear of no palliations, no excuses, no shuffling temporary expedients to put off the evil day, he insists upon their submitting to the full operation of the penalty incurred by the laws of God and of nature, nothing short of the utmost severity will satisfy him, ('tis death to spare) he will not bate them a jot of his argument, he makes them drain the unsavoury cup of misery to the very dregs.

In the same chapter, which is entitled 'Of the principal sources of the prevailing errors on population,' he says, " It has been observed that " many countries at the period of their greatest " populousness have lived in the greatest plenty, " and have been able to export corn ; but at

" other periods, when their population was very
" low, have lived in continual poverty and want,
" and have been obliged to import corn. Egypt,
" Palestine, Rome, Sicily, and Spain are cited
" as particular exemplifications of this fact ; and
" it has been inferred, that an increase of popu-
" lation in any state, not cultivated to the ut-
" most, will tend rather to augment than dimi-
" nish the relative plenty of the whole society,"
&c. After contradicting this inference without
giving any reasons against it, he goes on, " Scar-
" city and extreme poverty, therefore, may or
" may not accompany an increasing population,
" according to circumstances. But they must
" always accompany a permanently declining
" population; because there has never been,
" nor probably ever will be, any other cause
" than want of food, which makes the popu-
" lation of a country permanently decline. In
" the numerous instances of depopulation which
" occur in history, the causes of it may always be
" traced to the want of industry, or the ill-di-
" rection of that industry, arising from violence,
" bad government, ignorance, &c. which first
" occasions a want of food, and of course depo-
" pulation follows. When Rome adopted the
" custom of importing all her corn, and laying
" all Italy into pasture, she soon declined in
" population. The causes of the depopulation

" of Egypt and Turkey have already been al-
" luded to ; and in the case of Spain, it was
" certainly not the numerical loss of people,
" occasioned by the expulsion of the Moors ;
" but the industry and capital thus expelled,
" which permanently injured her population."
[I do not myself see, how the expulsion of
capital could *permanently* injure the population.]
" When a country has been depopulated by
" violent causes, if a bad government, with its
" usual concomitant, insecurity of property,
" ensue, which has generally been the case in
" all those countries which are now less peopled
" than formerly ; neither the food nor the po-
" pulation, will recover themselves, and the in-
" habitants will probably live in severe want."
&c. Yet Mr. Malthus elsewhere affects to consider all human institutions and contrivances as
perfectly indifferent to the question. We have
here, however, a truer account of the matter.
The state of population is evidently no proof of
what it might be : to judge whether it is more or
less than it might or ought to be, we must take
into consideration good and bad government,
the progress of civilization, &c. It is a thing
de facto, not *de jure*. It is not that rock,
against which whosoever sets himself shall be
dashed to pieces, but the clay moulded by the
potter into vessels of honour or dishonour,

With respect to Spain, it is allowed that her population is deficient, or short of what it might
be. The problem of political economy I take
to be, how far this is the case with respect to all
other countries, and how to remedy the defect ;
or how to support the greatest number of people in the greatest degree of comfort. But I
have said this more than once before.

To the same purpose I might quote Algernon
Sydney, who in his Discourses on government
gives the following account of the decline and
weakness of many of the modern states from
the loss of liberty.*

" I take Greece to have been happy and glo-
" rious, when it was full of populous cities,
" flourishing in all the arts that deserve praise
" among men ; when they were courted and
" feared by the greatest kings, and never as-
" saulted by any but to his own loss and confu-
" sion ; when Babylon and Susa trembled at the
" motion of their arms : and their valour, exer-
" cised in those wars and tumults, which our
" author [Filmer] looks upon as the greatest

---

* This is a work which I would recommend to every reader
of whatever party, not only for the knowledge it contains, but
for the purity, simplicity, and noble dignity of the style. It
smacks of the old Roman elevation,

" evils, was raised to such a power, that nothing
" upon earth was found able to resist them.
" And I think it now miserable, when peace
" reigns within their empty walls, and the poor
" remains of those exhausted nations, sheltering
" themselves under the ruins of the desolated
" cities, have neither any thing that deserves to
" be disputed among them, nor spirit or force to
" repel the injuries they daily suffer from a
" proud and insupportable master."

" The like may be said of Italy. Whilst it
" was inhabited by nations governing them-
" selves by their own will, they fell sometimes
" into domestic seditions, and had frequent
" wars with their neighbours. When they were
" free, they loved their country and were always
" ready to fight in its defence. Such as suc-
" ceeded well, increased in vigour and power;
" and even those which were the most unfortu-
" nate in one age, found means to repair their
" losses, if their government continued. While
" they had a property in their goods, they would
" not suffer the country to be invaded, since
" they knew they could have none, if it were
" lost. This gave occasion to wars and tumults;
" it sharpened their courage, kept up a good
" discipline, and the nations that were most ex-
" ercised by them, always increased in power

" and number : so that no country seems ever
" to have been of greater strength than Italy
" was when Hannibal invaded it, and after his
" defeat the rest of the world was not able to
" resist their valour and power. They some-
" times killed one another; but their enemies
" never got any thing but burying-places within
" their territories. All things are now brought
" into a very different method by the blessed
" governments they are under. The fatherly
" care of the king of Spain, the pope, and
" other princes has established peace among
" them. We have not in many ages heard
" of any sedition among the Latins, Sabines,
" Volsci, Equi, Samnites, and others. The
" thin, half-starved inhabitants of walls sup-
" ported by ivy fear neither popular tumults
" nor foreign alarms ; and their sleep is only in-
" terrupted by hunger, the cries of their chil-
" dren, or the howling of wolves. Instead of
" many turbulent, contentious cities, they have
" a few scattered, silent cottages ; and the
" fierceness of those nations is so tempered, that
" every rascally collector of taxes extorts, with-
" out fear, from every man, that which should
" be the nourishment of his family. And if
" any of those countries are free from these
" pernicious vermin, it is through the extremity
" of their poverty."

[How differently do people see things ! According to Mr. Malthus, this rascally tax-gatherer, this vile nuisance, is a very sacred sort of character, a privileged person, one of the most indispensable and active instruments in the procession of vice and misery, those harbingers of human happiness ; and all our reproaches and indignation should fall on the poor peasant, for bringing beings into the world whom he could not maintain, in " the face of the " clearest warning, and in defiance of the ex- " press command of God," as proved by the tax-book.   Our superficial politician was not aware (Mr. Matthus tells us that first appearances are very deceitful) that the produce of the husbandman's labour was much better employed in supporting the waste and extravagance of the rich, than in affording nourishment to his family, as this would only enable him to *rear* his family, which must operate as an encouragement to marriage, and this again would produce other marriages, and so on *ad infinitum*, to which unrestricted increase of population it is necessary to put a timely stop.]

" Even in Rome a man may be circum-
" vented by the fraud of a priest, or poisoned
" by one, who would have his estate, wife,
" whore, or child; but nothing is done that

" looks like violence or tumult. The gover-
" nors do as little fear Gracchus as Hannibal;
" and instead of wearying their subjects in
" wars," [We have not yet reached this pitch
of perfection] " they only seek by perverted laws,
" corrupt judges, false witnesses, and vexatious
" suits, to cheat them of their money and in-
" heritance. This is the best part of their con-
" dition. Where these arts are used, there are
" men, and they have something to lose; but
" for the most part, the lands lie waste; and
" they who were formerly troubled with the
" disorders incident to populous cities, now
" enjoy the quiet and peaceable estate of a
" wilderness.—Again, there is a way of killing
" worse than that of the sword; for as Ter-
" tullian says upon a different occasion, *vetare*
" *nasci est interficere*; those governments are in
" the highest degree guilty of blood, which by
" taking from men the means of living, bring
" some to perish through want, drive others out
" of the country, and generally dissuade men
" from marriage, *by taking from them all ways*
" *of supporting their families.*" [Our author,
we see, has not here put the cart before the
horse. He seems to have understood the necessity of food to population, though Mr.
Malthus's essay had not then been heard of.]
" Notwithstanding all the seditions of Flo-

" rence, and other cities of Tuscany, the hor-
" rid factions of Guelphs and Gibelines,* Neri,
" and Bianchi, nobles and commons, they con-
" tinued populous, strong, and exceeding rich ;
" but in the space of less than a hundred and
" fifty years, the peacable reign of the Medici
" is thought to have destroyed nine parts in
" ten of the people of that province. Among
" other things it is remarkable, that when Philip
" the second of Spain gave Sienna to the Duke
" of Florence, his embassador then at Rome
" sent him word, that he had given away more
" than six hundred and fifty thousand subjects ;
" and it is not believed there are now twenty
" thousand souls inhabiting that city and terri-
" tory. Pisa, Pistoia, Arezzo, Cortona, and
" other towns, that were then good and populous,

---

* I should like to know whether Mr. Malthus would go so far
as to say that all the wars and rebellions occasioned by religion,
that all the plots, assassinations, burnings, massacres, the perse-
cutions, feuds, animosities, hatreds and jealousy of different
sects, that the cruelty, bigotry, the pernicious customs, and
abominable practices of the Pagan and other superstitions, such
as human sacrifices, &c. whether all those mischiefs and enor-
mities of which religion has been made a tool, whether the
martyrdom of the first christians, the massacre of St. Bartho-
lomew, the fires of Smithfield, the expeditions to the holy land,
the Gunpowder Plot, the Inquisition, the long Parliament, the
Reformation and the Revolution,——Popery, Protestantism,
" monks, eremites, and friars, with all their trumpery" were the
offspring of the principle of population.

" are in the like proportion diminished, and
" Florence more than any. When that city
" had been long troubled with seditions, tumults,
" and wars, for the most part unprosperous, it
" still retained such strength, that when
" Charles the eighth of France, being admitted
" as a friend with his whole army, which soon
" after conquered the kingdom of Naples,
" thought to master them, the people, taking up
" arms, struck such a terror into him, that he
" was glad to depart upon such conditions as
" they thought fit to impose. Machiavel re-
" ports, that in the year 1298 Florence alone,
" with the Val d'Arno, a small territory belong-
" ing to that city, could, in a few hours, by the
" sound of a bell, bring together a hundred
" thousand well-armed men. Whereas now
" that city, with all the others in that province,
" are brought to such despicable weakness,
" emptiness, poverty, and baseness, that they
" can neither resist the oppressions of their own
" prince, nor defend him or themselves, if they
" were assaulted by a foreign enemy. The peo-
" ple are dispersed or destroyed, and the best
" families sent to seek habitations in Venice,
" Genoa, Rome, and Lucca. This is not the
" effect of war or pestilence : they enjoy a per-
" fect peace, and suffer no other plague than the
" government they are under. But he who has

" thus cured them of disorders and tumults
" does in my opinion deserve no greater praise
" than a physician, who should boast there was
" not a sick person in a house committed to his
" care, when he had poisoned all that were in it.
" The Spaniards have established the like peace
" in the kingdoms of Naples and Sicily, the
" West Indies, and other places. The Turks
" by the same means prevent tumults in their
" dominions. And they are of such efficacy in
" all places, that Mariò Chigi, brother to pope
" Alexander the seventh, by one sordid cheat
" upon the sale of corn, is said within eight
" years to have destroyed above a third part of
" the people in the ecclesiastical state. And
" that country, which was the strength of the
" Romans in the time of the Carthaginian wars,
" suffered more by the covetousness and fraud
" of that villain, than by all the defeats received
" from Hannibal, &c." Chap. ii. p. 223.

It will be worth the reader's while to turn to
Lord Kaims's account of the kingdom of Siam,
which, though one of the most fertile countries
in the world, is reduced to the lowest state of
poverty and wretchedness by the absurd and
tyrannical policy of its government. Some of
the finest districts that were formerly cultivated,
are now inhabited only by wild beasts. One of

the arts by which they preserve the balance of population in that country is, that the keeper of the king's menagerie is authorized to let loose the elephants into the gardens of all those within a given distance of the capital, who do not pay him a large fine yearly to be excused from this intrusion. Yet according to our Essayist, human institutions have a very slight influence on the happiness of a people, because they cannot alter the necessary ratios of the increase of food and population. It is probable, however, that some of the cases here cited, which seem to bear rather hard on Mr. Malthus's rule, might have led those hasty writers, whom he censures for their want of a due insight into the subject, to conceive an unjust prejudice against human institutions ; and perhaps some of my readers may also be led to suspect, from not comprehending fully the scope and connection of his arguments, that bad governments are not quite such innocent things, as Mr. Malthus would sometimes represent them. Is it necessary to press this subject any farther ? I do not pretend to be very deep-read in history, in the constitution of states, the principles of legislation, the progress of manners, or the immediate causes of the revolutions that have taken place in different countries. All that I can presume to bring to this question is a little stub-

born common sense, an earnestness of feeling, and
a certain familiarity with abstruse subjects, that
is not willingly or easily made the dupe of flimsy
distinctions. But without much learning in one's
self, it is easy to take advantage of the learning
of others. By the help of a common-place book,
which is all that is wanted in these cases (and
I am fortunate enough to have such a one by
me in the collections of " that honest chro-
nicler," James Burgh) I might soon swell the
size of these letters to a bulk, which the book-
seller would not like, by a number of striking
illustrations from the most celebrated authors.
I might make myself a splendid livery of the
wisdom of others. But I have no taste for this
pompous drudgery. However, to satisfy those
readers who are unable to discern the truth without the spectacles of facts, it will not be amiss
to refer to the opinions of a few of the writers,
who seem with sufficient clearness to have traced
the causes of the rise and fall of particular states
to principles quite independent on, which were
neither first set in motion nor afterwards regulated
by the principle of population, and the effects of
which were utterly disproportionate to the actual operation of that principle. After all, it is
impossible to answer a paradox satisfactorily.
The real answer consists of the feelings and observations of our whole lives ; and of course, it

must be impossible to embody these in any single statement. All that can be done in these cases is to set the imagination once more in its old track.

" Hear," says my authority, " the excellent
" Montague on the prevalence of luxury among
" the Romans."

‘ If we connect the various strokes interspersed
‘ through what we have remaining of the writ-
‘ ings of Sallust, which were levelled at the
‘ vices of his countrymen, we shall be able to
‘ form a just idea of the manners of the Romans
‘ in his time. From this picture, we must be con-
‘ vinced, that not only those shocking calami-
‘ ties, which the republic suffered during the con-
‘ test between Marius and Sylla, but those subse-
‘ quent and more fatal evils, which brought on
‘ the utter extinction of the Roman liberty and
‘ constitution, were the natural effects of that
‘ foreign luxury, which first introduced venality
‘ and corruption.’ [Now by *luxury* we may
understand a very great superabundance of the
good things of this life, either in the community at large or in certain classes of it, but it
cannot by any construction be made to signify
the general and absolute want of them. Luxury
in some classes may produce want in others,
but poverty is in this case the effect of the un-

equal distribution of the produce of the earth, not of its real deficiency. Or if by luxury we understand only certain exterior decorations or artificial indulgences, which have nothing to do with the real support of life, such as dress, furniture, buildings, pictures, gold and silver, rarities, delicacies of all kinds, every thing connected with shew and expence, (though all these things among the Romans being the effects not merely of leisure or of supernumerary hands, but of *power*, and foreign dominion, must imply a command over the more substantial necessaries of life) yet even in this sense the passion for luxury or for those indulgences (which is here said to have been one great instrument in the overthrow of the state) is certainly a very different thing from the passion of hunger, or want of food, Mr. Malthus's key to the solution of all problems of a political nature] ‘ Though the introduction of luxury ‘ from Asia preceded the ruin of Carthage in ‘ point of time, yet as Sallust informs us, ‘ the dread of that dangerous rival restrained ‘ the Romans within the bounds of decency ‘ and order. But as soon as ever *that obstacle* ‘ *was removed*, they gave a full scope to their ‘ ungoverned passions. The change in their ‘ manners was not gradual, and by little and ‘ little as before, but rapid and instantaneous.

' Religion, justice, modesty, decency, all re-
' gard for divine or human laws, were swept
' away at once by the irresistible torrent of
' corruption. The nobility strained their pri-
' vileges, and the people their liberty, alike
' into the most unbounded licentiousness.
' Every one made the dictate of his own will,
' his only rule of action. Public virtue, and
' the love of their country, which had raised
' the Romans to the empire of the universe,
' were extinct. Money, which alone could
' enable them to gratify their darling luxury,
' was substituted in its place. Power, do-
' minion, honours, and universal respect were
' annexed to the possession of money. Con-
' tempt, and whatever was the most reproachful
' was the bitter portion of poverty; and to be
' poor, grew to be the greatest of all crimes, in
' the estimation of the Romans. Thus wealth
' and poverty contributed alike to the ruin of
' the republic. The rich employed their wealth
' in the acquisition of power, and their power
' in every kind of oppression and rapine for the
' acquisition of more wealth. The poor, now
' dissolute and desperate, were ready to engage
' in every seditious insurrection, which pro-
' mised them the plunder of the rich, and set
' up both their liberty and country to sale, to
' the best bidder. The republic, which was the

' common prey to both, was thus rent to pieces
' between the contending factions. — A state so
' circumstanced must always furnish an ample
' supply of proper instruments for faction.   For
' as luxury consists in an inordinate gratifi-
' cation of the sensual passions, and as the
' more they are indulged, the more importunate
' they grow, the greatest fortune must at last
' sink under their insatiable demands.   Thus
' luxury necessarily produces corruption.   As
' wealth is necessary to the support of luxury,
' all those who have dissipated their private
' fortunes in the purchase of pleasure, will be
' ever ready to enlist in the cause of faction for
' the wages of corruption.   And when once the
' idea of respect and homage is annexed to the
' possession of wealth alone, honour, probity,
' every virtue and every amiable quality will be
' held cheap in comparison and looked upon as
' awkward, and quite unfashionable.   But as
' the spirit of liberty will yet exist in some de-
' gree, in a state which retains the name of
' freedom, even though the manners of that
' state should be generally depraved, an oppo-
' sition will arise from those virtuous citizens,
' who know the value of their birth-right, li-
' berty, and who will not submit tamely to the
' chains of faction.   Force will then be called
' in to the aid of corruption, a military govern-

' ment will be established on the ruins of the
' civil, and all commands and employments will
' be at the disposal of arbitrary, lawless power.
' The people will be fleeced to pay for their own
' fetters, and doomed, like the cattle, to unremit-
' ting toil and drudgery, for the support of their
' tyrannical masters.' [All this is evidently
erroneous, when we apply to it the touch-stone
of the theory of population. The people are
not fleeced and worked in this manner for the
benefit of those who fleece and work them, to
gratify any appetites or passions of theirs, it is
out of pure good-will to the poor wretches themselves, that they may live more at their ease, and
in a greater degree of affluence than they would
without this timely warning of the evils of poverty.] ' Or if the outward form of civil government
' should be permitted to remain, the people will
' be compelled to give a sanction to tyranny by
' their own suffrages, and to elect oppressors
' instead of protectors.—From this genuine por-
' trait of the Roman state it is evident that the
' fatal catastrophe of that republic, of which
' Sallust himself was an eye-witness, was the
' natural effect of the corruption of their man-
' ners ; and again, that this corruption was the
' effect of the introduction of foreign wealth
' and luxury. This fatal tendency was too
' obvious to escape the notice of those who had

' any regard for liberty and their ancient consti-
' tution. Many sumptuary laws were made to
' restrain the excesses of luxury; but these
' efforts were too feeble to check the overbearing
' violence of the torrent. Cato proposed a
' severe law, enforced by the sanction of an
' oath, against bribery and corruption at elec-
' tions; where the scandalous traffic of votes
' was established by custom, as at a public
' market. But he only incurred the resentment
' of both parties by that salutary measure. The
' rich, who had no other merit to plead but what
' arose from their superior wealth, thus found
' themselves precluded from all pretensions to the
' highest dignities. The electors abused, cursed
' and even pelted him as the author of a law
' which reduced them to the necessity of sub-
' sisting by labour. Corruption was arrived at
' its height, and those excesses which were
' formerly esteemed the *vices* of the people were
' now, by the force of custom, become the *man-*
' *ners* of the people. To pilfer the public money
' and to plunder the provinces by violence,
' though state crimes of the most heinous nature,
' were grown so familiar, that they were looked
' upon as no more than mere office perquisites.'
Really I am afraid that the reader will suspect
me of falsifying the historical record to write a
satire against our own times. Some of these

remarks are I confess *home* truths.   To a person
who has not that mysterious kind of penetration
which the author of the Essay possesses, they
carry more weight, and give a clearer insight into
the principles that operate in the decomposition
of states, than all Mr. Malthus's indiscriminate
and shadowy reasonings on the evils of population, which can no more prove any thing deci-
sively on the subject, than we can account for
the inequalities in the surface of the earth from
its being round.

The same author adds, ' Though there is a
' concurrence of several causes in the ruin of a
' state, yet, where luxury prevails, that parent of
' all our fantastic wants, ever craving, and ever
' unsatisfied, we may safely assign it as the lead-
' ing cause; since it ever was and ever will be
' the most baneful to public virtue. *As luxury*
' *is contagious from its very nature*, it will gra-
' dually descend from the highest to the lowest
' ranks till it has ultimately infected a whole
' people. — We see luxury gradually increasing
' and prevailing over the Roman spirit and vir-
' tue, till at length the contagion *even* reached
' ladies of the greatest distinction, who in imi-
' tation of the prince and his court, had their
' assemblies and representations in a grove,
' planted by the Emperor, where booths were

‘ built, and in them sold whatever incited to
‘ sensuality and wantonness. Thus was even
‘ the outward appearance of virtue banished
‘ the city, and all manner of avowed lewdness,
‘ depravity and dissoluteness introduced in its
‘ room, men and women being engaged in a
‘ contention to outvie each other in glaring
‘ vices, and scenes of impurity. Again.—About
‘ the time that the Roman republic was tottering
‘ to its fall, it was observed that there was an
‘ universal degeneracy of manners prevailing,
‘ particularly that the women were very scan-
‘ dalous in their behaviour at Rome, while those
‘ of the countries called by them barbarous were
‘ remarkably exemplary in this respect.’ Was
this difference wholly owing to the difference in
the state of population ? Or shall we believe
that the ladies of Roman knights, that the wives
and daughters of Emperors, that the mistresses
of those to whom the world was tributary, who
scattered pearls and gold among their followers,
who gave largesses of corn to the people, and
entertained them at ten thousand tables at a
time, who ate the tongues of peacocks and
nightingales, and the brains of parrots, whose
dogs were fed with the livers of geese, their
horses with raisins, and their wild beasts with
the flesh of partridges and pheasants, shall we
believe that these delicate creatures, who

dreamt of nothing but pleasure and feasting, who reclined on silken couches, whose baths were made of rose-water and wine, who scented the air with all the perfumes of the East, whose rich dresses were upborne by a train of waiting-women, and idle boys, were driven to the necessity of stimulating their passions by lewd exhibitions, and wanton dances, and lascivious songs, and soft music and obscene practices, because they were hindered from gratifying their honest desires in a lawful way by the difficulty of providing for their future offspring, or the pressure of population on the means of subsistence? Yet this is what we must be led to suppose from Mr. Malthus's theory, according to whom vice is the natural consequence of want, and want the effect of increasing population. For any one who is acquainted with the state of manners, and the mode of living among the great at Rome at this time to pretend that all this was owing to nothing but the advanced state of population, just as the rising or falling of the weather-glass depends on the pressure of the air outside, betrays a most astonishing ignorance of human nature. I think I am warranted in laying down the two following maxims; that luxury is itself an immediate cause of dissoluteness of manners; secondly, that example, particularly that of the great, has a powerful influence over manners,

Before I quit this subject of Roman luxury, I shall just mention a fact quoted by my author, which seems to contradict Mr. Malthus's notion that the luxuries of the rich do not in the least affect the condition of the poor. " The good Emperor Aurelius," says Burgh, " sold the " plate, furniture, jewels, pictures and statues " of the imperial palace, *to relieve the distresses* " *of the people*, occasioned by the invasion of " barbarians, pestilence, famine, &c. the value " of which was so great, that it maintained the " war for five years, beside other inestimable ex- " pences." If according to Mr. Malthus's reasoning on this subject in different parts of his work, every man's stomach can hold only a certain quantity of food, and what does not go into one man's stomach necessarily goes into some other's, that is, if every person has as large a share as it is possible he should have of the necessaries of life, I do not see what this moving of pictures and statues about, or setting them up to auction should have to do with the state of provisions, or how it should relieve the necessities of the poor. Mr. Malthus's reasonings are sometimes as remarkable for their simplicity as they are at others for their complexity. He sees things in the most natural or in the most artificial point of view, as he pleases. At one time, every thing comes round by a labyrinth of causes, and all the intricate secretions of the state ; at another time the whole science of political economy is reduced to a flat calculation of the size of a quartern loaf, and the size of the human stomach.

All authors (but Mr. Malthus) seem agreed that luxury has been fatal to the spirit of liberty, and that the loss of liberty has led to the loss of independence. " The welfare of " every country depends upon the morals of the " people. Though a nation may become rich " by trade, thrift, and industry, or from the ad- " vantages of soil and situation, or may attain " to great eminence and power either by force " of arms, or by the sagacity of their councils ; " yet when their manners are depraved, they " will decline insensibly, and at last come to " utter destruction. When a country is grown " vicious, industry decays, and the people be- " come unruly, effeminate, and unfit for labour. " Luxury, when introduced into free states, and " suffered to spread through the body of the " people was ever productive of that degene- " racy of manners, which extinguishes public " virtue, and puts a final period to liberty. " Thus the Assyrian empire sunk under the " arms of Cyrus with his poor but hardy Per- " sians. The extensive and opulent empire of

" Persia fell an easy prey to Alexander and a
" handful of Macedonians. And the Macedo-
" nian empire, when enervated by the luxury
" of Asia, was compelled to receive the yoke of
" the victorious Romans. The descendants of
" the heroes, philosophers, orators, and free ci-
" tizens of Greece are now the slaves of the
" Grand Turk. The posterity of the Scipios
" and Catos of Rome are now singing operas, in
" the shape of Italian eunuchs, on the English
" stage." *It should seem from the length of time
which these countries have remained in the
same degraded condition without a single effort
or even wish to relieve themselves from it, that
there must be other causes of the permanent
depression of states, and other channels of
transmission, by which the habits, and characters of the people, their customs and institutions,
are handed down through successive generations
without any hope of a change for the better, be·
sides the mechanical fluctuations in the principle
of population. If all laws, institutions, manners,
and customs were only so many *expressions* (as I
may say) of the power of that principle, kingdoms would rise and fall with the operation of
the checks provided for it ; their alternate renova-

* See the extracts from Davenant, Montague, and Boling-
broke.

tion and decay would be as regular as the ebbing and flowing of the tide; in proportion as they sank deep in wretchedness, they would tower to greater happiness and splendour ; the foundation of their future prosperity would be laid in the lowness of their fortune ; the exhausted state would rise, like the phœnix, out of its own ashes, and enter the career of liberty and glory in all its pristine vigour. But we do not find that the accounts in history correspond with the oscillations of Mr. Malthus's theory. We find through a long, dreary tract of time, during which our author's ratios must have been ascending and descending like buckets in a well, that the inhabitants of those devoted countries have remained just where they were,—in the lowest scale of human being. They have for a great many hundred years been undergoing the wholesome discipline of vice and misery without being the better for it, the iron yoke of necessity to which they have so long and patiently submitted does not seem ever to have been relaxed in their favour, and they have reaped none of those reversionary benefits which might be expected from slavery and famine. These powerful principles have not done much to rekindle in their breasts their ancient love of liberty, the glow of genius,—or to open a new field for the rapid increase of population. They have not

been favoured with any of those *ups* and *downs,*
those pretty whirls and agreeable vicissitudes of
good and evil, which Mr. Malthus describes as
the natural consequence of the principles on
which his machine of population is constructed.
This is a radical objection to his machine; it
shews plainly that it is not constructed on true
principles, that we cannot safely trust ourselves
in it, and will I hope deter us from getting up
into it.

" The Swiss keep the same unchanged cha-
" racter of simplicity, honesty, frugality, mo-
" desty, bravery. These are the virtues which
" preserve liberty. They have no corrupt court,
" no blood-sucking placemen, no standing ar-
" my, the ready instruments of tyranny, no am-
" bition for conquest, no debauching commerce,
" no luxury, no citadels against invasions and
" against liberty. Their mountains are their for-
" tifications, and every householder is a sol-
" dier, ready to fight for his country." This is
the account which Voltaire gives of that country. Since that time, it has fallen by a power
greater than its own, and paid with its liberty
for the folly and madness of the rest of Europe. I hope I shall not offend any of the sy-
cophants of power, any of the enlightened patriots of the day who regard the general dis-

tinctions of liberty and slavery as slight and
evanescent, by adding to my list of political
grievances foreign conquest as an evil, and an
evil that tends to no certain good.—I would
fain know from the adepts in the science of population whether according to that system it
would be an advantage to this country to be
conquered by the French. The necessary ratios
of the increase of food and population (which
according to our author are every thing,—he utterly rejects the idea that established governments can do any mischief) would of course remain the same ; and as to the practical part,
population would, if any thing, go on slower
than before. I cannot but think however that
most of my readers would in such a case anticipate the consequences which our political re-
former describes in his croaking old-fashioned
way as proceeding from another cause, the corruption of the people, and the abuses of government at home. " I see" he says, " my
" wretched country in the same condition as
" France is now." [This was written at a time
when it was the fashion for the English to reproach all other countries for their misery and
slavery, as they have since been in the habit of
hunting them down for their attempts at liberty.]
" Instead of the rich and thriving farmers, who
" now fill or who lately filled, the country with

" agriculture, yielding plenty for man and beast,
" I see the lands neglected, the villages and
" farms in ruins, with here and there a star-
" veling in wooden shoes, driving his plough,
" his team consisting of an old goat, a hide-
" bound bullock, and an ass, value in all forty
" shillings. I see the once rich and populous
" cities of England in the same condition with
" those of Spain; whole streets lying in rub-
" bish, and the grass peeping out between the
" stones in those which continue still inhabited.
" I see the harbours empty, the warehouses
" shut up, and the shop-keepers playing at
" draughts, for want of customers. I see our
" noble and spacious turnpike roads covered
" with thistles and other weeds, and hardly to
" be traced out. I see the studious men rea-
" ding the Political Disquisitions, and the his-
" tories of the eighteenth century, and exe-
" crating the stupidity of their fathers, who in
" spite of the many faithful warnings given
" them, sat still, and suffered their country to
" be ruined by a set of wretches, whom they
" could have crushed. I see the country de-
" voured by an army of 200,000 men. I see
" justice trodden under foot in the courts of
" justice. I see *Magna Charta*, the *Habeas*
" *Corpus* act, the bill of rights, and trial by
" jury, obsolete, and royal edicts and *arrets* set

" up in their place. I see the once respectable
" land-owners, tradesmen, and manufacturers
" of England sunk into contempt, and place-
" men and military officers the only persons of
" consequence, &c." I do not know but there
may be some staunch adherents to the new philosophy, some hyper-graduates in the school,
who would think such a state of things " a
" consummation devoutly to be wished." But
it is happy that where our reason leaves us, our
prejudices often come to our aid. Though
there may be some persons in this country who
would not care a fig for the Bastile, or letters
de cachet, there is no one who has not a just
dread of Buonaparte ; or who would not indig-
nantly spurn at the wretch who told him that
so long as the disproportion in the increase of
food and the increase of mankind continued, it
was of little consequence to him whether he was
subject to the yoke of a foreign tyrant, or governed by a mild and lawful sovereign.—It has
always been the custom for the English to extol
themselves to the skies as the freest and hap-
piest nation on the face of the earth. Ever
since I was a boy, I remember to have heard of
the trial by jury, Magna Charta, and the bill of
rights, of the Bastile in France, and the Inquisition in Spain, and the man in the Iron mask.
Now whether it is that I was a boy when I first

heard of these things, or that they carry some
weight and meaning in themselves, certain it is
that they have made such a strong and indelible
impression on my mind as totally to preclude
the effects of Mr. Malthus's philosophy.
Whether it is owing to the strength of my reason or my prejudices, I cannot receive the benefit of his new light. As these are some of
the strongest feelings I have, (though they may
perhaps be just as childish as those which I still
have in reading the story of Goody Two-Shoes,
or the Little Red Riding-hood) it occurred to
me to make some use of them in answer to Mr.
Malthus's challenge to shew that there is no
difference between one government and another
in the essentials of liberty and happiness. Or
I thought I might contrast the constitution of
this country with that of Denmark, where (says
Lord Molesworth) the peasants are as absolute
slaves as the negroes in Jamaica, and *worse fed.*
This seemed to be strong ground. But then I
recollected that the very same expression had
been applied by a person, whom it would be
unbecoming in me to contradict, to the peasants
in this country.* I also met with a passage

* See the ingenious and elegant defence of the Slave-Trade,
attributed in the newspapers to his Royal Highness the Duke of
Clarence. There is a magnanimity and noble ingenuousness

something to the same purpose in the Political
Disquisitions, which a little damped my patriotic eagerness. " A poor hard-working man,
" who has a wife and six children to maintain"
[what a wicked wretch !] " can neither enjoy
" the glorious light of heaven, nor the glim-
" mering of a farthing candle, without paying
" the window tax and the candle tax. He
" rises early and sits up late ; he fills the whole
" day with severe labour ; he goes to his flock-
" bed with half a belly-full of bread and cheese
" denying the call of natural appetite, that his
" wife and little starvelings may have the
" more." [Why he is very justly punished to
be sure. True ; but mark the sequel.] " In
" the mean while the exactors of these taxes
" are revelling at the expence of more money
" for one evening's amusement, than the
" wretched hard-working man (who is obliged
" to find the money for them to squander) can
" earn by half a year's severe labour." On the
whole, I was obliged to relinquish my project. I found that my picture must either
want effect, or be out of all keeping. And
besides the relations of things had not only

in the avowal of such a sentiment, which can only be expected
from those, who from the elevated superiority of their situation
can look down with contempt on the opinion of mankind, and
the vulgar notions of decency and order.

changed, but men's opinions had changed with them. An overcharged description of English liberty and continental slavery would not be at all to the taste of the times. It would sound like mere rant, and would come to nothing. But when I came to that fine representation of the effects of slavery, which Burgh has left us, with those exquisite figures of the old goat, the bullock and the ass, and the groupe of shop-keepers playing at draughts for want of something to do, I was determined to bring it in, cost what it would. At last, I bethought me of the expedient of an invasion,—at that word I knew that every true friend of his country would grow pale, would see the odious consequences of slavery in their native deformity, and turn with disdain from those vile panders to vice and misery, those sanguine enthusiasts of mischief, who would artfully reconcile them to every species of want, oppression, and unfeeling barbarity, as the necessary conse-- quences of the principle of population. So much more credit do we attach to names, than things !—The whole of the account of Denmark to which I have just referred, is well worthy of attention : I cannot forbear giving the following extract. " The consequence of " this oppression is that the people of Denmark

" finding it impossible to secure their property"
[from the tax-gatherers] " squander their little
" gettings, as fast as they can, and are irreme-
" diably poor.   Oppression and arbitrary sway
" beget distrust and doubts about the security
" of property ; doubts beget profusion, men
" chusing to squander on their pleasures what
" they apprehend may excite the rapaciousness
of⁹ their superiors ; and this profusion is the
" legitimate parent of that universal indolence,
" poverty and despondency, which so strongly
" characterize the miserable inhabitants of Den-
" mark.   When Lord Molesworth resided in
" that country, the collectors of the poll-tax
" were obliged to accept of old feather-beds,
" brass and pewter pans, &c. instead of money,
" from the inhabitants of a town, which once
" raised 200.000 rix dollars for Christiern IV.
" on twenty-four hours' notice.   The quar-
" tering and paying the king's troops is another
" grievance no less oppressive.   The boors are
" obliged to furnish the king and every little in-
" solent courtier with horses and waggons in
" their journeys, and are beaten like cattle.
" Consequently, Denmark, once very populous,
" is become thin of inhabitants ; as poverty,
" oppression, and meagre diet do miserably
" check procreation, besides producing diseases
" which shorten the lives of the few who are

" born." [How miserably short-sighted must our author have been not to perceive that these were great advantages!] " All this the rich " and thriving and free people of England may " bring themselves to, if they please" [by following up Mr. Malthus's theory.] " It is only " letting the court go on with their scheme of " diffusing universal corruption through all " ranks, and it will come of course."—There is one passage in this account, which malevolence itself cannot apply to the history of this country. " Before the government of Denmark was " made hereditary and absolute in the present " royal family, by that fatal measure in 1660, " the nobility lived in great splendour and afflu- " ence. *Now they are poor, and their number* " *diminished.*"

I shall conclude these extracts with the following passages, taken at random, which will at least serve to shew the strange prejudices that prevailed on the subject, before Mr. Malthus, like the clown in Shakespear, undertook to find out an answer that should explain all difficulties. " It must indeed be an answer of most mon- " strous size that fits all demands." But perhaps Mr. Malthus is by this time convinced, that " a thing may serve long, and not serve " ever."

" The richest soil in Europe, Italy, is full of
" beggars ; among the Grisons, the poorest
" country in Europe, there are no beggars.
" The bailage of Lugane is the worst country,
" the least productive, the most exposed to cold
" and the least capable of trade of any in all
" Italy, and yet is the best peopled. If ever
" this country is brought under a yoke like that
" which the rest of Italy bears, it will soon be
" abandoned, for nothing draws so many people
" to live in so bad a soil, when they are in sight
" of the best soil in Europe, but the easiness of
" the government." Burnet's Travels.

" Italy shews, in a very striking light, the ad-
" vantages of free government.*   The subjects
" of the Italian republics are thriving and
" happy.   Those under the Pope, the dukes of
" Tuscany, Florence &c. wretched in the ex-
" treme. — Lucca, to mention no other, is a re-
" markable instance of the happy effects of li-
" berty.   The whole dominion is but thirty
" miles round, yet contains, besides the city,
" 150 villages, 120,000 inhabitants, and all the
" soil is cultivated to the utmost.   Their magis-

---

* Mr. Malthus, for what reason I know not, in his account of
the state of population in the different countries of modern
Europe, has declined giving any account of the state of population in Italy.

" trates are re-elected every two months out of
" a body of nobility, who are chosen every two
" years." Modern Universal History. See
also A. Sydney as before quoted.—These differences cannot be accounted for by the length of
time or the force with which the principle of
population has operated in these states. The
countries are equally old, and the climate very
nearly the same.

" In England an industrious subject has the
" best chance for thriving, because the country
" is the freest. In the Mogul's dominions the
" worst, because the country is the most effec-
" tually enslaved."

" The title of freemen was formerly confined
" chiefly to the nobility and gentry, who were
" descended of free ancestors. *For the greatest
" part of the people* was restrained under some
" species of slavery, so that they were not their
" own masters." Spelman's Glossary.*—On

* Among other instances it is mentioned, that every vassal
was obliged to give the first night of his bride to the lord of
the manor, if he demanded it. It is hard to be sure for a man
to be cuckolded the very first night of his marriage But
even at present, though the formality of the thing is abolished,
there are very few husbands who are not tolerably certain of
being cuckolded by the first lord, or duke, who thinks it worth
his while to attempt it. It is some consolation to us poor devils

this passage my author remarks very gravely, " What has been in England may be again. If " liberty be on the decline, no one knows how " low it may sink, and to what pitch of slavery " and cruelty it may grow." Mr. Malthus's theory tends to familiarise the mind to such a change as the necessary effect of the progress of population. But this pretext is here clearly done away, as we have fought up to our present free, and flourishing state, in the *teeth* of this principle. Our progress has not been uniformly *retrograde*, as it ought to have been to make any thing of the argument.

" It is constantly (said a member in Queen Elizabeth's time) in the mouths of us all, that " our lands, goods and laws are at our prince's " disposal." We do not at present come *quite* up to the loyalty of this speaker.

" Nations have often been deceived into sla-" very by men of shining abilities." Perhaps

---

of authors, that we have no chance of getting a wife who is at all likely to meet with any such distinction. But if I were a snug tradesman or city-merchant, and had bargained for a sweet girl whose smile was Elysium, whose air was enchantment, and her looks all love,—I should be terribly afraid of the cocked hats at the opera. I should tremble at every coronet coach that passed the door, and should run mad at the sight of a prince's feather.

the late Mr. Burke was an instance of this. I
by no means insist that he was, because there
may be differences of opinion on that point.
But of this I am sure, that the effect of his
writings, good or bad, cannot be measured—by
the principle of population.

" A single genius changes the face and state
" of a whole country, as Gustavus Adolphus of
" Sweden, and Peter the great of Russia.
" Confucius produced a reformation in one of
" the oriental kingdoms in a few months."

" Commerce introduced by the czar Peter
" introduced luxury. Universal dissipation
" took the lead, and profligacy of manners suc-
" ceeded. *Many of the lords began to squeeze*
" *and grind the peasants to extort fresh supplies*
" *from them for the incessant demands of*
" *luxury*"—not of population.

" The extreme poverty occasioned by idle-
" ness and luxury in the beginning of Lewis
" XIII. of France filled the streets of Paris
" with beggars. The court disgusted at the
" sight, which indeed was a severe reproach on
" them, issued an order, forbidding all persons,
" on severe penalties, to relieve them, intending
" thereby to drive them out of the town, and

" not caring though they dropped down dead,
" before they could reach the country towns
" and villages." This was a project worthy
of the genius of Mr. Malthus.

" Government, according to Plato, is the
" parent of manners. One judicious regulation
" will often produce a very salutary effect on a
" whole people, as experimental philosophy
" shews us, that a wire will secure a castle
" from the once irresistible force of lightning.—
" Mankind may be brought to hold any prin-
" ciples and to indulge any practices, and again
" to give them up.—Is there any notion of
" right and wrong, about which mankind are
" universally agreed ? Is it not evident that
" mankind may be moulded into any shape ?
" How come we to know that antimony or
" quicksilver may, by chemical processes, be
" made to pass through twenty different states,
" and restored again to their original state ? Is
" it not by experiment ? Are not the various
" legislations, institutions, regulations of wise
" or designing statesmen, priests, and kings, a
" series of experiments, shewing that human
" nature is susceptible of any form or cha-
" racter ?" According to the most modern
discovery, these things never did, nor ever
will have any effect at all. The question is

simply, whether the state of food and the state
of population being the same, the different
causes here alluded to have not produced very
different results with respect to the degree both
of vice and misery existing in the world.*

" The great difference we see between the
" behaviour of the people called Quakers, and all
" others ; between English, Scotch, Irish,
" French, Spanish, Heathens, Mahometan,
" Christian, Popish, Protestant manners and
" characters, &c. the regular and permanent
" difference we see between the manners of all
" these divisions of mankind, shews beyond all
" doubt that the principles and habits of the
" people are very much in the power of able
" statesmen."

" Among the Lacedemonians there was no
" such crime as infidelity to the marriage-bed :
" yet Lycurgus in framing his laws had used
" no precaution against it, but the virtuous and
" temperate education he prescribed for the
" youth of both sexes.—The influence which
" education has on the manners of a people is so

* Even this is making a very large concession to Mr. Malthus.
The real points to be given are the possible power of produc-
tiveness in the earth and the necessary tendency of population to
increase.

" considerable that it cannot be estimated.
" But by *education* it is to be observed, we
" must understand not only what is taught at
" schools and universities, but the impressions
" young people receive from parents, and from
" the world, which greatly outweigh all that
" can be done by masters and tutors. Edu-
" cation, taken in this enlarged sense, is almost
" all that makes the difference between the
" characters of nations; and it is a severe satire
" on our times, *that the world makes most young*
" *men very different beings from what those who*
" *educated them intended them to be.*" This
last remark is I think of the utmost force and
importance; and has never been sufficiently
attended to by those who prate most fluently
and triumphantly about the inherent perversity
of human nature. A young man is seldom
tainted by the world, till he becomes dependent on it. I have known several persons
who I am sure have set out in life with the utmost purity of intention, and a noble ingenuousness of mind, and were prepared to act on
very different principles from those, which they
found prevailing in the world. Is the fault in
this case in the wood, or in the carver? Is it
in the stuff, or in the mould, in which it is
cast? The difficulty seems to be, how to get
a better mould.

" Aristotle lays down very strict rules con-
" cerning the company young people may be al-
" lowed to keep, the public diversions they may
" attend ; the pictures they may see, and against
" obscenity, intemperance, &c. And the eighth
" book of his politics is employed wholly on
" education, in which he shews, that youth
" ought to be strongly impressed with the idea
" of their being members of a community,
" whose good they are to prefer to their private
" advantage in all cases where they come in
" competition. He commends the wisdom of
" the Spartans in paying such attention to this
" great object. Such is the delicacy of this old
" Heathen, that he hesitates about the propriety
" of young men's applying to music, as being
" likely to enervate the mind."

" Lycurgus did not allow the Spartans to tra-
" vel, lest they should be tainted by the man-
" ners of other nations." I do not chuse to
name all the vices that have been imported into
this country within the last fifty years by the
aid of foreign travel. Vice is unfortunately of
a very tenacious quality, and there is no quaran-
tine against the epidemics of the mind. In return, however, we have learned to converse, to
dress, and dance better than we used to do.

" At Sparta, the poets could not publish any
" thing without a license; and all immoral
" writings were prohibited. A very wise man*
" said he believed, if a man were permitted
" to make all the ballads, he need not care who
" made the laws of a nation. The ancient le-
" gislators did not pretend to reform the man-
" ners of the people without the help of the
" poets."

" The grave Romans did not allow a person
" of character to dance! It was a saying
" among them, no one dances unless he is
" drunk or mad."

" In the old English laws, we find punish-
" ments for wanton behaviour, as touching the
" breasts of women, &c.—By the ancient laws
" of France, the least indecency of behaviour
" to a free woman, as squeezing the hand,
" touching the arm or breast, &c. was punish-
" able by fire."† What odd, sour, crabbed notions must have prevailed in those days! Not
squeeze a lady's hand! No—a much more
agreeable latitude of behaviour is allowed at
present: we are as much improved in our notions of gallantry as of liberty. The polite

---

* Fletcher of Saltoun.   † Spelman's Glossary.

reader will not suspect me of a design to hold up the shocking manners of our ancestors as models of imitation in the present day ; I only mention them to shew what a wide difference there may be in the notions of decency and propriety at different times !

If a stranger, on entering a large town, London for example, should be struck with that immense number of prostitutes, " who elbow us " aside in all our crowded streets," and not well knowing how to account for this enormous abuse, should apply to a disciple of the modern school for some explanation of it, he would probably be told with great gravity, *That it was a necessary consequence of the progress of population, and the superior power of that principle over the increase in the means of subsistence.*— If Mr. Malthus, contented to follow in the track of common sense, and not smitten with the love of dangerous novelty, had endeavoured to trace that torrent of vice and dissipation which threatens to bear down every principle of virtue and decency among us to the chief sources pointed out by other writers, to the particular institutions of society, to the prevalence of luxury, the inequality of conditions, the facility of gratifying the passions from the power of offering temptation, and inducements to accept it, the disproportion between the passions excited in individuals, and their situation in life, to books, to education, the progress of arts, the influence of neighbouring example, &c. these are all causes, which, as they are arbitrary and variable, seem as if they could be counteracted or modified by other causes ; they are the work of man, and what is the work of man it seems in the power of man to confirm or alter. We see distinctly the source of the grievance, and try to remedy it : hope remains, the will acts with double energy, the spirit of virtue is not broken. Our vices grow out of other vices, out of our own passions, prejudices, folly, and weakness : there is nothing in this to make us proud of them, or to reconcile us to them ; even though we may despair, we are not confounded. We still have the theory of virtue left : we are not obliged to give up the distinction between good and evil even in imagination : there is some little good which we may at least wish to do. Man in this case retains the character of a free agent ; he stands chargeable with his own conduct, and a sense of the consequences of his own presumption or blindness may arouse in him feelings that may in some measure counteract their worst effects ;

he may regret what he cannot help : the life, the pulse, the spring of morality is not dead in him ; his moral sense is not quite extinguished. But our author has chosen to stagger the minds of his readers by representing vice and misery as the necessary consequences of an abstract principle, of a fundamental law of our nature, on which nothing can be effected by the human will. This principle follows us wherever we go ; if we fly into the uttermost parts of the earth, it is there : whether we turn to the right or the left, we cannot escape from it. O rather for that warning voice, that once cried aloud, *Insenses qui vous plaignez sans cesse de la nature, apprenez que tous vos maux vous viennent de vous !* As however I deny the sufficiency of our author's all-pervading principle, I may be required to point out more particularly what I conceive to be the real and determining causes of the decay of manners. I do not know that I can mention any that do not come under the heads already alluded to, but if I must give a short answer, I should say,—Great towns, great schools, dress, and novels. These things are not regulated exactly by the size of the earth, and yet must be allowed to have some influence on manners. To instance only in the two last. Is it to be wondered at that a young raw ignorant girl, who is sent up from the country as a milliner's or mantua-maker's apprentice, and stowed into a room with eight or ten others, who snatch every moment they can spare from caps and bonnets, and sit up half the night to read all the novels they can get, and as soon they have finished one, send for another, whose heart, in the course of half a year, has been pierced through with twenty beaux on paper, who has been courted, seduced, run away with, married and put to bed under all the fine names that the imagination can invent to as many fine gentlemen, who has sighed and wept with so many heroes and heroines that her tears and sighs have at last caused in her a defluction of the brain, and a palpitation of the heart at the sight of every man, whose fancy is love-sick, and her head quite turned, should be unable to resist the first coxcomb of real flesh and blood, who in shining boots and a velvet collar accosts her in the shape of a lover, but who has no thoughts of marrying her, because if he were to take this imprudent step, he must give up his shining boots and velvet collar, and the respect they procure him in the world? Zaleucus ordained that no woman should dress herself gorgeously, unless she was a prostitute. If I were a law-giver, and chose to meddle in such matters, I would ordain that no woman should expose her shape publicly, unless she were a prostitute.—The female form is more proper for child-bearing, than for public exhibition: this secret analogy, when coupled with modesty and reserve, is however its greatest charm. The strange fancy-dresses, the perverse disguises, the counterfeit shapes, the stiff stays, and enormous hoops worn by the women in the time of the Spectator gave an agreeable scope to the imagination. The greedy eye and rash hand of licentiousness were repressed. The senses were never satisfied in an instant. Love was entangled in the folds of the swelling handkerchief, and the desires might wander for ever round the circumference of a quilted petticoat, or find a rich lodging in the flowers of a damask stomacher. There was room for years of patient perseverance, for a thousand thoughts, fancies, conjectures, hopes, fears, and wishes. There seemed no end to difficulties and delays: to overcome so many obstacles was the work of ages. A *wife* had then some meaning it: it was an angel concealed behind whalebone, flounces, and brocade. The transition from a mistress in masquerade to a wife in wedding sheets was worth venturing for: now it is nothing, and we hear no more of faithful courtships, and roman-

tic loves. A woman can be *but* undressed.—
The young ladies we at present see with the
thin muslin vest drawn tight round the slender
waist, and following with nice exactness the
undulations of the shape downwards, disclosing
each full swell, each coy recess, obtruding on
the eye each opening charm, the play of the
muscles, the working of the thighs, and by the
help of a walk, of which every step seems a
gird, and which keeps the limbs strained to the
utmost point, displaying all those graceful in-
volutions of person, and all those powers of fascinating motion, of which the female form is
susceptible—these moving pictures of lust and
nakedness, against which the greasy imaginations of grooms and porters may rub themselves, running the gauntlet of the saucy looks
and indecent sarcasms of the boys in the street,
staring at every ugly fellow, leering at every
handsome man, and throwing out a lure for
every fool (true Spartan girls, who if they were
metamorphosed into any thing in the manner of
Ovid, it would certainly be into valerian !) are the
very same, whose mothers or grand-mothers
buried themselves under a pile of clothes,
whose timid steps hardly touched the ground,
whose eyes were constantly averted from the
rude gaze of the men, and who almost blushed

at their own shadows. " Of such we in romances read." It does not require any great spirit of divination to perceive that this change in appearance must imply some change in manners. Is this change then owing entirely to the increased pressure of the principle of population, or have not French fashions, French milliners, and French dancing-masters had some hand in producing it?*—Mr. Malthus inveighs with great severity against squalid poverty, and the vices produced by filth and rags. I allow the justice of his remarks, and think that the condition of the poor in this respect is one of the chief nuisances of society. After giving the poor a scrubbing with a coarse towel in the manner he has done, it would not have been amiss if he had taken a clean white clerical pocket-handkerchief, and applied it to wipe off the rouge from the cheeks of painted prostitution, or thrown it as a covering over the polished neck and ivory shoulders of ladies of high quality. The bishop of London would have praised the attempt. Mr. Malthus might have distinguished between the involuntary rents, and the unlucky loop-holes

* Have Dryden's Fables, the New Eloise, or the Memoirs of Fanny Hill never added any thing to the pressure of the principle of population, without any reference to the parish registers of deaths and marriages?

which sometimes appear in a poor girl's petticoat, and the elegant dishabille and studied nakedness of high life. The dirt that sticks to a wench's face in cleaning a saucepan is I think likely to have less effect on the character than the red paste daubed on the cheeks before a looking-glass, to give *animation* to the eyes. The contempt which dirt and poverty excite must destroy all moral sensibility. Must not the glare of fashion and the perpetual intoxication of personal vanity have the same effect? The poor grovel in disagreeable sensations, the rich wanton in voluptuous ones. The passions are not more likely to be inflamed by stale porter, the screams of a fiddle, and the clattering of a hornpipe at a hop in St. Giles's, than by the elegant liqueurs, the soft sounds of the clarionet and hautboy, and the languishing movements of walses, allemandes, and minuets *de la cour* at a ball in St. James's. A fair, or an opera may equally turn the head of any silly girl that goes to one. Of the two, a tune on the salt-box would be got over sooner than Narcissus and the Graces. The tawdry prints to be seen in garrets, and the ballads sung at the corners of streets do not much improve the morals of the people : but I put it to the conscience of our sentimental divine, whether the Wanton Wife of

Bath, or the tall captain with his arm round the
chambermaid's waist, or Jemmy Jessamy loll-
ing on the sofa with his mistress, may be expected to produce more accidents than those
luscious collections of the poets, or those grave
scripture-pieces, or classical *chef-d'œuvres* of
Venus and Adonis, of Leda with her Swan,
Nymphs, Fawns, and Satyrs, which gentlemen
of fortune keep in their houses for the instruction of their wives and daughters. Mr.
Malthus is convinced that no young woman
brought up in nastiness and vulgarity, however
virtuous she may seem, can be good for any
thing at twenty: I confess I have the same
cynical opinion of those, who have the good
fortune to be brought up in the obscene refinements of fashionable life.

I never fell in love but once; and then it was
with a girl who always wore her handkerchief
pinned tight round her neck, with a fair face,
gentle eyes, a soft smile, and cool auburn locks.
I mention this, because it may in some measure account for my temperate, tractable notions of this passion, compared with Mr. Malthus's. It was not a raging heat, a fever in
the veins: but it was like a vision, a dream,
like thoughts of childhood, an everlasting hope,

a distant joy, a heaven, a world that might be. The dream is still left, and sometimes comes confusedly over me in solitude and silence, and mingles with the softness of the sky, and veils my eyes from mortal grossness. After all, Mr. Malthus may be right in his opinion of human nature. Though my notions of love have been thus aerial and refined, I do not know that this was any advantage to me, or that I might not have done better with a few of our author's ungovernable transports, and sensual oozings. Perhaps the workings of the heart are best expressed by a gloating countenance, by mawkish sentiments and lively gestures. Cupid often perches on broad shoulders, or on the brawny calf of a leg, a settlement is better than a love-letter, and in love not minds, but bodies and fortunes meet. I have therefore half a mind to retract all that I have said, and prove to Mr. Malthus that love is not even so intellectual a passion as he sometimes admits it to be, but altogether gross and corporal.

I have thus attempted to answer the different points of Mr. Malthus's argument, and give a truer account of the various principles that actuate human nature. There is but one advantage that I can conceive of as resulting from the admission of his mechanical theory on the subject, which is that it would be the most effectual recipe for indifference that has yet been found out. No one need give himself any farther trouble about the progress of vice, or the extension of misery. The office of moral censor, that troublesome, uneasy office which every one is so ready to set up in his own breast, and which I verily believe is the occasion of more unhappiness than any one cause else, would be at an end. The professor's chair of morality would become vacant, and no one would have more cause than I to rejoice at the breaking up for the holidays; for I have plagued myself a good deal about the distinctions of right and wrong. The pilot might let go the helm, and leave the vessel to drift carelessly before the stream. When we are once convinced that the degree of virtue and happiness can no more be influenced by human wisdom than the ebbing and flowing of the tide, it must be idle to give ourselves any more concern about them. The wise man might then enjoy an Epicurean languor and repose, without being conscious of the neglect of duty. Mr. Malthus's system is one, " in which " the wicked cease from troubling, and in which " the weary are at rest." To persons of an irritable and nervous disposition, who are fond

of kicking against the pricks, who have tasted
of the bitterness of the knowledge of good and
evil, and to whom whatever is amiss in others
sticks not merely like a burr, but like a pitch-
plaister, the advantage of such a system is in-
calculable.—

Happy are they, who live in the dream of
their own existence, and see all things in
the light of their own minds ; who walk by
faith and hope, not by knowledge ; to whom
the guiding-star of their youth still shines from
afar, and into whom the spirit of the world has
not entered ! They have not been " hurt by
the archers," nor has the iron entered their
souls. They live in the midst of arrows, and
of death, unconscious of harm. The evil thing
comes not nigh them. The shafts of ridicule
pass unheeded by, and malice loses its sting.
Their keen perceptions do not catch at hidden
mischiefs, nor cling to every folly. The example
of vice does not rankle in their breasts, like
the poisoned shirt of Nessus. Evil impressions
fall off from them, like drops of water. The yoke
of life is to them light and supportable. The
world has no hold on them. They are in it,
not of it ; and a dream and a glory is ever about
them.

EXTRACTS

FROM THE ESSAY ON POPULATION.

WITH A COMMENTARY, AND NOTES.

———————

I INTENDED to have added another Letter on the principle of population as affecting the laws of property, and the condition of the poor. But I found it impossible to combat some of Mr. Malthus's opinions without bringing vouchers for them. I might otherwise seem to be combating the chimeras of my own brain. There are some instances of perverse reasoning so gross and mischievous, that without seeing the confidence with which they are insisted on, it seems a waste of time to contradict them. The reader may perhaps have had something of this feeling already. By throwing the remainder of the work into the form of Extracts with notes I shall at least avoid the imputation of ascribing to Mr. Malthus singularities he never dreamt of, and have an opportunity of remarking upon some incidental passages, which appeared to me liable to objection in the perusal. My remarks will be confined almost entirely to the two last books of the work.

" M. Condorcet's *Esquisse d'un tableau historique des*
" *progres de l'esprit humain*, was written, it is said, under
" the pressure of that cruel proscription which termi-
" nated in his death. If he had no hopes of its being
" seen during his life, and of its interesting France in
" his favour, it is a singular instance of the attachment
" of a man to principles, which every day's experience
" was, so fatally for himself, contradicting. To see the
" human mind, in one of the most enlightened na-
" tions of the world, debased by such a fermentation
" of disgusting passions, of fear, cruelty, malice,
" revenge, ambition, madness, and folly, as would
" have disgraced the most savage nations in the most
" barbarous age, must have been such a tremendous
" shock to his ideas of the necessary and inevitable
" progress of the human mind, that nothing but the
" the firmest conviction of the truth of his prin-
" ciples, in spite of all appearances, could have
" withstood."

Mr. Malthus in his pick-thank way, here takes
occasion to sneer at Condorcet for his attachment to
principles, which, he asserts, every day's experience
was contradicting. As this of mine is not a pick-
thank work, I must take the liberty of observing, as
I have never read M. Condorcet's work, that if his
ideas of the future progress of the human mind were
the same as those of other writers on the subject,
that debasement of character, and that mass of disgusting passions, which developed themselves in the
events to which Mr. Malthus here alludes, were the
strongest confirmation of the necessity of getting rid
of those institutions which had thus degraded the

human character, and under which such passions had been fostered: for to say that the progress of the human mind, in spite of those institutions, was necessary and inevitable, or that there were no such passions as fear, cruelty, malice, revenge, &c. belonging to the character generated by the old system in France (in which an immediate change could not be expected without a miracle) would have been such a contradiction to common sense, and to all their own favourite schemes of reform, as no madman in the height of revolutionary madness was ever guilty of. All that could ever be pretended by the advocates of reform was that there were capacities for improvement in the mind, which had hitherto notwithstanding the advantages of knowledge been thwarted by human institutions. The contradiction rests therefore not with Condorcet, but with our author. The same objection has been often made, and often refuted. But there are some reasoners who care little how often a fallacy has been exposed, if they know there are people who are still inclined to listen to it.

" This posthumous publication is only a sketch of " a much larger work which he proposed should be " executed. It necessarily wants, therefore, that " detail and application, which can alone prove the " truth of any theory." [This remark I cannot admit. I do not think for instance that any detail or application is necessary to prove the truth of Mr. Malthus's general principle of the disproportion between the power of increase in population, and in the productions of the earth, or to shew the bad consequences of an unrestricted increase of population.] " A few observations will be sufficient to " shew how completely this theory is contradicted, " when it is applied to the real and not to an imaginary " state of things." [The *contre-sens* implied in this expression is not a slip of the pen, but a fixed principle in Mr. Malthus's mind. He has a very satisfactory method of answering all theories relating to any imaginary alterations or improvements in the condition of mankind, by shewing what would be the consequences of a certain state of society, if no such state of society really existed, but if every thing remained just as it is at present. He thinks it sound sense and true philosophy to judge of a theory which is confessedly imaginary or has never been realized by comparing it " with the real and not with an imaginary state of " things." That is, he does not adopt the necessarian maxim that men will be always the same while the circumstances continue, but he insists upon it that they will 'be always the same, whether the circumstances are the same or not. Some instances have already appeared of this in the foregoing work. The following passage may serve as another instance. After supposing Mr. Godwin's system of equality to be realized to its utmost extent, and the most perfect form of society established, he exclaims, " this would " indeed be a happy state; but that it is merely an " imaginary state with scarcely a feature near the " *truth*, the reader, I am afraid, is already too well " convinced." Mr. Godwin himself was I apprehend very well convinced that this imaginary state

was very different from the truth or from the present
state of things, when he wrote his book to shew how
much better the one *would be* than the other *is*. He then
goes on, " Man cannot live in the midst of plenty.
" All cannot share alike the bounties of nature.
" Were there no established administration of pro-
" perty, every man would be obliged to guard with
" force his little store. Selfishness would be trium-
" phant. The subjects of contention would be per-
" petual," &c. If there were no established administration of property, while men continued as selfish as
they are at present, (which is I suppose what Mr.
Malthus means by applying the theory *to the real
state of things*) the consequences here mentioned
would no doubt follow. But it is supposed that there
is no established administration of property, because
the necessity for it has ceased or because selfishness is
not triumphant, but vanquished. This is the supposition. Mr. Malthus however persists, that were there
no established administration of property, " every man
" would be obliged to guard with force his little store
" since selfishness would still be as triumphant as ever."
This is contrary to all the received rules of reasoning.
He then proceeds to examine, how long Mr. Godwin's
theory if once realized might be expected to last,
and how soon the present vices of men would dis-
compose this *perfect* form of society, concluding
very wisely that " a theory that will not admit of ap-
" plication cannot possibly be just." True: if a man
tells you that a triangle has certain properties, he is
bound to make good this theory with respect to a triangle, but not with respect to a circle.—The outcry

which Mr. Malthus here makes about experience is
without any meaning. It is evident that we cannot
make this word a rule in all cases whatever. For instance, if a man who is in the habit of drinking a
bottle of brandy every day of his life and consequently enjoys but an indifferent state of health, is
advised by his physician to leave off this practice,
and told that *on this condition* he may recover his
health and appetite, it would not be considered as a
proof of any great wisdom in the man, if he were to
answer this reasoning of his physician by applying it
to the real, and not to an imaginary state of things,
or by saying, " The consequences you promise me
from submitting to your regimen are indeed very
desirable ; but I cannot expect any such consequences
from it : I have always been in very bad health
from the habit I have constantly been in of drinking
brandy ; and it would be contrary to the experience of my whole life to suppose, that I should
receive any benefit from leaving it off." In like manner, I conceive that it is not from any great depth of
philosophy, but from the strength of his attachment
to the good things of this life, that Mr. Malthus makes
so many ill-judged appeals to experience. He is
afraid of launching into the empty regions of abstraction, he stands shivering on the brink ; or if he
ventures a little way, soon turns back again,
frightened out of his wits, and muttering something
about population. His imagination cannot sustain
for a moment the idea of any real improvement or
elevation in the human character, but instantly drops
down into the filth of vice and misery, out of which

it had just crawled. His attempts at philosophy put me in mind of the exploits of those citizens who set out on a Sunday morning to take an excursion into the country, resolved to taste the fresh air, and not be confined for ever to the same spot, but who get no farther than Paddington, White Conduit-house, or Bagnigge-wells, unable to leave the smoke, the noise and dust, to which they have so long been used! Mr. Malthus is a perfect *cockney* in matters of philosophy.

M. Condorcet, allowing that there must in all stages of society be a number of individuals who have no other resource than their industry, or that " there exists a necessary cause of inequality, of " dependence and even of misery,* which menaces " without ceasing the most numerous and active " class of the community," proposes to establish a fund, which should assure to the old an assistance, produced in part *by their own former savings,* and partly by the savings of others, who die before they reap the benefit of it; and that this fund might extend to women and children, who had lost their husbands or fathers, and afford a capital to young beginners, sufficient for the developement of their industry. To those who have not fathomed all the depths and shoals of the principle of population, this

---

* Mr. M. always translates the word *misere* or want misery, and has adopted it as the burthen of his song. He has made a very significant use of this equivoque in many parts of his work.

plan seems feasible enough. Mr. Malthus's cautious reserved humanity, his anxious concern about the support of the aged, the infirm, the widow, and the orphan, his wish to give every encouragement to industry, and above all, his regard for the rights and independence of his fellows, lead him to see nothing but difficulties and objections in the way of such a plan.

" Such establishments may appear very promising
" upon paper; but when applied to real life, they
" will be found to be absolutely nugatory. M. Con-
" dorcet allows, that a class of people which main-
" tains itself entirely by industry is necessary to
" every state. Why does he allow this? No other
" reason can well be assigned, than because he con-
" ceives, that the labour necessary to procure sub-
" sistence for an extended population, will not be
" performed without the goad of necessity. If by
" establishments, upon the plans that have been men-
" tioned, this spur to industry be removed; if the
" idle and negligent be placed upon the same footing
" with regard to their credit, and the future support
" of their wives and families, as the active and in-
" dustrious, can we expect to see men exert that
" animated activity in bettering their condition,
" which now forms the master-spring of publick
" prosperity. If an inquisition were to be established
" to examine the claims of each individual, and to
" determine whether he had, or had not, exerted
" himself to the utmost, and to grant or refuse

" assistance accordingly, this would be little else
" than a repetition upon a larger scale, of the Eng-
" lish poor laws, and would be completely de-
" structive of the true principles of liberty and
" equality."

This passage only shews the shyness of our author's
benevolence. He will hear of no short-cuts or obvious
expedients for bettering the condition of the poor.
All his benefits are extracted by the Cæsarean operation.—In the first place, he contradicts himself. He
first supposes that labour cannot be performed without
the *goad of necessity,* and then affirms that it is *the prospect of bettering their condition,* that makes men exert
themselves, and forms the master-spring of public
prosperity. But why is it necessary that the idle and
negligent should be put upon the same footing with
the industrious, with respect to their credit, the support of their families, &c.? As to the first of these,
it is proposed to be only temporary, to serve as a beginning, and if a proper use is not made of it, the
goad of necessity, to which Mr. Malthus is so ready
to resort on all occasions, will soon begin to do its
office. As to the second object, the support of a
surviving family, in case of accidents, did Mr. Malthus
never hear of any distress produced in this way, but
in consequence of the idleness and negligence of the
deceased? Is not a poor family necessarily reduced
to distress by the death of the husband, let his industry
and sobriety have been never so great, and even
reduced to greater distress in proportion to his industry,
as they must miss his help the more? Besides, it

is not likely that the witholding this assistance from a
man's family after his death will be any inducement
to the idle and negligent to exert themselves, when the
sight of the actual distress in which their families are
involved by their ill conduct has no effect upon them.
I see no objection to proportioning the allowance to
the old, or to those who have had time to make a provision for themselves, to the contributions they have
really made to the fund in a given length of time. This
would be a sufficient test of the validity of their pretensions, as they could not contribute largely, without
proportionably straitening themselves, and the idle and
profligate are not very apt to part with their present gains
to provide for any speculative uncertainties or future difficulty. (Mr. Malthus may measure the support allotted
to their families in the same way.) While the distinction of the idle and industrious continued, and while it
was necessary to encourage the one and discountenance
the other, I do not understand what objection there can
be to this mode, or how it would trench upon the true
principles of liberty and equality. True equality supposes equal merit and virtue. But Mr. Malthus is
alarmed at this scheme, because, he says, it is little else
than a repetition on a larger scale of the English poor
laws. If the English poor laws are formed upon this
principle, I should, I confess, be very sorry to see
them abolished.

" Were every man sure of a comfortable provision
" for a family, almost every man would have one ; and
" were the rising generation free from the ' killing frost'

" of misery, population must increase with unusual
" rapidity."

This is an utter falsification of the argument, as I
have already shewn. Every man could not be sure of
a comfortable provision for a family, unless this provision existed, and I see no reason why the rising generation should not be free from the killing frost of misery, at least while they can. To argue that our enlightened posterity will feel " secure that the general
" benevolence will supply every deficiency," is to suppose
them strangely unacquainted with the principles of
Mr. Malthus's Essay.

" The period when the number of men surpass their
" means of subsistence' has long since arrived." p. 357.

This I must deny. That the period of the utmost
degree of populousness would have arrived long ago,
if nothing had prevented it, I am very ready to grant.
But that it has ever actually arrived, is another question. Because population would have arrived at its
greatest possible or desirable height long before our
time, if it had not been kept back by any artificial and
arbitrary checks, is that any reason why it should never
attain that height, or should not now be suffered to go
on, though those checks have always operated to
keep it back much more than was necessary, viz.
below the level not only of the possible, but of
the *actual* means of subsistence or produce of the
earth? As to the period when the world is likely
to maintain the greatest possible number of inhabi-

tants in the greatest possible comfort, I have no notion
that it will ever arrive at all. If however it should
ever arrive, it must be in consequence either of a gradual or immediate complete improvement in the state
of society. If this improvement is gradual, the increase in population will be so too, and will not
reach its farthest limit till a considerably remote period;
if the improvement is sudden and rapid, still it must be
some time before the operation of the new system of
things will have overcome all obstacles, and completely
peopled the earth. So that in either case the event
seems a good way off. The danger of arriving at this
point does not therefore appear to be " immediate or
" imminent," but doubtful and distant.

Mr. Malthus in his examination of Condorcet's arguments, in favour of the indefinite prolongation of
human life, (one of those absurdities against which no
good reason can be given, but that it shocks all common sense) shews considerable ingenuity, mixed np
with a great deal of that minute verbal logic, to which
he seems to have accustomed his mind, and which is
perpetually leading him into erroneous methods of
reasoning, even when he happens to be right in his
conclusions. As in the following passages.

" Variations from different causes are essentially dis-
" tinct from a regular and unretrograde increase. The
" average duration of human life will, to a certain de-
" gree, vary, from healthy or unhealthy climates, from
" wholesome or unwholesome food, from virtuous or

" vicious manners, and other causes ; but it may be
" fairly doubted, whether there has been really the
" smallest perceptible advance in the natural duration of
" human life, since first we had any authentic history
" of man. The prejudices of all ages have, indeed,
" been directly contrary to this supposition.

Now this statement is very unsatisfactory, to say
the least. For the only reason that can be given why
the causes here mentioned, on which Mr. M. allows
that the duration of human life depends, have not
produced a regular and permanent effect *must be,*
that they themselves have neither been regular nor
permanent. The mere fact, therefore, of the variableness in the length of human life proves nothing
but the variableness of those moral and artificial
causes, which are supposed to have some influence
on our physical constitution. But Condorcet supposes a regular advance to be made in these causes,
and that an indefinite advance in some of them (as
the knowledge of medicine for instance) is probable,
will hardly be disputed. The question (in this point
of view) of the necessary duration of human life is not
properly a question of fact, or history, but depends
on a comparison of the present circumstances of
mankind with their past circumstances, and (on
the probability that may thence appear of preventing
or counteracting those maladies and passions which
are most unfavourable to long life. That our reason
may sometimes get the start of our experience is
what no one can deny. Thus when the art of printing was first discovered it required no great stretch

of thought to perceive that knowledge and learning would soon become more generally diffused than they had hitherto been, though till this event no perceptible or regular progress had ever been made. Those who reason otherwise are a kind of stereographic reasoners who take things in the lump without being able to analyse or connect their different principles. Experience is but the alphabet of reason. With respect to the general shortness of human life compared with what it was in the first ages of mankind, this fact seems rather against Mr. Malthus, for if there is no certain date, no settled period to human life, beyond which it cannot hold out, but that it has varied from a thousand to a hundred years, so far there is no reason why we should not tread back our steps, or even go beyond the point from which we set out. There is no fixed limit: the present length of human life is not evidently a general law of nature. The mere naked fact of its never exceeding a certain length at present is just as decisive against its ever having been longer, as it is against its ever being longer in future. Mr. Malthus argues about human life, as Hume argues about miracles.

" It will be said, perhaps, that the reason why " plants and animals cannot increase indefinitely in " size, is, that they would fall by their own weight. " I answer, how do we know this but from expe- " rience? from experience of the degree of strength " with which these bodies are formed. I know that " a carnation, long before it reached the size of a " cabbage, would not be supported by its stalk; but

" I only know this from my experience of the weak-
" ness, and want of tenacity in the materials of a
" carnation stalk. There are many substances in
" nature, of the same size, that would support as
" large a head as a cabbage.

" The reasons of the mortality of plants are at
" present perfectly unknown to us. No man can say
" why such a plant is annual, another biennial, and
" another endures for ages. The whole affair in all
" these cases, in plants, animals, and in the human
" race, is an affair of experience ; and I only con-
" clude that man is mortal, because the invariable
" experience of all ages has proved the mortality
" of those materials of which his visible body is
" made.

" What can we reason but from what we know."

This is making use of words without ideas. It is endeavouring to confound two things essentially distinct,
because the same lax expression may be applied to
them both. It is an attempt to deprive men of their
understanding, and leave them nothing but the use of
their senses, by a trick of language. Does it follow
because all our knowledge may be traced in some way
to something which may be called *experience*, that all
our conclusions are nothing but an affair of memory ?
Does Mr. Malthus know of only one sort of experience ? Is there not a blind and a rational experience ?
Is it not one thing merely to know a fact, or a number
of facts, and another to know the *reason* of them ? Or
if our philosopher is determined to intrench himself
behind a word, is there not a knowledge founded on the

experience of certain positive results, (which often ex-
tends no further than those results) and a knowledge
founded on the experience of certain general principles
or laws, to which all particular effects are subject ? Mr.
Malthus seems to insinuate that the knowledge of the
general law or principle adds nothing to the knowledge
of the fact, because both are equally an affair of experience. He might as well assert that a ligature of iron
would not strengthen a deal plank, because they are
both held together by the same law of cohesion.
The fact expresses nothing more than the actual
co-existence of certain things in certain circumstances,
and while all those circumstances continue, no
doubt the same consequences will follow . But we
know that they are hardly ever the same, and the question is, which of them is necessary to produce the effect talked of. This the *reason* points out, that is, it
points out a relation between certain things, which has
been found to hold not merely in the given circumstances, but in all others, which is properly the relation
of cause and effect. Our idea of cause and effect is
not derived from our immediate but from our *compa-*
rative experience : it is only by taking our experience
to pieces, by seeing what things are, or are not necessarily connected together in different circumstances,
that we learn to reason with clearness and confidence
on the succession of events.

The succession of events is not the same thing as the
succession of cause and effect. By assigning a reason
for a thing, I mean then being able to refer it to a general rule or principle collected from and proved by an
infinite number of collateral instances, and confirming

the particular fact or instance to which it is applied. It is drawing together the different ramifications of our experience, and winding them round a particular bundle of things, and tying them fast together. Thus suppose we have never seen a carnation of the size of a cabbage : does it follow that we never shall, or that there can be no such thing ? We might say, I know no *reason* why a flower of a certain shape, colour, &c. should not reach a certain size, but that it has never been so within my knowledge. This might however be owing to the soil, culture, or a thousand circumstances, which are not invariable.—But the moment the reason is given (supposing it to be a good one) namely, the connection between the contexture and weight, (though this reason is also derived indirectly from the general fund of our experience) there is an end at once of the question. To suppose a flower to grow to a greater height than it could support from the slenderness of the stalk would be to suppose what never happened not only with respect to that particular flower, the carnation, but with respect to any other flower, or plant, or animal, or any other body whatever. We know that climate has such an effect that what are plants with us, in the tropical climates become large trees : but the necessary proportion between the size or weight of the plant, and the strength of the stalk that is to support it, is what no change of soil or climate can supersede, unless we could supersede the law of gravitation itself. The mere experimental or historical proof is here then buttressed up by the general rule, or reason of the thing.—I have always seen a stone fall to the ground ; I remember a house

always to have stood where it does ; a hill has never
stirred from the place where I first saw it. Is the inference to be drawn from these different cases equally
certain ? Am I to conclude that the house will last as
long as the mountain, because I have the same positive evidence of their permanence ? No : because
though I have never seen any alteration in that particular house, I have seen other houses pulled down
and built up ; and besides, from the size of the objects, the shape and nature of the materials, I know
that one of them may be very easily destroyed,
whereas nothing but some great convulsion in nature
is ever likely to destroy the other or remove it from
its place. Our particular experience is only to be
depended on, as it is explained and confirmed by
analogy to other cases, viz. by a number of other
facts of the same kind, or by general observation.
Secondly, the aggregate of our experience with respect to any given class of events is constantly
over-ruled by the *reason of the case,* viz. by our
knowledge of cause and effect, by the intelligible,
explicit connections of things, and by considering
whether the principles concerned in the production
of a series of events, (forming a body of facts, or
the concrete mass of our experience) are resolvable
into a simple law of nature operating universally,
unchangeably, without ever being suspended for a
moment, (as for instance, the law of gravitation
which holds equally of all bodies in all cases, and
can never be separated from our reasonings upon
them) or whether the event has been owing to a
combination of mixed causes, which do not always

act alike and with equal force, or the effect of which depends upon circumstances, which we know may be altered, (as in the case of soils, climates, methods of culture,* &c. to return to the former example). Suppose a rock to have stood for ages on the summit of a mountain. Am I sure that it will stand there always? Yes, if nothing happens to prevent it. But can I be sure that nothing will ever remove it, because nothing has ever done so hitherto? On the contrary, I know that if a man points a cannon against it, it will be shattered to pieces in an instant, though it has stood there for ages, and though there is not at present the least appearance of a change in it. Here then my experience is of no avail against my reason. In one sense of the word, it is all thrown away, and goes for nothing. To judge rationally, I must take other circumstances into the account, the effects of gunpowder, &c. The resistance made by the rock will depend upon its hardness, not upon the length of time it had stood there. Our experience then is not one thing, or any number of things, taken absolutely or blindly by themselves, but a vast collection of facts, and what is of infinitely more importance, of rules, founded upon those facts, bearing one upon another, and perpetually modified by circumstances. It is not upon any single fact or class of facts, or on any single rule, but on the combination of all these, and the manner in which they balance and control one another, that our decisions must ultimately rest. It is from

* The engrafting of trees might be mentioned as an instance in point.

this rational and abstracted experience that we obtain any certain results, and infer from the altered relation of causes and events, that things will happen which never happened before. The future is contained in the past, only as it grows out of the same powers in nature, but acting in different situations, and producing different practical results by invariable laws. To apply all this to the question. If it is allowed that the improvements in physic have an influence on the duration of human life, and that these improvements may go on indefinitely, I do not think Mr. Malthus's answer a conclusive one that no considerable progress will ever be made in this respect, because none has hitherto been made. If the improvements in science have not hitherto been regular and permanent, it cannot be expected that any advantages depending on them should have been so: nor does the past history of mankind in this instance furnish a rule for our future conjectures, inasmuch as in all that relates to the permanence and general diffusion of knowledge, a new turn has been given to the question (as before observed) by the invention of printing. This single circumstance, which was matter of mere accident, may be said in many respects to have given a new aspect to human affairs; to say that it has not yet produced the effects predicted from it, when it has had no time to produce them, is like saying, that the repeated blows of a battering-ram will not break down a stone-wall, because for the two or three first blows it does not begin to move. The true question is, whether the cause is adequate to the effect ascribed to it, that is, whether its operation is of a sufficiently general and powerful nature to produce a correspondent general change in the circumstances of mankind. I think it will hardly be denied that printing may be applied with great success as an instrument for the propagation of vice: may it not then be made use of to give currency to the principles of virtue? At any rate, to deny that it is a means of diffusing and embodying knowledge is to deny that such a contrivance exists at all, or that books will be more generally read, or less liable to be lost from the facility with which they are multiplied. While therefore Mr. Malthus allows certain moral habits, and the state of physical knowledge in a great measure to determine the length of human life, he cannot object on any allowed principles of philosophy to M. Condorcet's employing these causes as intermediate links in a chain of argument to establish the probability of the gradual approach of mankind---to a state of immortality. The error does not lie in M. Condorcet's general principles of reasoning, but in the wrong application of them; though I do not know that I could detect the error better than Mr. Malthus has done. What I have endeavoured to shew in these hasty remarks is that the admission of the rule laid down by our author, that in our calculations of the future, we are to attend to nothing but the general state of the fact hitherto, without giving any weight to the actual change of collateral circumstances, or the existence of any new cause which may influence the state of that fact, would overturn every principle, not

only of sound philosophy, but of the most obvious
common sense.* I dissent equally from M. Condorcet's paradoxical speculations and from Mr. Malthus's
paradoxical answers to them. It would be unfair not
to add that Mr. Malthus has made one good distinction
on the subject, between an unlimited and an indefinite improvement. It is the old argument of the
Heap, and is here stated with considerable effect, and
novelty of appearance. The conclusion of Mr. Malthus's argument on this idle question is a sensible and
pleasant account of the matter. After all, I do not
quite dislike a man who quotes Bickerstaff so well.

" It does not, however, by any means, seem impos-
" sible, that by an attention to breed, a certain degree
" of improvement, similar to that among animals,
" might take place among men. Whether intellect
" could be communicated may be a matter of doubt :
" but size, strength, beauty, complection, and perhaps
" even longevity, are in a degree transmissible. The
" error does not seem to lie, in supposing a small de-

* Dr. Paley, of whose depth or originality I have in general
but a slender opinion, has made one very shrewd and effectual
observation in reply to Hume's argument upon miracles; which
is, that according to Hume's reasoning, miracles must be *equally*
inadmissible and improbable, whether we believe in a superin-
tending Providence or not. There must therefore be some
fallacy in an argument, which completely sets aside so material
a consideration. I would recommend this answer, which I
think a true and philosophical one, to Mr. Malthus's attention,
as it may perhaps lead him " to new-model some of his argu-
" ments" about experience.

" gree of improvement possible, but in not discrimi-
" nating between a small improvement, the limit of
" which is undefined, and an improvement really un-
" limited. As the human race, however, could not be
" improved in this way, without condemning all the
" bad specimens to celibacy, it is not probable, that
" an attention to breed should ever become general;
" indeed, I know of no well-directed attempts of the
" kind, except in the ancient family of the Bick-
" erstaffs, who are said to have been very successful in
' whitening the skins, and increasing the height of
" their race by prudent marriages, particularly by that
" very judicious cross with Maud the milk-maid, by
" which some very capital defects in the constitutions
" of the family were corrected.

Mr. Malthus afterwards adds, " When paradoxes of
" this kind are advanced by ingenious and able men,
" neglect has no tendency to convince them of their
" mistakes. Priding themselves on what they conceive
" to be a mark of the reach and size of their own
" understandings, of the extent and comprehen-
" siveness of their views; they will look upon this
" neglect merely as an indication of poverty, and
" narrowness, in the mental exertions of their con-
" temporaries; and only think, that the world is not
" yet prepared to receive their sublime truths."—This
is said *bitingly* enough. For my own part, I conceive
that the world is neither prepared to receive, nor re-
ject, nor answer them, nor decide any thing about them
but that they are contrary to all our notions of things,

which, till we know more about the matter, is perhaps a sufficient answer.

" Mr. Godwin at the conclusion of the third chap-
" ter of his eighth book, speaking of population, says,"
' There is a principle in human society, by which
' population is perpetually kept down to the level of
' the means of subsistence. Thus, among the wan-
' dering tribes of America and Asia, we never find,
' through the lapse of ages, that population has so
' increased as to render necessary the cultivation of
' the earth.' " This principle, which Mr. Godwin
" thus mentions as some mysterious and occult cause,
" and which he does not attempt to investigate, has
" appeared to be the grinding law of necessity—
" misery, and the fear of misery."

There is a want of clearness here. The cause
which Mr. Malthus thus explains so accurately has
still something dark and mysterious about it. With
respect to the savage tribes Mr. Malthus states in
another place, that it is not owing to the backwardness
of population that agriculture has never become necessary, but to the want of agriculture that population
has never increased among them. The passage is
worth quoting. " It is not, therefore," he says, " as
" Lord Kaimes imagines, that the American tribes
" have never increased sufficiently to render the
" pastoral or agricultural state necessary to them;
" but, from some cause or other," [Mr. Malthus also
deals in occult causes] " they have not adopted in any
" great degree these more plentiful modes of pro-

' curing subsistence, and therefore, cannot have
" increased so as to have become populous. If hunger
" alone could have prompted the savage tribes of
" America to such a change in their habits, I do not
" conceive that there would have been a single nation
" of hunters and fishers remaining; but it is evident,
" that some fortunate train of circumstances, in addi-
" tion to this stimulus, is necessary for this purpose;
" and it is undoubtedly probable, that these arts of
" obtaining food, will be first invented and improved
" in those spots that are best suited to them, and
" where the natural fertility of the situation," [Is
not the soil of America sufficiently fertile ?] " by
" allowing a greater number of people to sub-
" sist together, would give the fairest chance to
" the inventive powers of the human mind."—
Here then we see " the grinding law of necessity"
converted into a " fortunate train of circumstances,"
so that we have a fact arising from a *necessary cause*,
and that necessary cause depending on an *accident*.
The population is kept down to the level of the
means of subsistence, but not to *what it is*, by the
law of necessity; since there are ways and means of
raising that level, and the population along with it.
Notwithstanding all the misery, and all the fear of
misery, which Mr. Malthus describes as thus
operating to keep population down to its proper
level, he is altogether unwilling to lighten their pressure, or to extend the benefits of that fortunate train
of circumstances and of those more plentiful modes
of obtaining food beyond their present necessary
limits. Nothing can exceed his jealousy on this point.

He is apprehensive lest some speculative philosopher should take it into his head " to exterminate the " inhabitants of the greatest part of Asia and Africa'' on a principle of humanity. He proposes rather " to " civilize and direct the industry of the various tribes " of Tartars and Negroes, as a work of considerable " time, and as having little chance of success." He looks with an enlightened concern at the encroachments daily made by the thriving population of the colonies on the deserts and uncultivated plains of North America, grieving to see the few scattered inhabitants driven " from their assigned and native dwel- " ling-place," and foreseeing that by this means the whole population of that vast continent will be some time or other completely choaked up! It is, I know, a painful object to Mr. Malthus (I cannot tell how it happens) to see plenty, comfort, civilisation and numerous swarms of people succeed to want, ignorance, famine, misery, and desolation. Those who are the well-wishers of the happiness of mankind (among which number I reckon Mr. Malthus one) are always diverted from their projects by their own delicacy and scruples. Those who wish to enslave or destroy them never boggle at difficulties, or stand upon ceremony!

Mr. Malthus says that the principle, by which population is perpetually kept down to a certain level is the grinding law of necessity—misery and the fear of misery. This may be true of the savage tribes there spoken of, but if he means to apply it generally, " it is not in any degree near the truth."

At this rate, all those who do not formally set about propagating their species ought to be restrained by want or the fear of it. Is this the fact? Misery or the fear of misery may be the check to population among the poor, but it cannot be the check to it among the rich. Yet we do not find that the rich, any more than the poor, regularly marry and get children. If this were the case, the rich would long ago have multiplied themselves into beggars. They would all have descendants, and those descendants would have others, till the world would not have room for such a number of poor gentlemen. All their wealth would be turned into rags, and they would be glad of a crust of bread. The world would be one great work-house.* There must therefore be some other principle which checks population among the higher classes, and makes them stop short within many degrees of actual poverty, besides " misery and the fear of misery." They do not even come within sight of misery: the fact is that they

---

* It is to no purpose to object, that they would hinder the poor from increasing in proportion. This would be merely a negative check,—preventing the increase on one side, but setting no bounds to it on the other. Besides, not having the poor to work for them, they must work for themselves. Neither can it be said that property is a fluctuating thing, that changes hands, and passes from the rich to the poor and from the poor back again to the rich, still keeping up the same inequality; for the greatest wealth would soon be melted down by the principle of population, and it is only by the accumulation and transmission of property in regular descents that any great inequality can subsist. Mr. Malthus wishes to preserve the balance of society by hindering the poor from marrying ; perhaps it would be preserved as effectually by forcing the rich to marry.

are as unwilling to descend from the highest pitch
of luxury as the poor are to sink into the lowest
state of want.—Mr. Malthus by asserting in this
careless manner that population can only be checked
by misery or the fear of misery, gains a main point.
He has always a certain quantity of misery *in bank*,
as you must put so much salt in your porridge, and
so many poor devils standing on the brink of
wretchedness, as a sort of out-guard or forlorn
hope, to ward off the evils of population from the
society at large. Thus the enemy is sure to be de-
feated, before it can make any impression on the
body of the community. This would be very well
if we had to deal with an external, and not with an
internal enemy. But is it the poor then only, who
are subject to this disease of population? Are the
rich quite proof against the evils of this all-pervading principle, this inevitable law of nature? If
the account which Mr. Malthus gives of that principle were true, its ravages could no more be
checked by devoting a certain class of the community to glut " its ravenous maw," than you could
keep the plague out of a house by placing some one
at the door to catch it. Either misery and the dread
of misery are not absolutely necessary to keep population within due bounds, or nothing short of the
general spread of misery and poverty through the
whole community could save us from it. Mr. Malthus
tries to shut the gates of mercy on mankind by an ill-
natured manœuvre! From the little trouble our author
gives himself about the application of his arithmetical
and geometrical ratios to the rich, and his confidence in

the method of inoculating the poor only by way of prevention, one would suppose that the former hadno concern in the affair: that " they neither marry " nor are given in marriage;" but leaving the vulgar business of procreation to their inferiors, only look on to see that they do not overstock the world. Why no, says Mr. Malthus, I have always insisted on *vice* as one of the necessary checks to population; and though in the upper ranks of life, the restraints on marriage cannot be said to be imposed by misery or the fear of misery, yet it cannot be denied that these restraints lead to a great deal of vice and profligacy, which answer the purpose just as well.— There is one merit which I shall not deny to Mr. Malthus, which is, that he has adapted his remedies with great skill and judgment to the different tempers, habits, and circumstances of his patients. In his division of the evils of human life, he has allotted to the poor *all* the misery, and to the rich *as much vice as they please!* These last will I daresay be very well satisfied with this distribution.—These remarks sufficiently shew that we cannot apologize for all the misery there is in the world by saying, that nothing else can put a stop to the evils of population; nor for all the vice by saying, that it is the alternative of misery. It cannot be pretended, that no one would ever indulge in vicious gratifications, but from the apprehension of reducing himself to want by having a family.— " But he cannot maintain them in a certain style."— True: vice then is a very convenient auxiliary to pride, vanity, luxury, artificial distinctions, &c. but it is not a resource against want. I once knew an instance of a gentleman and lady who had a very romantic passion for each other, but who could not afford to marry because they could only muster seven thousand pounds between them. Were they not to be pitied? What could they do in this case? Why, the lady no doubt would behave with all the wonted fortitude of her sex on the occasion: but the poor man must certainly be driven into vicious courses. Oh! no: I had forgot he was a clergyman; and his cloth would not admit of any such thing. Vice does not therefore seem to be *always* a necessary consequence of the obstacles to marriage. Moral restraint is always practicable, where the opinion of the world renders it necessary. At all events, I conceive that either one or the other of Mr. Malthus's remedies may be dispensed with: they are not *both* necessary. By his own account, (as formerly seen) extreme poverty is a very ineffectual bar to population; and as to vice, if it could be administered in doses, proportioned to the occasion, so much and no more, it might be an excellent cure; but the misfortune is, that when it once begins, there is no end of it. To change my metaphor, it takes the bit in its mouth, and sets off at a glorious rate, without the least spur from necessity, always keeping as much a-head of the occasion, as Mr. Malthus's geometrical series keeps a-head of his arithmetical one. Some persons may perhaps argue, that there is a natural connection between vice and misery, inasmuch as without the temptation of want among the poor, the vices of the rich would lack proper objects to exercise themselves upon : so that, there being no one to offer temptation to, and no one having any very great temptations to offer, people would be forced to marry among their *equals*, unless the trifling consideration of not being able to provide immediately for a large family should induce them to moderate their passions for a while. This is an argument which I shall not controvert: the disturbing that beautiful harmony and dependence which at present subsists betwen vice and misery would certainly lead us back in a great measure to all the evils which Mr. Malthus anticipates as arising out of a state of excessive virtue and happiness, and the most perfect form of society.

I shall here quote at large Mr. Malthus's account of the origin of the distinctions of property as necessarily arising from the pressure of population on the means of subsistence, and from that principle solely. I shall mark what I think the most noticeable parts in italics, and make some observations at the end.

 " It may be curious to observe in the case that " we have been supposing, how some of the prin- " cipal laws, which at present govern civilized so- " ciety, would be successively dictated by the most " imperious necessity. As man, according to Mr. " Godwin, is the creature of the impressions to which " he is subject, the goadings of want could not con- " tinue long before some violations of public or pri- " vate stock would necessarily take place. As these

" violations increased in number and extent, *the more*
" *active and comprehensive intellects of the society would*
" *soon perceive,* that while population was fast increas-
" ing the yearly produce of the country would shortly
" begin to diminish. The urgency of the case would
" suggest the necessity of some immediate measures
" being taken for the general safety. Some kind of
" convention would then be called, and the dangerous
" situation of the country stated in the strongest
" terms. *It would be observed, that while they lived in*
" *the midst of plenty it was of little consequence who*
" *laboured the least, or who possessed the least, as every*
" *man was perfectly willing and ready to supply the*
" *wants of his neighbour. But that the question was no*
" *longer whether one man should give to another that*
" *which he did not use himself*; *but whether he should*
" *give to his neighbour the food which was absolutely*
" *necessary to his own existence. It would be represented*
" *that the number of those who were in want very greatly*
" *exceeded the number and means of those who should*
" *supply them*; that these pressing wants, which from
" the state of the produce of the country, could not
" all be gratified, had occasioned some flagrant viola-
" tions of justice; that these violations had already
" checked the increase of food, and would, if they
" were not by some means or other prevented, throw
" the whole community into confusion : that im-
" perious necessity seemed to dictate, that a yearly
" increase of produce should, if possible, be obtained
" at all events ; that in order to effect this first great
" and indispensable purpose it would be advisable to
" make a more complete division of land, and to

" secure every man's property against violation by the
" most powerful sanctions.

" It might be urged perhaps, by some objectors,
" that as the fertility of the land increased, and va-
" rious accidents occurred, the shares of some men
" might be much more than sufficient for their sup-
" port; and that when the reign of self-love was
" once established, *they would not distribute their sur-*
" *plus produce without some compensation in return.* It
" would be observed in answer, that this was an in-
" convenience greatly to be lamented; but that it
" was an evil which would bear no comparison to the
" black train of distresses which would inevitably be
" occasioned by the insecurity of property ; *that the*
" *quantity of food which one man could consume, was*
" *necessarily limited by the narrow capacity of the hu-*
" *man stomach*; *that it was not certainly probable that*
" *he should throw away the rest*; *and if he exchanged*
" *his surplus produce for the labour of others, this would*
" *be better than that these others should absolutely*
" *starve.*

" It seems highly probable therefore, that an ad-
" ministration of property *not very different from that*
" *which prevails in civilized states at present* would be
" established as the best though inadequate remedy
" for the evils which were pressing on the society.

" The next subject which would come under dis-
" cussion, intimately connected with the preceding,
" is the commerce of the sexes. It would be urged

" by those who had turned their attention to the *true*
" *cause of the difficulties under which the community*
" *laboured, that while every man felt secure that all his*
" *children would be well provided for by general benevo-*
" *lence, the powers of the earth would be absolutely*
" *inadequate to produce food for the population which*
" *would inevitably ensue*; that even if the whole atten-
" tion and labour of the society were directed to this
" sole point, and if by the most perfect security of
" property, and every other encouragement that
" could be thought of, the greatest possible increase
" of produce were yearly obtained ; yet still the
" increase of food would by no means keep pace with
" the much more rapid increase of population ; that
" some check to population therefore was imperiously
" called for ; that the most natural and obvious check
" seemed to be to make every man provide for his
" own children ; that this would operate in some
" respect as a measure and a guide in the increase of
" population, as it might be expected that no man
" would bring beings into the world for whom he
" could not find the means of support ; that where
" this notwithstanding was the case, it seemed neces-
" sary for the example of others, that the disgrace
" and inconvenience attending such a conduct should
" fall upon that individual who had thus inconsider-
" ately plunged himself and his innocent children into
" want and misery.

" The institution of marriage, or at least of some
" express or implied obligation on every man to sup-
" port his own children, seems to be the natural re-

" sult of these reasonings in a community under the
" difficulties that we have supposed.

" When these two fundamental laws of society,
" the security of property, and the institution of mar-
" riage were once established, inequality of conditions
" must necessarily follow. Those who were born
" after the division of property would come *into a*
" *world already possessed.* If their parents from hav-
" ing too large a family were unable to give them
" sufficient for their support, what could they do in
" a world where every thing was appropriated? We
" have seen the fatal effects that would result to so-
" ciety if every man had *a valid claim to an equal*
" *share of the produce of the earth.* The members of
" a family which was grown too large for the original
" division of land appropriated to it, *could not then*
" *demand a part of the surplus produce of others as a*
" *debt of justice. It has appeared that from the inevit-*
" *able laws of human nature some human beings will be*
" *exposed to want. These are the unhappy persons who*
" *in the great lottery of life have drawn a blank. The*
" *number of these persons would soon exceed the ability of*
" *the surplus produce to supply. Moral merit is a very*
" *difficult criterion except in extreme cases. The owners*
" *of surplus' produce would in general seek some more*
" *obvious mark of distinction; and it seems to be both*
" *natural and just, that except upon particular occasions*
" *their choice should fall upon those who were able, and*
" *professed themselves willing to exert their strength in*
" *procuring a further surplus produce, which would at*
" *once benefit the community, and enable the proprietors*

" to afford assistance to greater numbers.   All who were
" in want of food would be urged by imperious necessity
" to offer their labour in exchange for this article, so ab-
" solutely necessary to existence. The fund appropriated
" to the maintenance of labour would be the aggregate
" quantity of food possessed by the owners of land be-
" yond their own consumption.   When the demands upon
" this fund were great and numerous it would naturally
" be divided into very small shares.   Labour would be
" ill paid.   Men would offer to work for a bare sub-
" sistence; and the rearing of families would be
" checked by sickness and misery.   On the contrary,
" when this fund was increasing fast; when it was
" great in proportion to the number of claimants, it
" would be divided in much larger shares.   No man
" would exchange his labour without receiving an ample
" quantity of food in return.   Labourers would live in
" ease and comfort, and would consequently be able to
" rear a numerous and vigorous offspring.

" On the state of this fund the happiness or the de-
" gree of misery, prevailing among the lower classes
" of people in every known state, at present chiefly
" depends; and on this happiness or degree of misery
" depends principally the increase, stationariness, or
" decrease of population.

" And thus it appears, that a society constituted
" according to the most beautiful form that imagina-
" tion can conceive, with benevolence for its moving
" principle instead of self-love, and with every evil
" disposition in all its members corrected by reason,

" *not force, would from the inevitable laws of nature,*
" *and not from any original depravity of man, or of*
" *human institutions, degenerate in a very short period*
" *into a society constructed upon a plan not essentially*
" *different from that which prevails in every known state*
" *at present; a society divided into a class of pro-*
" *prietors and a class of labourers, and with self-love*
" *for the mainspring of the great machine*; we may,
" therefore, venture to pronounce with certainty,
" that if Mr. Godwin's system of society were esta-
" blished in its utmost perfection, instead of myriads
" of centuries, not thirty years could elapse before
" its utter destruction from the simple principle of
" population."

Not to insist on the absurdity, with which Mr.
Malthus seems to be enamoured, of believing that
the change here predicted would be the consequence
of the inevitable laws of nature, not of any inherent
depravity in the human mind, when it is evident that
the whole mischief originates in the folly and headstrong passions of the individuals composing this
extraordinary society, all the members of which are
actuated by the purest motives of reason and virtue,
I shall at once suppose a state of society not indeed
perfect, but equal, and with self-love, and a little
common sense, instead of benevolence and perfect
wisdom, for its moving principles; and see whether
it would not be possible for such a state of practical
equality, admitting neither poverty nor riches, to
last more than " thirty years, before its *utter destruction from the simple principle of population.*" The

question is, if I understand it rightly, how that principle *alone* (I do not enter into the general structure, foundations, or purposes of civil society, I propose to examine the question only as a branch of political economy, or as it relates to the physical sustenance of mankind, which is the point of view in which Mr. Malthus has treated it) how I say that principle imperiously requires, that there should be one class of the community, ready to perish of want except as they are kept from it by severe and unremitting exertion, and another class living in ease and luxury for no other purpose than to keep the good things of this life from the first class, because if they were admitted to a share of them they would be immediately subjected to greater want and hardships than ever. It is to be remembered that Mr. Malthus here pretends to bring forward a new theory of property; to have added the key-stone to the arch of political society, which, he says, was in danger of falling without it; to enforce the rights of the rich, and set aside the claims of the poor as false and unfounded; and by shewing how the distinctions of property are immediately connected with the physical nature and very existence of mankind in a way that had not been supposed before, to point out the necessity of arming the law with new rigour, and steeling the heart with fresh obduracy to second the decisions of his pragmatical philosophy. The laws of England recognise the right of the poor man to live by his labour; Mr. Malthus denies this right, and holds it up to ridicule. The question is, which of them we shall believe. I shall therefore examine the subject freely, having so good an authority on my side.

All that I can find Mr. Malthus has discovered is, that it would be necessary in the progress of society, in order to stave off the evils of population, to make a regulation, that every man should be obliged to work for a subsistence, and to provide for his own children. A great matter truly! But having allowed to Mr. Malthus that these two regulations would be *necessary* in the common course of things, I cannot at the same time help thinking that they would also be *sufficient*—to avert the approach of famine, which is the point at issue. I can easily understand if every man had a valid claim to an equal share of the produce of the earth, that this abstract unqualified right would lead to great inconveniences—but not when that abstract right is clogged with the condition, that he should work for his share of it. I can also admit that I can have no claim to the surplus produce of another without some compensation in return. This would certainly be hard. But it does not appear (upon the face of the argument) how I should therefore have no claim to the produce of my own industry; or how any other person has a right to force me to work for him without making me what compensation I think fit. *He* has a right to his estate, *I* have a right to my labour. As to any produce, whether surplus or not, which he may raise from it, he has a right to keep it to himself; as to that which I raise for him, it seems to be a subject of voluntary agreement. Again, if a man who is as industrious as myself, and equally reaps the benefit of his industry chuses to have the additional solace of a wife and family, as he has all the *fun*, I see no reason why he should not have all the trouble; it is neither fair nor equal that I should make a drudge of myself, or be put to inconvenience for the sake of his amusements. Let us see then how the argument stands in this stage of it. The reason which appeared for not allowing to every man a valid claim to an equal share of the produce of the earth was, that the admission of such a claim would only be an excuse for idleness. The extravagant, the worthless, and indolent would thus prey upon the honest and laborious part of the community. (We are supposing a case where every evil disposition and original depravity had *not* been completely eradicated by reason and philosophy.) Even if no such characters existed, they would hardly fail to be produced by having such fine encouragement given them. On the other hand, if every one was at liberty to saddle his neighbour or the community with as many children as he pleased, there would either be no sufficient check to the inordinate increase of population, or at least any one person who got the start in the race of matrimony would have it in his power to deprive the others of their right to the surplus produce of their labour by claiming it for his family. It is necessary then to prevent the imposition of any one's fastening himself and children on another for support, that there should be a certain *appropriation of the common stock*; that is, that each man's claim upon it should be in proportion to the share he had in increasing it. The next consideration is whether with this hold upon him, you would not be able to make him effectually exert himself, and at the same time prevent him from having more children than he could maintain, the same all-powerful stimulus of self-interest equally counteracting his indolence and his indiscretion. Mr. Malthus says that the true cause of the difficulties under which the community would labour, would be the excessive tendency to population, arising from the security felt by every man that his children would be well provided for by the general benevolence: by taking away this security then, and imposing the task of maintaining them upon himself, you remove the only cause of the unavoidable tendency of population to excess, and of all the confusion that would ensue, by making his selfishness and his indolence operate as direct checks on his sensual propensities. He would be tied to his good behaviour as effectually as a country fellow is at present by being bound in a penalty of twenty pounds to the parish for every bastard child that he gets. If every man's earnings were in proportion to his exertions, if his share of the necessaries, the comforts, or even the superfluities of life were derived from the produce of his own toil, or ingenuity, or determined by equitable *compensation*, I cannot conceive how there could be any greater security for regularity of conduct and a general spirit of industry in the several members of the community, as far as was consistent with health and the real enjoyment of life. If these principles are not sufficient to ensure the good order of society in such circumstances, I should like to know what are the principles by which it is enforced at present. They are nothing more than the regular connection between industry and its reward, and the additional charge or labour to which a man necessarily subjects himself by being encumbered with a family. The only difference is in the proportion between the reward, and the exertion, or the rate at which the payment of labour is fixed. So far then we see no very pressing symptoms of the dissolution of the society, or of any violent departure from this system of decent equality, from the sole principle of population. Yet we have not hitherto got (in the regular course of the argument) so far as the distinction of a class of labourers, and a class of proprietors. It may be urged perhaps that nothing but extreme want or misery can furnish a stimulus sufficiently strong to produce " the labour necessary for the support of " an extended population," or counteract the principle of population. But Mr. Malthus himself admits that " the most constant and best directed ef- " forts of industry are to be found among a class of " people above the class of the wretchedly poor," among those who have something to lose, and something to gain, and who, happen what will, cannot be worse off than they are. He also admits that it is among this middling class of people, that we are to look for most instances of self-denial, prudence, and a competent resistance to the principle of population. I do not therefore understand either the weight or consistency of the charge which he brings against Paine of having fallen into the most fundamental errors respecting the principles of government by confounding the affairs of Europe with those of America. If the people in America are not forced to labour (and there are no people more industrious) by extreme poverty, if they are not forced to be prudent (and their prudence is I believe equal to their industry) by the scantiness of the soil, or the unequal distribution of its produce, no matter whether the state is old or new, whether the population is increasing or stationary, the example proves equally in all cases that wretchedness is not the *sine qua non* of industry, and that the way to hinder people from taking *desperate* steps is not to involve them in despair. The current of our daily life, the springs of our activity or fortitude, may be supplied as well from hope as fear, from " cheerful and confident " thoughts" as the apparition of famine stalking just behind us. The merchant attends to his business, settles his accounts, and answers his correspondents as diligently and punctually as the shop-keeper. The shop-keeper minds his customers, and puffs off his goods, tells more lies, is a greater drudge, and gets less for his pains than the merchant. The shoe-black piques himself upon giving the last polish to a gentleman's shoes, and gets a penny for his trouble. In all these cases, it is not strictly the proportion between the exertion and the object, neither hope nor fear in the abstract, that determines the degree of our exertions, but the balance of our hopes and fears, the *difference* that it will make to us in our situation whether we exert ourselves to the utmost or not, and the impossibility of turning our labour to any better account that habitually regulates our conduct.* We all do the best for ourselves that we can. This is at least a general rule.—But let us suppose, though I do not think Mr. Malthus has thrown any new or striking light on the way, in which such a change would be brought about, that it is found necessary to make a regular division of the land, and that a class of proprietors and a class of labourers is consequently established. Let us see in this case what proportion of the surplus produce of the ground might be supposed to fall to the share of the labourer, or whether if any thing more was allowed him than what was just enough to keep him alive and enable him to stagger through the tasks of the day, both rich and poor (but especially the latter) would not suffer grievously from all such impious and inhuman attempts, as our author afterwards calls them, to reverse the laws of nature, or decrees of Providence (which you please) " by which some human beings are " inevitably exposed to want." I shall argue the question solely on the ground stated by Mr. Malthus. I shall suppose that every proprietor has an absolute right to his property, and to the *whole* produce of his own exertions. There are two other questions to be

---

* Thus the shop-keeper cannot in general be supposed to be actuated by any fear of want. His exertions are animated entirely by the prospect of gain, or advantage. Yet how trifling are his profits compared with those of the merchant. This however does not abate his diligence. It may be said that the advantage is as great to him. That is, it is the greatest in his power to make; which is the very thing I mean to say. In fact we are wound up to a certain pitch of resolution and activity almost as mechanically as we wind up a clock.

considered, namely, whether the right to the labour of others and to the produce of their labour attaches to the possession of the soil, secondly, if that is not the case, to what proportion of the produce of the ground the labourer is naturally entitled by his exertions. Mr. Malthus infers that from the establishment of the two fundamental laws, security of property, and the institution of marriage, inequality of conditions must necessarily follow. I confess I do not see this necessary consequence. I would ask, upon what plea Mr. Malthus succeeded in establishing these two fundamental laws, but because they were necessary and competent to stimulate the exertions and restrain the passions of the community at large, that is, to maintain a general practical equality, to regulate each person's indulgences according to their industry, to lay an even tax upon every man, and thus prevent the return of fraud, violence, confusion, want and misery. Grant that the most fatal effects would result to society, if every man had a valid claim to *an equal share* of the produce of the earth; it by no means follows that the same fatal effects would result to society from allowing to every man a valid claim to a share of the produce of the earth *proportioned* to his labour. Yet I doubt whether any great inequality could subsist, while each man had this valid claim. It is one thing to have a right to the produce of your own exertions, and another to have a right to the produce of the earth, that is, of the labour of others. It is so far from being fair to apply the same reasoning to these two things, that the evils which would be the necessary consequences of the one, cannot possibly result from the other. The one is a direct contradiction to the other. It is on this distinction in fact, that all property and all society is originally founded. By making it equally the interest of each individual to exert himself, you in all probability secure an equal degree of industry and comfort in each individual. At least, a society formed upon this plan would have as fair a chance of realising all the advantages of which it was capable, with as few deviations from the original direction and design, as a society, where only a less degree of equality was *possible*, would have of coming up to its original idea. Industry and regularity of behaviour must gain ground, where these habits were enforced by the general example of the whole society, and where the sacrifice to be made was less, and the reward more certain. I might appeal to the history of all countries in proof of this. Industry flourishes most in those countries, where there is the greatest equality of conditions, and where in consequence instances of extreme distress can rarely occur. The excessive depression of the lower class of the community can only (by taking away the spring of hope, and making it nearly impossible for them to fall lower,) dishearten industry, and make them regardless of consequences. It cannot be laid down as an axiom, that you animate industry, in proportion as you take away its reward. It may be said that the poor will not go through extreme hardships but from the fear of starving. I know no reason why such hardships are necessary but because one

man is obliged to do the work of several.—These
general observations are not set aside by supposing
the right of property to be established. All that I
can understand by a right of property is a right in
any one to cultivate a piece of land, be it more or
less, and a right at the same time to prevent any one
else from cultivating it, or reaping the produce.
This, in whatever way a man comes by it, is the
utmost extent of this right. " Those who were
" born after the division of property," says Mr.
Malthus, " would come into *a world already possessed.*"
[How the whole world should come to be possessed
immediately after the division of property I do not
understand.] " If their parents, from having too
" large a family, were unable to give them sufficient
" for their support, what could they do in a world,
" where every thing was appropriated?" [Just now
the world, and at present, *every thing in it* is appropriated.] " We have seen the fatal effects that would
" result to society, if every man had a valid claim to
" an equal share of the produce of the earth." [This
has been answered.] " The members of a family
" which was grown too large for the original division
" of land appropriated to it could not then demand
" a part of the *surplus produce of others* as a debt of
" justice." [Certainly not. They would have no
right to it, because one man would have no right to
another man's property; but that right, as far as relates to the surplus produce, is not backed by the
necessity of the case, as Mr. Malthus would lead us
to suppose, or because every thing is already appropriated.] " It has appeared that, from the inevitable

" laws of human nature, some beings will be exposed
" to want." [That is the question.] " The number
" of those persons would soon exceed the ability of
" the *surplus produce* to supply." I believe so, if
they depended on the surplus produce of the labour of
the rich to supply them. But the long and the short
of it is that these laborious landholders, these owners
of surplus produce, finding that their own exertions
could not supply all their own wants, and at the
same time keep pace with their benevolence to those
unhappy persons, who in the great lottery of life
had drawn a blank, would call to their aid such of
these as professed themselves able and willing to
exert their strength in procuring a *further surplus produce*, which would enable the proprietors to afford
assistance to greater numbers, that is, out of the
produce of their own labour, not out of that of the
proprietors. To hear Mr. Malthus talk, one would
suppose that the rich were really a very hard-working, ill-used people, who are not suffered to enjoy
the earnings of their honest industry in quiet by a
set of troublesome, unsatisfied, luxurious, idle people called *the poor*. Or one might suppose that a
landed estate was a machine that did its own work;
or that it was like a large plum-cake, which the
owner might at once cut up into slices, and either
eat them himself, or give them away to others, just
as he pleased. In this case I grant that the poor
might be said to depend entirely upon the bounty or
surplus produce of the rich; and as they would have
no trouble in procuring their share but merely that
of asking for it, their demands would no doubt be a

little unreasonable, and in short, if they were complied with, the estate, the surplus produce, or the plumb-cake (call it which you will) would soon be gone. The question would no longer be " whether " one man should g ve to another that which he did " not use himself: but whether he should give to his " neighbour the food which was absolutely necessary " to his own existence." But I cannot admit that they would be reduced to any such necessity merely from allowing to the labourer as much of the additional produce of the ground as he himself had really *added* to it. I repeat that I do not see how a man's reaping the produce, and no more than the produce of his industry, can operate as an inducement to idleness, or to the excessive multiplication of children, when notwithstanding all his industry it is impossible he should provide for them without either diminishing his own comforts, or if the population is already full, plunging them and himself into want and misery. This addition to the argument is like a foil to a sword —it prevents any dangerous consequences. If I say to a number of people, that they may each of them have as much of a heap of corn as they desire, the whole of it would very soon be bespoke, but if I tell them that they may each of them have as much as they can *carry away* themselves, there might be enough to load them all, and I might have plenty left for my own consumption. The ability and the willingness of a man to labour, (when these are made the general foundation of his claim to the produce of the earth) at once set bounds to his own rapacious demands, and effectually limit the population.—If Mr. Malthus had shewn that nothing but extreme misery can excite to industry or check population, he would then have shewn the necessity of such a state. But if it has appeared in various ways that there is no connection between these things, or that if there is, it is directly contrary to what Mr. Malthus supposes it, then he has failed in his attempt to regulate the price of labour by the principle of population, or to prove that this should be fixed so low, as only just to keep the labourer from starving. Certainly any advance in the price of labour, or a more equal distribution of the produce of the earth would enable a greater number of persons to live in comfort, and would increase population; but it is the height of absurdity, as I have shewn over and over again, to suppose that it would lead to an excessive or unrestricted increase; as if by making people acquainted with comfort and decency, you were teaching them to fall in love with misery. This is the real jut and bearing of the question. The author of the Essay, to assist his argument, transposes the question. He represents the labouring class of the community as a set of useless, supernumerary paupers, living on charity, or on the labour of the industrious proprietor. If this representation had any foundation, I should be ready to admit that these interlopers had no claim on any part of *the surplus produce of others as a debt of justice.* They must owe every thing to favour, and would be entirely at the mercy of their benefactors. Every reader must perceive, how little this account is in any degree near the truth. The case is not that of a person both willing and able to labour for himself, and imparting freely to

another, who had done nothing to deserve it, a part of
the surplus produce of the soil, but of a person bar-
gaining with another to do all his work for him, and
allowing him as a bribe part of the produce of
his own labour in return. It is not therefore
a question of right any more than it is a question
of expediency, but a question of power on one side,
and of necessity on the other. On the degree of
power, or on that of the necessity, and on nothing
else, will the price of labour depend. Mr. Malthus
somewhere talks of a man's having no right to subsistence when his labour will not *fairly* purchase it.
This word *fairness* conveys to my ears no meaning
but that of the struggle between power and want, just
spoken of. " A man," he says, " born into a world
" already possessed, if the society do not want his
" labour, has no claim of *right* to the smallest portion
" of food." This is, as if the question was of an individual, pestering a laborious community for a job,
when they do not want his assistance, and not of the
laborious part of the community demanding a small
portion of food or the means of subsistence out of the
surplus produce of their labour as *a fair compensation*
for their trouble! I sometimes think that abstruse
subjects are best illustrated by familiar examples, and
I shall accordingly give one. Suppose I have got
possession of an island which I either took from some-
body else, or was the first to occupy. But no matter
how I came by it, I am in possession of it, and that is
enough. Suppose then I see another person coming
towards it either in a canoe (these questions are
always first decided in a state very nearly approaching

a state of nature) or swimming from some other island as I conceive either with intent to drive me from it, or to defraud me of the produce of my labour. Now even allowing that I had more than enough for myself, that part of my surplus produce was devoured by fowls or wild beasts, or that I threw it for sport into the sea, yet I should contend that I have a right, a strict right in one sense of the word, to take out a long pole, and push this unfair intruder from the shore, and try to sink his boat or himself in the water to get rid of him, and defend my own *right*. But suppose that instead of his coming to me, I go to him, and persuade him to return with me; and that when I have got him home, I want to set him to work to do either part or the whole of my business for me. In this case I should conceive that he is at liberty either to work or refuse working just as he thinks proper, to work on what terms he thinks proper, to receive only a small part, or the half, or more than half the produce as he pleases; or if I do not chuse to agree to his terms, I must do my work myself. What possible right have I over him? His right to his liberty is just as good as my right to my property. It is an excellent *cheveux-de-fris*, and if he is as idle as I am lazy, he will make his market of it. I say then that this original right continues in all stages of society, unless where it has been specifically given up; and acts as a counterpoise to the insolence of property. If indeed the poor will work for the rich at a certain rate, they are not bound to employ others who demand higher wages, or a greater number than they want: but as it is plain that they must either work themselves, or get others to work for them,

over whom they have no right whatever, I contend that
the mass of the labouring community have always a
right to *strike*, to demand what wages they please;
the least that they can demand is enough to support
them and their families; and the real contest will be
between the aversion of the rich to labour, and of
the poor to famine. This seems to be the philosophy
of the question. It is also the spirit of the laws of
England, which have left a provision for the poor;
wisely considering, no doubt, that they who received their all from the labour of others were bound
to provide out of their superfluities for the necessities of such as were in want. If it be said that this
principle will lead to extreme abuse in practice, I
answer, No, for there is hardly any one, who will
live in dependence, or on casualties, if he can help
it. The check to the abuse is sufficiently provided
in the miserable precariousness and disgusting nature
of the remedy. But if from the extreme inequality
of conditions, that is, from one part of the community having been able to engross all the advantages of society to themselves, so that they
can trample on the others at pleasure, the poor
are reduced so low in intellect and feeling as
to be indifferent to every consideration of the kind,
neither will they be restrained from following their
inclinations by Mr. Malthus's grinding law of necessity, by the abolition of the poor laws, or by the
prospect of seeing their children starving at the doors
of the rich. It is not by their own fault alone that
they have fallen into this degradation: those who
have brought them into it ought to be answerable for

some of the consequences. The way to obviate those consequences is not by obstinately increasing the pressure, but by lessening it. It is not my business to inquire how a society formed upon the simple plan above-mentioned might be supposed to degenerate in consequence of the different passions, follies, vices, and circumstances of mankind, into a state of excessive inequality and wretchedness : it is sufficient for my purpose to have shewn, that such a change was not rendered necessary by the sole principle of population, or that it would not be absolutely impossible for a state of actual equality to last " thirty years" without producing the total overthrow and destruction of the society. Equality produces no such maddening effects on the principle of population, nor is it a thing, any approaches to which must be fatal to human happiness, and are universally to be dreaded. The connection therefore between that degree of inequality, which terminates in extreme vice and misery, and the necessary restraints on population, is not so obvious or indissoluble, as to give Mr. Malthus a right to " qualify" the luxuries of the rich, and the distresses of the poor as the inevitable consequences of the fundamental laws of nature, and as necessary to the very existence of society. I shall here take the liberty of quoting the two following passages from Mr. Malthus's Essay, which seem exactly to confirm my ideas on the subject, only better expressed, and stated in a much neater manner. " In most countries, among the " lower classes of people, there appears to be some- " thing like a standard of wretchedness, a point be-

" low which, they will not continue to marry and
" propagate their species. This standard is different
" in different countries, and is formed by various
" concurring circumstances of soil, climate, govern-
" ment, degree of knowledge, and civilization, &c.
" The principal circumstances which contribute to
" raise it, are, liberty, security of property, the
" spread of knowledge, and *a taste for the conveni-*
" *ences and the comforts of life.* Those which con-
" tribute principally to lower it are despotism and
" ignorance." For what purpose did Mr. Malthus
" write his book? " In an attempt to better the
" condition of the lower classes of society, our ob-
" ject should be to raise this standard as high as
" possible, by cultivating a spirit of independence, a
" decent pride, and a taste for cleanliness and com-
" fort among the poor. These habits would be best
" inculcated by a system of general education and,
" when strongly fixed, would be *the most powerful*
" *means of preventing their marrying with the prospect*
" *of being obliged to forfeit such advantages; and*
" *would consequently raise them nearer to the middle*
" *classes of society."* Yet Mr. Malthus elsewhere
attempts to prove that the pressure of population on
the means of subsistence can only be kept back by a
system of terror and famine, as the pressure of a
crowd is only kept back by the soldiers' bayonets.
I have thus endeavoured to answer the *play of words,*
by which Mr. Malthus undertakes to prove that the
rich have an absolute right to the disposal of the
whole of the surplus produce of *the labour of others.*
After this preparation, I shall venture to trust the

reader's imagination with the passages, in which he tries to put down private charity, and to prove the right of the rich (whenever they conveniently can) to starve the poor. They are very pretty passages.

" There is one right, which man has generally
" been thought to possess, which I am confident he
" neither does, nor can, possess, a right to subsis-
" tence when his labour will not *fairly* purchase it.
" Our laws indeed say, that he has this right, and
" bind the society to furnish employment and food
" to those who cannot get them in the regular mar-
" ket; but in so doing, they attempt to reverse the
" laws of nature; and it is, in consequence, to be
" expected, not only that they should fail in their
" object, but that the poor who were intended to be
" benefited, should suffer most cruelly from this in-
" human deceit which is practised upon them.

" A man who is born into a world already pos-
' sessed, if he cannot get subsistence from his pa-
" rents on whom he has a just demand, and if the
" society do not want his labour, has no claim of
" *right* to the smallest portion of food, and, in fact,
" has no business to be where he is. At nature's
" mighty feast there is no vacant cover for him.
" She tells him to be gone, and will quickly execute
" her own orders, if he do not work upon the com-
" passion of some of her guests. If these guests get
" up and make room for him, other intruders imme-
" diately appear demanding the same favour. The

" report of a provision for all that come, fills the
" hall with numerous claimants. The order and
" harmony of the feast is disturbed, the plenty that
" before reigned is changed into scarcity; and the
" happiness of the guests is destroyed by the spec-
" tacle of misery and dependence in every part of
" the hall, and by the clamorous importunity of
" those, who are justly enraged at not finding the
" provision which they had been taught to expect.
" The guests learn too late their error, in counter-
" acting those strict orders to all intruders, issued by
" the great mistress of the feast, who, wishing that
" all her guests should have plenty, and knowing
" that she could not provide for unlimited numbers,
" humanely refused to admit fresh comers when her
" table was already full." This is a very brilliant
description, and a pleasing allegory. Our author
luxuriates in the dearth of nature: he cannot contain his triumph: he frolics with his subject in the
gaiety of his heart, and his tongue grows wanton in
praise of famine. But let us examine it not as a
display of imagination, but as a piece of reasoning.
In the first place, I cannot admit the assertion that
" at nature's mighty feast there is no vacant cover
" for the poor man." There are plenty of vacant
covers but that the guests at the head of the
table have seized upon all those at the lower end,
before the table was full. Or if there were no
vacant cover, it would be no great matter, he only
asks for the crumbs which fall from rich men's tables, and the bones which they throw to their dogs.
" She (nature) tells him to be gone, and will quickly

" execute her own orders, if he do not work on the
" compassion of some of the guests." When I see
a poor old man, who after a life of unceasing labour
is obliged at last to beg his bread, driven from the
door of the rich man by a surly porter, and half a dozen
sleek well-fed dogs, kept for the pleasure of their
master or mistress, jumping up from the fire-side, or
bouncing out of their warm kennels upon him, I am,
according to Mr. Malthus, in the whole of this scene,
to fancy nature presiding in person and executing her
own orders against this unwelcome intruder, who as
he is bent fairly double with hard labour, and can
no longer get employment in the regular market, has
no claim of *right* (as our author emphatically expresses it) to the smallest portion of food, and in
fact has no business to be where he is. The preference which is often given to the inferior animals
over the human species by the institutions and customs of society is bad enough. But Mr. Malthus
wishes to go farther. By the institutions of society
a rich man is at liberty to give his superabundance
either to the poor or to his dogs. Mr. Malthus will
not allow him this liberty, but says that by the laws
of nature he is bound to give it to his dogs, because if we suffer the poor to work upon our compassion at all, this will only embolden their importunity, " and the order and harmony that before
" reigned at nature's feast will be disturbed and
" changed into want and confusion." This might probably be the consequence, if the rich, or the chief
guests had provided the entertainment for themselves;
or if nature, like a liberal hostess, had kindly pro-

vided it for them, at her own proper cost and expence, without any obligations to the poor. It might be necessary in this case for those who had either provided the feast, or been expressly invited to it, to keep a pretty strict hand over those idle and disorderly persons, to whose importunity there was no end. But the question really is, not whether all those should be supplied who press forward into the hall without having contributed any thing to the plenty that abounds, but whether after the different guests have contributed largely, each of them having brought his share and more than his share, the proprietors of the mansion have a right to turn them all out again, and only leave a few scraps or coarse bits to be flung to them out of the windows, or handed to them outside the door. Or whether if every man was allowed to eat the *mess* which he had brought with him in quiet, he would immediately go out, and bring in half a dozen more, so that he would have nothing left for himself, and the hall would be instantly overcrowded. This statement is, I believe, considerably nearer the truth than Mr. Malthus's. And if so, we can have little difficulty in deciding whether there is any ground for Mr. Malthus's apprehensions of the danger of raising the condition of the poor, or relieving the distresses to which, in their present unnatural and unnecessary state of degradation, they are unavoidably subject. " The spectacle of misery and dependence" never arises from the scantiness of the provision, or from the nearly equal shares, in which it is divided, giving encouragement to a greater number of applicants ; for those helpless intruders, against whom Mr.

Malthus issues such strict orders, namely the *rising generation*, never come into the world till they are sent for, and it is not likely that those who find themselves warm in their seats with every thing comfortable about them and nothing to complain of, should when there is really no room for fresh comers, send for more people to shove them out of their places, and eat the victuals out of their mouths. " The " Abbé Raynal has said that, ' Avant toutes les loix " sociales l'homme avoit le droit de subsister.' He " might with just as much propriety have said, that " before the institution of social laws, every man had " a right to live a hundred years. Undoubtedly he had " then, and has still, a good right to live a hundred " years, nay a thousand *if he can*, without interfering " with *the right of others to live* ; but the affair, in both " cases, is principally an affair of power, not of right. " Social laws very greatly increase this power, by ena- " bling a much greater number to subsist than could " subsist without them, and so far very greatly enlarge " *le droit de subsister*; but neither before nor after the " institution of social laws, could *an unlimited number* " *subsist*; and before, as well as since, he who ceased " to have *the power*, ceased to have *the right*." In this passage Mr. Malthus " sharpens his understanding " upon his flinty heart." The logic is smart and lively and unembarrased : it is not encumbered with any of the awkward feelings of humanity. After all, he misses his aim. For his argument proves that the right of subsistence or one man's right to live is only limited by its interfering with the right of others to live : that is, that a man has then only no right to live, when there is nothing for him to live upon; in which case the question becomes an affair of power, not of right. But it is not the question whether the proprietor should starve himself in order that the labourer may live; but whether the proprietor has a right to live in extravagance and luxury, while the labourer is starving. As to his absolute right to the produce of the soil, that is to say, of the labour of others, we have seen that he has no such right either to the whole of the surplus produce, or to *as much of it as he pleases.* With respect then to the share of the produce which the labourer has a right to demand, " it is not " likely that he should exchange his labour, without " receiving a *sufficient* quantity of food in return," to enable him to live, unless the right of the proprietor to exact the labour of others on what terms he chuses, is seconded by a kind of power, which has very little connection with the power of the earth to bring forth no more produce. As to the right of the rich, in a moral point of view, wantonly to starve the poor, it is I think best to say nothing about it. Social institutions, on which our author lays great stress as enlarging the power of subsistence and the right along with it, do not deny relief to the poor. For this very reason Mr. Malthus wishes to shoulder them aside, in order to make room for certain regulations of his own, more agreeable to *the laws of nature and the principle of population.* A little farther on he says, " As a previous step even to any considerable altera- " tion in the present system, which would *contract* or " stop the increase of the relief to be given, it ap- " pears to *me* that we are bound in justi e and honour

" *formally to disclaim the right of the poor to support.*"
It would be more modest in Mr. Malthus to let them
disclaim it for themselves. But it appears that the
reason for *contracting* the relief afforded them by the
present system, and denying the right altogether, is
that there is no subtistence for an unlimited number.
As to the point at which it may be prudent or proper
for the rich to withhold assistance from the poor, I
shall not enquire into it. But I shall dispute Mr. Malthus's right to thrust the poor man out of existence
because there is no room for him " at nature's mighty
" feast," till he can give some better reason for it than
that there is not room for an *unlimited number !*—The
maintainance of the needy poor is a tax on the inequality of conditions and the luxuries of the rich,
which they could not enjoy but in consequence of
that general depression of the lower classes which
continually subjects them to difficulties and want. It
is a *douceur* to keep them quiet, and prevent them
from enforcing those more solid, and important
claims, not interfering with the right of property, but
a direct consequence of the right of personal freedom,
and of their right to set their own price on their own
exertions, which would raise them above the reach of
want, and enable them to maintain their own *poor.*
But they cannot do this without a general combination
of the labouring part of the community; and if any
thing of this kind were to be attempted, the legislature we know would instantly interfere to prevent it.
I know indeed that the legislature assumes a right to
prevent combinations of the poor to keep themselves
above want, though they *disclaim* any right to med-

dle with monopolies of corn, or other combinations *in the regular course of trade,* by which the rich and thriving endeavour to grind the poor. But though the men of property have thus retained the legislature on their side, Mr. Malthus does not think this practical security sufficient: he thinks it absolutely necessary to recur to first principles; and that they may see how well qualified he is to act as chamber counsel in the business, he makes them a present of his Essay, written expressly for the purpose, and containing a new institute of the laws of nature, and a complete theory of population, in which it is clearly proved that the poor have no right to live any longer than the rich will let them. In this work which those to whom it is addressed should have bound in morocco, and constantly lying by them as a text-book to refer to in all cases of difficulty, it is shewn that there is no injustice in forcing the poorer classes to work almost for nothing, because they have no right to the produce of their labour, and no inhumanity in denying them assistance when they happen to be in want, because they ought not to be encouraged in idleness. Thus armed with " metaphysical aid,"and conscience-proof, the rich will I should think be able very successfully to resist the unjust claims of the poor—to a subsistence!

Neither the fundamental laws of property then, nor the principle of population seem to imply the necessity of any great inequality of conditions. They do not even require the distinction of rich and poor, much less do they imply the right of the rich to starve the poor. What shews that there must be some radical defect in our author's reasoning is, that a substantial equality does really prevail in several countries, where the right of property is established, and where the *principle of population* has been known to exist for a great length of time. Property may certainly be made a handle for power; and that power may, and does almost constantly lead to abuse, I mean to want and wretchedness. But neither the power nor the abuse is any part of the original right; and the original end and design of the right itself, namely to procure a sufficient supply for the actual population, and to prevent an unlimited increase of population, is just as well, or indeed much better answered *wi hout*, than *with* the abuse.— But perhaps we have mistaken Mr. Malthus all this while. Perhaps he only wishes to secure to the rich their original right, which is to reserve a certain share of the produce for their own use; and to prevent their being driven out of house and home by the poor, under pretence of population. He seems to say in one place, that the fund appropriated to the maintenance of labour is the aggregate quantity of food possessed by the owners of land beyond what is necessary for their own immediate consumption. He says this, or something like it. In this case, it is evident, that " no man would be forced to ex-" change his labour without receiving an ample " quantity of food in return." At this rate the labourer would be as rich, only not so idle as the proprietor. The only difference between them would be that one of them would get his share for nothing, and the other would be obliged to work for it. It would in fact be a common fund divided equally between the rich and poor, or more properly speaking, between the sleeping and the acting partners in this joint-concern. If so, I do not see what the poor could have to complain of, as, if they were ever in want, it must be owing to their own idleness, extravagance, and imprudence, and they would deserve to be punished. Now Mr. Malthus is ready to prove with a pair of compasses that this is always the state of the case. The poor are always just as well off as the rich, if it is not their own fault, and the want in which they are sometimes plunged is not owing to an unequal division of the shares among as many as can possibly subsist, but to the folly of pushing population beyond the verge of subsistence. By this means there is nothing left for those who come last, who have consequently no right to be where they are, because there is nothing for them. " The quantity " of food" (says Mr. Malthus) " which one man can " consume is necessarily limited by the narrow ca- " pacity of the human stomach; it is not certainly " probable that he should throw away the rest; " and if he exchange his surplus produce for the " labour of others, this is better than that these " others should absolutely starve." Here then we see the necessary limits of the inequality of conditions, or of the almost imperceptible difference in the advantages wh ch the rich have over the poor. But is there really then no difference between being gorged and *not* being starved, between eating venison and turtle-soup, and drinking three bottles of

wine a-day, and living on crusts of bread and water? Is it physically impossible that one man should
eat more than does him good, or that another
should not get his full share? But it may be asked,
what advantage can it be to the rich to consume
more than they want? None. But the food which is
thus misapplied, might be of great use to the poor.
Is there no such thing as waste in great houses,
which must considerably diminish the disproportion
between the quantity of food, and the narrow capacity of the human stomach? When I consider
that the rich are neither a bit taller, nor stouter, nor
born with larger stomachs than other men, it does
indeed seem at first sight a little extraordinary that
they should make such havoc in the world as they
do. But the wonder vanishes the instant we recollect that crowd of dependents always dangling about
them, who intercept the surplus produce long before it can reach the labourer, and who instead of
dividing his toil with the husbandman, or sharing in
other tasks not less useful or necessary are maintained by the distresses and hardships of the poor.
A rich man has not only himself and his family to
keep, but he has to keep his gentleman, his valet,
his butler, his cook, his coachman, his groom, his
horses, his hounds, his ornamental gardener, his ar-
chitect, his upholsterer, his jeweller, his silversmith,
his man's-mercer, and haberdasher, his pimps, para-
sites, and players, his poets, painters, and musi-
cians, not to mention a hundred more, who are of no
service on the face of the earth, nor have any mortal
thing to do—but to tend upon his person, to dress

his hair, to brush his clothes, or air his shirt, to run on his errands, to do his jobs, to manage his affairs, to please his taste, to pamper his appetites, to study his humours, to follow his steps, to fawn and cringe and bow and smile as he directs. All these persons depend entirely on the bounty of their patron; and though they do nothing to increase the produce of the ground, they do not devour it the less eagerly, and it may be supposed that they make a good gap in it. In the mean time, the productive labourer, and hard-working mechanic are straitened in their circumstances, and doomed to unremitting toil and drudgery, that these hangers-on of the rich may live at their ease, or contribute only to the vanity and convenience of their employers. This as I understand it is the pinch of the grievance.—The rich man has not only to supply his own wants, but the wants of those who depend upon him, and who do nothing to support either him or themselves. He is something in the situation of a balance-master, who undertakes to support twenty men, some on his head, some on his shoulders, and others suspended from different parts of his body: his own weight is nothing: it is the weight of those who hang upon him that makes the rich man a burthen to the poor. I see a little old emaciated man riding on a poney along the street, and a stout healthy, well looking man riding behind him at some distance, who follows him like his puppet, who turns as he turns, and whenever he passes him touches his hat in a respectful manner. What is the meaning of this? It is a nobleman, and his servant.

The man is as well-fed, as comfortably clothed, and as well-mounted as his master: what makes all the difference is, that there are thirty or forty gradations of society between them, each looking up with envy, or down with contempt on the other, as they have more or less power over the necessaries and conveniences of life not for themselves, but others, and so can hire the respect of a certain number of dependents. So little can we judge of the state of society in the mechanical way pointed out by Mr. Malthus. But it is time to proceed with my author.

" As Mr. Godwin seems disposed to understand, and " candidly to admit the truth of, the principal argu- " ment in the essay, I feel the more mortified, that he " should think it a fair inference from my positions, " that the political superintendents of a community " are bound to exercise a paternal vigilance and care " over the two great means of advantage and safety to " mankind, misery and vice; and that no evil is more " to be dreaded than that we should have too little " of them in the world, to confine the principle of " population within its proper sphere." [This I think a fair statement of the argument.] " I am at a " loss to conceive what class of evils Mr. Godwin " imagines is yet behind, which these salutary " checks are to prevent." [It is not Mr. Godwin's business, but our author's to find out such a class of evils.] " For my own part, I know of no stronger " or more general terms than vice and misery; and

" the sole question is, respecting a greater or less
" degree of them. The only reason why I object to
" Mr. Godwin's system, is, my full conviction that
" an attempt to execute it, would very greatly
" increase the quantity of vice and misery in
" society."

Be it so. But still Mr. Malthus thinks a less degree of them necessary to prevent a greater; and it
therefore seems a fair inference from his positions to
say, that the greatest care ought to be taken, not to
diminish the necessary quantity. He approves much
of the things in his own mind, but he does not like
to hear them called by their names in a disre-
spectful way. He does not like the odium attached
to them.

" Mr. Godwin observes, that he should naturally
" be disposed to pronounce that man strangely in-
" different to schemes of extraordinary improvement
" in society, who made it a conclusive argument
" against them, that, when they were realized, they
" might peradventure be of no permanence and du-
" ration. And yet, what is morality, individual or
" political, according to Mr. Godwin's own defini-
" tion of it, but a calculation of consequences?"
[This, I must say, is a very *abortive* kind of argu-
ment]. " Is the physician the patron of pain, who
" advises his patient to bear a present evil, rather
" than betake himself to a remedy, which, though
" it might give momentary relief, would afterwards
" greatly aggravate all the symptoms?" [The real

case is of a physician, who tells his patient he must not get well, and endeavours to keep him from doing so, because if he were once in perfect health, he would be subject to more violent returns of his disorder]. " Is the moralist to be called an enemy " to pleasure, because he recommends to a young " man just entering into life, not to ruin his health " and patrimony in a few years, by an excess of pre- " sent gratifications, but to economize his enjoy- " ments, that he may spread them over a longer " period?" [Our Essayist would advise the young man to neglect his affairs, and ruin his health, because by a contrary method his estate would increase so that he would not be able to manage it, and it would be thrown into complete and total disorder, at the same time that his improved health and spirits would urge him to plunge into much greater excesses, than, if his constitution were debilitated in time, he would be capable of committing]. " Of " Mr. Godwin's system, according to the present ar- " guments by which it is supported, it is not enough " to say, *peradventure* it will be of no permanence: " but we can pronounce *with certainty* that it will be " of no permanence : and under such circumstances an " attempt to execute it would unquestionably be a " great political immorality." According to the *present* arguments against it, this has not appeared to be the case.

" The permission of infanticide is bad enough, " and cannot but have a bad effect on the moral " sensibility of a nation; but I cannot conceive any " thing much more detestable, or shocking to the

" feelings, than any direct regulation of this kind,
" although sanctioned by the names of Plato and
" Aristotle." Mr. Malthus in this passage very properly gives way to his feelings, which are, in my
opinion, a much better test of morality than a calculation of consequences. At the same time, he would
himself make a law to starve the children of the
poor, because their parents are not able to maintain.
Mr. Malthus's humanity is of the *intermittent* sort.
The mention of the Chinese, of Plato or Aristotle,
has a great effect in bringing the fit on: at the mention of population or the poor-laws it vanishes in an
instant, and " he is himself again."—I hope I shall
sometimes be allowed to appeal to my feelings
against Mr. Malthus's authority, as he dissents from
that of Plato and Aristotle on the same *unphilosophical* plea, and to look upon those arguments as
narrow and superficial, which pay no regard to the
" moral sensibility of a nation;" the more so as the
system of morality prevailing at present is built upon
the natural affections and common feelings and habitual prejudices of mankind, not, as Mr. Malthus
pretends, on pure reason, or a dry calculation of
consequences. Our author's plan is addressed neither
to the *head*, nor *heart*. It retains the common sym-
pathies of our nature only to shock and insult them,
and engrafts the vices of a bad heart on a perverted
understanding.

Mr. Malthus defies Mr. Godwin to point out a
method, by which it is possible " to limit the num-

" ber of children to each prolific marriage." According to his theory, there seems no way but by
having a constable in the room, and converting bed-
chambers into a kind of lock-up houses.— Speaking
of the possibility of delaying the gratification of the
passion between the sexes, he says,

" If the whole effect were to depend merely on a
" sense of duty, considering the powerful antagonist
" that is to be contended with, in the present case,
" I confess that I should absolutely despair. At the
" same time, I am strongly of opinion that a sense
" of duty, superadded to a sense of interest, would
" by no means be without its effect. There are
" many noble and disinterested spirits, who, though
" aware of the inconveniences which they may bring
" upon themselves by the indulgence of an early
" and virtuous passion, feel a kind of repugnance
" to listen to the dictates of mere worldly prudence,
" and a pride in rejecting these low considerations.
" There is a kind of romantic gallantry in sacrificing
" all for love, naturally fascinating to a young mind;
" and, to say the truth, if all is to be sacrificed, I
" do not know, in what better cause it can be done.
" But if a strong sense of duty could, in these in-
" stances, be added to prudential suggestions, the
" whole question might wear a different colour. In
" delaying the gratification of passion, from a sense
" of duty, the most disinterested spirit, the most
" delicate honour, might be satisfied. The romantic
" pride might take a different direction, and the dic-
" tates of worldly prudence might be followed with

" the cheerful consciousness of making a virtuous
" sacrifice."

I am happy to learn that Mr. Malthus has been
able to reconcile the sense of duty and interest with
the gratification of his favourite passion. By preaching the virtue of celibacy with such success to
others, he found it no longer necessary to practise
it himself. He is not the first philosopher who extracted the flames of love out of ice. We read of
such a one in Hudibras. I should be sorry to scanda-
lize the modest reader; but really whenever I think
of our author's escape from the consequences of his
own doctrine in a wife, it puts me in mind of St.
Francis's triumph over his desires,

> " Which after in enjoyment quenching,
> " He hung a garland on his engine."

This St. Francis was as great an adept as our author
in the cold-sweat of the passions.

There is no end of Mr. Malthus's paradoxes. I
come now to his attempts to prove that in proportion as you raise the wages of the poor, you take
away their livelihood.

" Suppose, that by a subscription of the rich, the
" eighteen-pence, or two shillings, which men earn
" now, were made up five shillings, it might be
" imagined, perhaps, that they would then be able
" to live comfortably, and have a piece of meat
'" every day for their dinner. But this would be a

" very false conclusion. The transfer of three addi-
" tional shillings a day to each labourer would not
" increase the quantity of meat in the country.
" There is not at present enough for all to have a
" moderate share. What would then be the conse-
" quence? The competition among the buyers in
" the market of meat, would rapidly raise the price
" from eight pence or nine pence, to two or three
" shillings in the pound, and the commodity would
" not be divided among many more than it is at
" present. When an article is scarce, and cannot
" be distributed to all, he that can shew' the most
" valid patent, that is, he that offers the most
" money, becomes the possessor. When subsis-
" tence is scarce in proportion to the number of
" people, it is of little consequence, whether the
" lowest members of the society possess two shil-
" lings or five. They must, at all events, be re-
" duced to live upon the hardest fare, and in the
" smallest quantity."

Again, some pages after he says, " The question
" is, how far, wealth has a tendency to better the
" condition of the labouring poor. It is a self-evi-
" dent proposition that any general advance in the
" price of labour, the stock of provisions remaining
" the same, can only be a nominal advance, as it
" must shortly be followed by a *proportional* rise in
' provisions. The increase in the price of labour
" which we have supposed, would have no perma-
" nent effect therefore in giving to the labouring

" poor a greater command over the necessaries of
" life."

On these two passages which explain the drift of
our author's reasonings pretty clearly, I shall remark, first, that wealth is nothing but the power of
securing to yourself the fruits of the earth, or com-
manding the labour of others. The more equal distribution of wealth, or the throwing a greater quantity of money *(bona fide)* into the hands of the poor
must therefore enable them to procure either a
greater share of provisions or of the labour of others,
or both. This I hold to be an axiom, as far as I can
comprehend the subject. But Mr. Malthus says that
if the wages of the poor were raised to double or
treble what they are at present, this in the firs
place would not increase the quantity of meat in
the market, nor the share which the labourer would
have of it, because any advance in the price of labour must be followed by a *proportional* rise in provisions. This word is equivocal. To make out the
argument, the rise ought to be not only proportional
but equal to the rise of wages, which it evidently
would not be. But Mr. Malthus is willing to ex-
clude the possibility of bettering the condition of
the poor, even in theory, by an *equivoque*, or any
thing else. But to put an end to this miserable
quackery, I would ask, whether if the rich were to
divide their incomes with the poor, the latter would
be any the richer for it. To say in this case, that
the good things of the world would not be shared
more equally among them, is flat nonsense. But

any approach to a more equal division of wealth must lessen the difference between the rich and the poor *proportionally.* It is true that the lowest members of the community will still live upon the hardest fare, and in the smallest quantity: but their fare will be less hard and in larger quantities than it used to be, *in proportion* to the advance in the price of labour.

" It may at first appear strange, but I believe it " is true, that I cannot by means of money, raise " the condition of a poor man, and enable him to " live much better than he did before, without pro- " portionably depressing others in the same class. " If I retrench the quantity of food consumed in my " house, and give him what I have cut off, I then " benefit him without depressing any but myself " and family, who perhaps may be well able to " bear it. If I turn up a piece of uncultivated " land, and give him the produce, I then benefit " both him and all the members of society, because " what he before consumed is thrown into the com- " mon stock, and, probably, some of the new pro- " duce with it. But if I only give him money, sup- " posing the produce of the country to remain the " same, I give him a title to a larger share of that " produce than formerly, which share he cannot " receive without diminishing the shares of others. " It is evident, that this effect in individual in- " stances must be so small as to be totally imper- " ceptible; but still it must exist, as many other ef-

" fects do, which, like some of the insects that
" people the air, elude our grosser perceptions.

It will be sufficient to ask in answer to this passage,
whether when I give away my money to another, I do
not necessarily retrench the quantity of food or other
things consumed in my own house, and give him what
I have cut off. I give him a title to a larger share of the
common produce by diminishing *my own* share. It does
not matter to the community whether he or I spend
the money: the only difference that it makes is
between ourselves.—Mr. Malthus seems to have a
notion that the rich are never the worse for their
charities.

" Supposing the quantity of food in any country,
" to remain the same for many years together, it
" is evident, that this food must be divided according
" to the value of each man's patent, or the sum of
" money which he can afford to spend in this com-
" modity so universally in request. It is a demon-
" strative truth, therefore, that the patents of one
" set of men could not be increased in value, with-
" ', out diminishing the value of the patents of some
" other set of men."

At any rate, then, the poor would be enabled to
contend with the rich. The increased value of the
patents of the poor would necessarily diminish the
value of the patents of the rich. In order to outbid
them, they must make some other sacrifices, which
they will not always be willing to do. Food to the rich

is in a great measure an article of luxury: to the poor it is a necessary ; and the one, about which they are chiefly concerned. Many a *petit-maitre*, and ape of fashion goes without his dinner to pay for his coat, or go to the play, " where he picks clean teeth," &c.

" No person, I believe, will venture to doubt, that,
" if we were to give three additional shillings a day
" to every labouring man in the kingdom, as I before
" supposed, in order that he might have meat for his
" dinner, the price of meat would rise in the most
" rapid and unexampled manner.

Mr. Malthus here creeps on. He first spoke of a number of individuals as having a certain sum given them. He now includes every labouring man in the kingdom. Because if we were to give five shillings a day to five hundred thousand men, the remaining five hundred thousand might be the worse for it, therefore he would have us suppose that the same or greater mischiefs would follow from giving the same sum to the whole number, or in fact from doing away that very inequality, which was the only source of the mischief. To suppose that we can allow five shillings a-day to five hundred, or ten hundred thousand people without retrenching from our own superfluities, or that we can distribute our own patents among others without diminishing our own number, is one of those perversities which I shall not attempt to answer. If the labourer with his three shillings extra is only able to purchase an ounce of meat, this will be an advantage to him. Let the rise be what it will, the rich man will evidently be less able to out-bid him than he is at present, and the rise can only be in proportion to his capacity to out-bid him.   Besides, it is not to be supposed that his additional gains would all be laid out in meat, but in articles of trade, &c. which would be rendered cheaper by the neglect of the rich, or in proportion to the run upon provisions.   To assert generally that increasing the wages of the poor does not give them a greater command over the necessaries of life, is as much as to say that if they were forced to work for nothing, and could get nothing to eat, this would lower the markets, and they would be much better off than they were before.   It would be looked upon as an insult, rather than a consolation, to tell them that they ought to be contented with the cheapness of provisions, and to consider that allowing them any thing for their labour, would only raise the price of meat by enabling them to buy some of it to satisfy their hunger.

How things being cheap or dear, or how there being much or little to spare, proves that that much, or little will not be divided according to the ability of different people to pay for it, is beyond my comprehension.   It is ridiculous.   It is saying that the money of a poor man will not *pass*, even when he has it.   If the poor in consequence of having more money, or being richer could not draw to themselves a greater portion of food, there could be no room for competition, nor for an increase in the price or the demand.

" The poor who were assisted by their parishes had no reason whatever to complain of the high price of grain ; because it was the excessiveness of this price, and this alone, which, by enforcing such

" a saving, left a greater quantity of corn, for the con.
" sumption of the lowest classes, which corn, the pa-
" rish allowances enabled them to command." [Yet
Mr. Malthus has just tried to persuade us, that the
increased price of provisions, occasioned by the competition of the poor, does not enforce any retrench-
ment of the superfluities of the higher classes, or
leave a greater quantity of corn, for the consumption
of the lower classes]. " The greatest sufferers in the
" scarcity were undoubtedly the classes immediately
" above the poor; and these were in the most marked
" manner depressed by the excessive bounties given
" to those below them." [It is better that these
classes should be depressed than those below them,
because they can bear it better. Is it an argument
that because the pressure of a scarcity does not fall
directly upon those who can bear it best, viz. the very
rich, that it should therefore fall upon those, who can
bear it least, viz. on the very poor? Unless Mr. Malthus can contrive to starve some one, he thinks he
does nothing.] " This distribution by giving to the
" poorer classes a command of food, so much greater
" than their degree of skill and industry entitled
" them to, in the actual circumstances of the country,
" diminished, exactly in the same proportion, that
" command over the necessaries of life, which the
" classes above them, by their superior skill and in-
" dustry, would naturally possess." [Is a man then
to starve on account of his want of skill? To tack
industry to skill as if the lowest classes did not work
the hardest is impudence indeed]. " And it may be
" a question, whether the degree of assistance which

" the poor received, and which prevented them from
" resorting to the use of those substitutes, which, in
" every other country, on such occasions, the great
" law of necessity teaches, was not more than over-
" balanced by the severity of the pressure on so
" large a body of people from the extreme high pri-
" ces, and the permanent evil which must result from
" forcing so many persons on the parish, who before
" thought themselves almost out of the reach of
" want.

It is a contradiction to say, that the poor were forced
on the parish by the assistance they received from it.
If they were to be denied this assistance from a tender regard for their morals and independence, it is a
pity that the same disinterested motives, joined to the
" severe pressure" of the high prices on the classes
above the poor, did not induce some of *them* to con-
descend to the use of those cheap and wholesome
substitutes recommended by Mr. Malthus, by which
means they would have saved their own pockets, and
not have " forced so many persons on the parish."

" If we were to double the fortunes of all those
" who possess above a hundred a year, the effect on
" the price of grain would be slow and inconsidera-
" ble ; but if we were to double the price of labour
" throughout the kingdom, the effect, in raising the
" price of grain, would be rapid and great."

I do not see the harm of this rise. It would be in
consequence of, and would denote the number of
bellies that were filled that had not been filled before.

Mr. Malthus in this passage seems to prefer a little evil to a great good.

" The parish rates and the prodigious sum ex-
" pended in voluntary charity, must have had a most
" powerful effect in raising the price of the neces-
" saries of life, if any reliance can be placed on the
" clearest general principles, confirmed as much as
" possible by appearances. A man with a family, has
" received, *to my knowledge*, fourteen shillings a week
" from the parish." [Shocking to be sure.] " His
" common earnings were ten shillings a week, and his
" weekly *revenue*, therefore, twenty-four. Before the
" scarcity, he had been in the habit of purchasing
" a bushel of flour a week with eight shillings per-
" haps, and consequently had two shillings out of his
" ten, to spare for other necessaries. During the
" scarcity, he was enabled to purchase the same
" quantity at nearly three times the price. He paid
" twenty-two shillings for his bushel of flour, and
" had, as before, two shillings remaining for other
" wants." [Good : but does Mr. Malthus deny that
the scarcity would of itself have raised the price of
wheat ? And in that case if the labourer had had no
addition to his " weekly revenue," instead of having
the large sum of two shillings at the end of the week
to lay out in other necessaries, he would have had nothing. Perhaps Mr. Malthus is ready to prove, that
half a bushel of corn will go farther with a poor family in a time of scarcity than a whole one, because
they would husband it more carefully]. " Such in-
" stances could not possibly have been universal,
" without raising the price of every wheat much

" higher than it really was during any part of the
" dearth. But similar instances were by no means in-
" frequent, and *the system itself, of measuring the relief
" given by the price of grain, was general.*"

I cannot conceive of any better rule. But the gentleman is alarmed at the *voluntary* contributions ex-
torted from the rich. After all, I do not see how the
rich would suffer by their great charity, if, as our
author says, the poor got nothing by it. I would ask,
were the rich ever in danger of starving in the late
scarcity, and were not the poor in danger of it, and
would they not have starved, but for the assistance
given to them ? Is it better that the poor should
starve than that the rich should be at the expence of
relieving them? Or if the pressure in scarce times
falls on the middle classes, have they to complain, that
they, in whom " life and death may always be said
" to contend for victory," are still just kept alive, or
that the sleek and pampered continue to fatten on the
distresses of others? The false feeling which runs
through all Mr. Malthus's reasonings on this subject is,
that the upper classes cannot be expected to retrench any
of their superfluities, to lie at the mercy of the seasons,
or to contribute any thing to the general necessity, but
that the whole burthen of a scarcity ought to fall on
those whom Mr. Malthus calls " the least fortunate
" members of the community," on those who are most
used to distress, and in whom the transition is easy
and natural from poverty to famine ! " They lay
" heavy burthens on the poor and needy, which they
" will not touch with one of their fingers." Would

it not be worth our author's while to comment on this
text, and shew how little it has been understood ?—I
remember to have heard of but one instance of a real,
effectual, and judicious determination in the rich to
retrench idle and superfluous waste and expence, some
years ago at a time when the poor were *in want of bread.*
It originated in a great and noble family, where seventy
or eighty servants were kept, and where twenty or thirty
guests of the first distinction " fared sumptuously
" every day." These humane and enlightened persons, struck with the difference between their own
good fortune, and the necessities of others, came to a
resolution that the pieces of bread which they left at
dinner should neither be thrown nor given away, but
that the bread-baskets should be divided into little
compartments with each person's name affixed to
them, where he could conveniently put the piece of
bread which he left, and have it *saved* till the next
day. This humane example was much talked of in
the neighbourhood, and soon after followed by several
of the gentry, who got their bread-baskets divided
into little compartments with the different names affixed, and eat the pieces of bread which they left one
day, the day after—so that the poor were thus placed
completely out of the reach of want!

Mr. Malthus next talks about the embarrassments
of commerce, returning cheapness, &c. Now I do
not see, according to his doctrine, what cheapness has
to do with the question. He says, every thing depends
on the quantity of provisions in the country, and that
this being given, all the rest follows as a matter of

course. What then does it signify whether you call a piece of paper one pound or two, if you can get a proportionable quantity of food for your money.?

" If instead of giving the temporary assistance of
" parish allowances, which might be withdrawn on the
" first fall of price, we had raised universally the wages
" of labour, it is evident, that the obstacles to a dimi-
" nution of the circulation, and to returning cheap-
" ness, would have been still further increased ; and
" the high price of labour would have become per-
" manent, without any advantage whatever to the la-
" bourer,"—or disadvantage to the proprietor.

" There is no one that more ardently desires to see
" a real advance in the price of labour than myself;
" but the attempt to effect this object by forcibly
" raising the nominal price, which was practised to a
" certain degree, and recommended almost universally
" during the late scarcities, every thinking man must
" reprobate as puerile and ineffectual."

" The price of labour, when left to find its natural
" level, is a most important political barometer, ex-
" pressing the relation between the supply of pro-
" visions, and the demand for them; between the
" quantity to be consumed, and the number of con-
" sumers; and taken on the average, independently
" of accidental circumstances, it further expresses,
" clearly, the wants of the society respecting popu-
" lation; that is, whatever may be the number of
" children to a marriage necessary to maintain exactly

" the present population, the price of labour will be
" just sufficient to support this number, or be above
" it, or below it, according to the state of the real
" funds for the maintainance of labour, whether sta-
" tionary, progressive, or retrograde. Instead, how-
" ever, of considering it in this light, we consider it
" as something which we may raise or depress at
" pleasure, something which depends principally
" upon his majesty's justices of the peace. When
" an advance in the price of provisions already ex-
" presses that the demand is too great for the supply,
" in order to put the labourer in the same condition
" as before, we raise the price of labour, that is, we
" increase the demand, and are then much surprised
" that the price of provisions continues rising. In
" this, we act much in the same manner, as if, when
" the quicksilver in the common weather-glass stood
" at *stormy*, we were to raise it by some forcible
" pressure to *settled fair*, and then be greatly as-
" tonished that it continued raining."

This is certainly a most excellent illustration. As
to the argument itself, it is all false and hollow.
With respect to the rise in the price of provisions
consequent on the rise of wages, I am not I confess
at all concerned about it, so that the labourer is still
enabled to purchase the same *necessary* quantity as
before. All that is wanted is that the one should
keep pace with the other. What the natural level of
the price of labour is, otherwise than as it is regulated
by the positive institutions of society, or as I have
before stated, by the power of one set of men, and

the wants of another is—likᵉ many other things in this book of Mr. Malthus's—what I do not understand. If we are to believe him, the whole is a trick. There is a pretence of sacrificing something for the relief of the poor in hard times, and then the next thing is to render that relief ineffectual, by out-bidding them, by lowering the value of money, by creating artificial wealth, and other methods. If then the rich are so entirely masters of the price of labour, that they can render it real or nominal as they please, and take good care never to lose by it in the end, I should like to know how this most important political barometer has any relation to real plenty or want; how it expresses any thing more than the will of the rich and great; or the miserable pittance they are willing to allow out of the support of their own extravagant and ostentatious establishments to the maintainance of the mass of the people. It does indeed express the relation between the supply of provisions, and the demand for them, &c. supposing that a certain number of people are to consume four or five times as much (either in quantity or quality) as the others; and that this proportion is unalterable and one of the laws of nature. It further expresses the wants of the society respecting population, while this division continues, or that degree of poverty, beyond which it is impossible for people to subsist at all. The object in a scarcity is not however to stop the ordinary process of population, but to alleviate the distresses of those already in existence, by a more equal distrbution of the real funds for the maintainance of labour. By these funds Mr. Malthus means any arbitrary division of the produce of the ground, which the rich find it convenient to make, and which the poor are forced to take up with as better than nothing. But the real funds for the maintenance of labour are the produce of labour. According to Mr. Malthus, they are not the produce itself, but what happens to be left of it, as the husks only and not the corn are given to the swine.

" The number of servants out of place, and of " manufacturers wanting employment during the " late scarcities, were melancholy proofs of the " truth of these reasonings. If a general rise in the " wages of labour had taken place proportioned to " the price of provisions, none but farmers and a " few gentlemen could have afforded to employ the " same number of workmen as before. Additional " crowds of servants and manufacturers would have " been turned off; and those who were thus thrown " out of employment, would, of course, have no " other refuge than the parish. In the natural order " of things, a scarcity must tend to lower, instead " of to raise, the price of labour."

This natural order has been already explained to mean a very artificial order. Our ingenious author is a great admirer of moral analogies. He sticks to the old proverb, those that have little shall have less. " The most laborious and deserving part of the com- " munity" are to bear the brunt of all distress, *ordinary and extraordinary*. He will not suffer the positive regulations of society, which carry inequality of conditions as far almost as it can go in common cases, to relax a little in their favour in extreme cases, so as not to push them quite out of existence. I know no reason why in the natural order of things a scarcity should tend to lower, instead of raising the price of labour, but upon that common principle that the weakest are to go to the wall. The rich forsooth are a privileged class, out of the reach of fortune, " whose solid virtue the shot of " accident or dart of change can neither graze nor " pierce." In the rest of this passage, Mr. Malthus quarrels with his own favourite system, with those capricious and arbitrary institutions, in consequence of which those who ministered only to the vanity or artificial wants of the rich will in times of difficulty be turned adrift and reduced to want, or else saddled as an additional weight on the common labourer, who had enough to do to support them and their employers under the most favourable circumstances.

GENERAL ANSWER.—I wish Mr. Malthus to state explicitly whether he means that the rise in the price of labour should be nominal or real. He has shifted his ground four or five times on the subject in the course of the chapter, now supposing it to be a mere non-entity, and now fraught with the most terrible consequences, famine, and God knows what. But it seems to me, that if nominal, it must be nugatory, and therefore innocent; and that if real, it must be proportionably beneficial. For if real, it must throw a greater quantity of the necessaries or comforts of life into the hands of those who most want them, and take them from those who are oppressed with their superfluities. For suppose the quantity of food and the quantity of money to be fixed, given quantities (unless we suppose both, there is no reasoning about the matter) and that an additional price is given for labour: let us suppose farther that this raises the price of provisions. It is evident in this case, that the rich having less money to give, and being obliged to give more for their former luxuries, will be obliged to retrench somewhere. This must be either in provisions, or other things. First, they may retrench in the article of provisions. This will evidently leave a greater plenty for others, who stand very much in need of them; and their additional wages will be laid out in supplying themselves with what they could not otherwise have obtained. Secondly, they may retrench in articles of furniture, dress, houses, &c. and there will consequently be less demand for these things. Well then, in the first place, with regard to provisions, the poor will be no worse off in this respect than if there had been no advance in the price, for it is not to be supposed that if the rich are so attached to the luxuries of the belly as notwithstanding the increased price to buy the same quantity as ever, that they would have bought less, if the price had continued lower. They would have engrossed the markets at all events. On the other hand, they must retrench their expences in other things, in superfluities of different kinds, which will thus fall into the hands of the poor, who having been excluded from the meat-market can only lay out their additional wages in providing themselves with household conveniences, good clothes, tables, chairs, &c. What should they do with their money? It is supposed that they cannot get a morsel of meat with it: and it is not to be expected that they should throw it away. Sooner than do this, they might spend it in buying smart buckles for their shoes, or garters and ribbons for their sweethearts. The labour of the mechanic, inasmuch as it is not wanted by the great, will go to enrich the lower classes. The less they are employed by the rich, in consequence of " a more equal distribution of the money of the " society," the better able they will be to employ one another. The farmer's servant will employ the mechanic with the same money with which the farmer or his landlord would have employed him: if he has the same wages as before, he will have as much to do; or if his wages are doubled, and he has only half as much to do, this will be a proportionable relief to him on the score of labour, and would be no prejudice to his earnings as he would get the same wages for doing half as much work. But there is no occasion to suppose any such slackness in the demand for labour. The proportion between the money, the productive and mechanical labour in the community, would remain the same : and the rise in the wages of the labouring manufacturer and mechanic to be real and effectual ought to be paid out of the profits of the master and proprietor. In this case, the demand would be the same: and it would evidently be his interest to employ the same number of men that he did before, as though he would get less by each of them, he must get more, the more

hands he employs, as long as the demand continues.*
If however our rich men and manufacturers should
grow sulky upon the occasion, and take it into
their heads to hoard their money in order to spite
the poor, thus driving them altogether out of employ,
I conceive the best use that can be made of this
hoarded wealth would be to transfer it to the poor's
fund, for the relief of those who are willing to work,
but not to starve. On the whole, and in every view
of the subject it appears to me that any addition to
the price of labour must as far as it goes, be an advantage to the labourer, and that the more general
and permanent it is, the greater will be the benefit to
the labouring class of the community. The rise of
wages would certainly take from the pomp and
luxury of the rich, and it would as certainly and in
the same proportion add to the comforts of the poor.
I am not here recommending such a change. I only
contend that it would follow the distribution of wealth;
and that it is absurd to say that the poorer a man is,
the richer he will be.

* The immediate rise in the price of manufactured articles
upon any rise in the price of labour is either a foolish impa-
tience of loss, or a trick to make the labourer refund his own
earnings by paying more for what he wants himself, and by
being *pigeoned* by others that they may be able to pay the additional price. It has nothing to do with a fair and liberal determination to raise the price of labour, which of itself, and if
not immediately counteracted by the power and artifices of the
rich, must always tend to the benefit of the labouring part of
the community.

Mr. Malthus's acuteness amounts to a species of second-sight, whenever there is a question of famine. Thus he demonstrates that this must be the necessary consequence of fixing a maximum in a time of scarcity. Now I do not see this necessary consequence, because if it were fixed at a certain height above the common price in proportion to the deficiency, this would check the too rapid consumption. Or even without supposing this, as it would be necessary to have some kind of law or order of the police to enforce the observance of a maximum, and make the farmers and dealers bring their corn to market, the quantities in which it was brought forward might be regulated in the same way as the price. Besides. I do not believe that people would starve themselves with their eyes open, whether the police interfered or not. As to the epithets of illiberal, unjust, and narrow policy which some people may apply to such a measure, I would ask them whether fixing the assize of bread in London is not just the same thing. But cornfactors, forestallers and regraters are a set of people whose liberal notions place them above the law, who ought not to be looked upon in the same light with every little scurvy knavish bread and biscuit baker, nor cramped in their generous exertions to economize the public resources, and save the poor from famine at the latter end of the year—by starving them in the beginning. With respect to the parallel which Mr. Malthus attempts to establish between fixing a maximum, and raising the price of labour, I am so unfortunate as not to perceive it. He sometimes argues against raising the price of labour because it

would give the poor no greater command over the
provisions than before; he here talks as if it would
enable them to devour every thing before them. I
think neither of these suppositions is true. The high
price of corn in proportion to other things will always make people unwilling to lay out more in that
way than they can help, and will consequently diminish the consumption. As to famine, people will
look many ways, before they submit to it.

" Independently of any considerations respecting a
" year of deficient crops, it is evident, that an increase
" of population, without a proportional increase of
" food, must lower the value of each man's *earnings*.
" The food must necessarily be distributed in smaller
" quantities, and consequently, a day's labour will pur-
" chase a smaller quantity of provisions.

Why of earnings more than property? Mr. Malthus would have this considered as an elementary or
philosophical work. Yet he looks only at the flattering side of his subject. A day's labour will purchase a less quantity of provisions, but a day's idleness will purchase the same. In this case idleness
and industry are plaintiff and defendant; and the
verdict is in favour of idleness, and industry is not
only cast, but pays the costs.—It is all very well.

" The quantity of provisions consumed in work-
" houses, upon a part of the society, that cannot in
" general be considered as the most valuable part,"
[or in other houses on footmen, &c. who are not the

most respectable kind of paupers] " diminishes the
" shares that would otherwise belong to more indus-
" trious and more worthy members, and thus in the
" same measure, forces more to become dependent.

" Fortunately for England, a spirit of independence
" still remains among the peasantry. The poor laws
" are strongly calculated to eradicate this spirit." [Is
it the man who reduces me to beggary, or he who affords me relief, that lowers my condition and breaks
my spirit?] " They have succeeded in part; but
" had they succeeded as completely as might have
" been expected, their pernicious tendency would not
" have been so long concealed.

It would have been discovered sooner, if Mr. Malthus had read Mr. Wallace's book sooner.

" The parish laws of England *appear* to have con-
" tributed to raise the price of provisions, and to
" lower the real price of labour." [Our author's demonstrations are delusive appearances. What must
his *appearances* be ? Shall we take them for demonstrations ?] They have therefore contributed to im-
" poverish that class of people whose only possession
" is their labour. It is also difficult to suppose, that
" they have not powerfully contributed to generate
" that carelessness and want of frugality observable
" among the poor, so contrary to the disposition ge-
" nerally to be remarked among petty tradesmen and
" small farmers. The labouring poor, to use a vulgar
" expression, seem always to live from hand to mouth.

" Their present wants employ their whole attention;
" and they seldom think of the future. Even when
" they have an opportunity of saving, they seldom
" exercise it; but all that they earn beyond their
" present necessities, goes, generally speaking, to the
" alehouse. The poor laws may, therefore, be said
" to diminish both the power, and the will, to save,
" among the common people, and thus to weaken
" one of the strongest incentives to sobriety and
" industry, and consequently to happiness."

This passage is remarkable. It may be asked in
the first place, whether the parish laws are not
equally open to petty tradesmen and small farmers,
as to the poor. If so, they cannot account for the
difference observable between them. I shall therefore, as far as this very striking contrast goes, put
the poor laws out of the question; and say that the
difference in their behaviour can arise from nothing
but the difference in their situations, from the
greater hardships imposed on the labouring part of
the community, from their different prospects in life,
and the little estimation in which they are held.
Mr. Malthus accounts for the carelessness and lazi-
ness of the poor from their casting a sheep's-eye at
the work-house. No: they are to be accounted for
from that poverty and depression which makes the
work-house a temptation to them. We cannot say
of those who are seduced by the prospect of a work-
house—" Alas from what height fallen!" Mr. Malthus
proposes to remove this dazzling object out of their
way; to make them indulge in larger views of things by

setting before them the prospect of their wives and
children starving, in case of any accident to themselves, and to stimulate their industry by lowering
their wages. The poor live from hand to mouth, because, in general, they have no hopes of living in any
other way. They seldom think of the future, because they are afraid to think of it. Their present
wants employ their whole attention. This is their
misfortune. Others have better luck. They have no
time to think of wind-falls. Mr. Malthus may take
his glass of wine after dinner, and his afternoon's nap,
when, having got the Essay on Population out of his
head, queen Mab " comes to him with a tythe-pig's
" tail, tickling the parson as he lies asleep:—then
" dreams he of another benefice." The poor cannot
indulge in such pleasing speculations. If what they
earn beyond their immediate necessities goes to the
ale-house, it is because the severe labour they undergo
requires some relaxation, because they are willing to
forget the *work-house*, their old age, and the prospect
of their wives and children starving, and to drown
care in a mug of ale, in noise, and mirth, and laughter,
and old ditties, and coarse jokes, and hot disputes;
and in that sense of short-lived comfort, independence and good-fellowship, which is necessary to relieve the hurt mind and jaded body. But all these,
when our author's system is once established, " shall
" no more impart,

" An hour's importance to the poor man's heart."

No human patience can submit to everlasting toil
and self-denial. The prospect of mere physical com-

fort is not a match for continued physical suffering: and the lower classes of the people have no other motives to animate them to bear up against the ills of life, in habits of moral reflection, in the pursuits and example of the rich, or in the *real* respect and credit attached to their own good behaviour. You reduce them almost to the condition of brutes, and then grudge them their coarse enjoyments: you make machines of them, and then expect from them firmness, resolution, the love of independence, the fruits of an erect and manly spirit. Mr. Malthus, like the Sphinx, destroys his victims by the help of riddles; and makes a snare of impossibilities. As to the workmen and mechanics in manufacturing towns (to say nothing of the closeness and unwholesomeness of their occupations, which would go a good way in accounting for " their drunkenness and dissipation") the noise and turbulence in which they live, and their being crowded together as they are must unfit them for enjoying the quiet and stillness of domestic life: they are glad to escape from the contempt which their " squalid appearance" excites in the well-dressed mob who walk the streets, and hide their greasy clothes and smutched faces in the nearest pot-house; and to say the truth, with respect to those of them who are married, the hard features, the disjointed shapes, the coarse limbs, the carking countenances, and ill-humour of their wives, occasioned by the fretful wants of a set of squalling children, cannot be supposed to prove so attractive to them, as " the symmetry of person, the " vivacity, the voluptuous softness of temper, the

" affectionate kindness of feeling, the imagination,
" and the wit" which in Mr. Malthus's opinion con-
stitute the charm of the sex. After all, are the
higher classes a bit better than their inferiors? Are
drinking and dissipation confined to the poor? As Mr.
Malthus ingenuously observes, " Our Doctors Com-
" mons and the lives that many married men [of the
" better sort] are known to lead sufficiently prove the
" reverse of this." I believe it will hardly be proposed to make moral merit a rule for the division of
the good things of fortune. The only difference in
the vices of the rich and the poor is, that the rich can
afford theirs better. Nevertheless they set up for cen-
sors and reformers of the morals of the poor. I remember to have seen a red-faced swag-bellied bishop (such another as Father Paul in the Duenna)
who could drink his two bottles of wine without being affected, belch out a severe reprimand against a
poor labouring man, who was staggering home after
drinking a quart of small beer. As to our author's plan
of *starving* the poor out of their vices, I must say (all
circumstances considered) that I think it, in the first
place, an impudent proposal, because their execu-
tioners are no better than themselves; in the second
place, a silly proposal, because, if not literally followed up, it must evidently defeat itself; in the third
place, a malignant proposal, because if it were strictly
put in practice, it could only produce despair and
sullen insensibility among the poor, and destroy all
traces of justice or humanity among the rich; in the
fourth place, a lying proposal, because it is contrary
to Mr. Malthus's own reasonings, who in many places

has shewn that the only way to improve the condition of the poor is not by urging them to extremity, but by raising them above want, by inspiring them with a respect for themselves, and a taste for the comforts and decencies of life by sharing in them.

" That the poor (says Mr. Malthus) employed in " manufactures consdier parish assistance as a *reason* " why they may spend all the wages which they earn, " and enjoy themselves while they can, *appears to be* " *evident,* from the number of families that upon the " failureof any great manufactory, immediately fall " upon the parish." This is an assumption of the question. Our author here confounds the fact and the reason together. It appears evident that the manufacturer often spends his earnings as he gets them, but not that he does so in the hope that his family may go to the parish after his death. " A man who might not " be deterred from going to the alehouse from the " consideration that on his death or sickness he " should leave his wife and family upon the parish, " might yet hesitate in thus dissipating his ear- " nings if he were assured that in either of " these cases *his family must starve,* or be left " to the support of casual bounty." Now it has appeared that his conduct is regulated by motives and circumstances which have nothing to do with what happens to his wife and children after his death. It may therefore be questioned whether the catastrophe proposed by Mr. Malthus would have the desired effect. But certainly it could not have this effect as long as there was a dependence on casual bounty: and to stop up this resource it would be absolutely necessary to call in the aid of the magistrate to prevent the indiscreet and unavailing interference of private charity, and execute the sentence of the law of nature and the law of God on his wife and hapless progeny, justly doomed to starve for the neglect of their parent. What effect this would have on the " moral sensibility of the nation" I leave to Mr. Malthus to determine with his well-known penetration and humanity. " The suffering a poor family to " perish of want is bad enough: but I cannot con- " ceive of any thing much more detestable or shocking " to the feelings than any direct regulation of this " kind, by whatever name it is sanctioned." Mr. Malthus may perhaps object that I have quoted him unfairly; and applied to the *organizing the starving of a family* what he applied to the direct regulation of *infanticide*,—a very different thing! Unfortunately, I have not sufficient delicacy of *verbal* feeling to be able to find out the difference.—Now I recollect, however, what shocked Mr. Malthus so much in speaking of infanticide was the supposition that the parents were to be forced to destroy their own children, when they thought they could maintain them: according to our author's mode of starving a family, the society are only to stand by and prevent others from affording them assistance. Here we see there is not that direct violation of the parental affection which, says Mr. Malthus, is the principal aggravation of the other case. He explains the grounds of this distinction in another part of his work. " If," says he, " the " parents desert their child, *they* ought to be answer- " able for the crime. The infant is, comparatively

" speaking, of no value to the society *, as others
" will immediately supply its place. Its principal
" value is on account of its being the object of one
" of the most delightful passions in human nature—
" parental affection. But if this value be disregarded
" by those who are *alone* in a capacity to feel it, the
" *society* cannot be called upon to put itself in their
" place and has no further business in its protection,"
than just to see that its parents do not ill-use, or kill or
eat it. Nothing can be plainer than the inference
from these premises. The society, which is bound to
prevent or punish the least barbarity in parents towards
their children, because they are to them an object of
a very delightful passion, may exercise any barbarity it pleases on them itself, because it is not in a
capacity to feel this affection towards them. It is not
only not called upon to put itself in their place, but
is bound to prevent others from doing so, and thus
reversing the laws of nature, by which " the child
" is confided exclusively to its parents." It is only,
says our author, by extinguishing every spark of humanity in the breasts of the community towards the
children of others, that the ties of parental affection can
ever exist in their full force, or be expected " to re-
" main in the state in which nature has left them." Mr.
Malthus may therefore in his zeal for the growth of
parental affection, and the entire suppression of com-

---

* This is something like Mr. Godwin's saying, he does not
regard a new-born infant with any peculiar complacency. They
both differ from the founder of the Christian religion, who has
said, Bring unto me little children. But modern philosophers
scorn to pin their faith on musty sayings.

mon humanity as subversive of it, very consistently
brand every attempt of the society to make the parents accomplices in starving their children, as the
greatest injustice, though we may very heroically
proceed to starve them ourselves, repeating after this
high-priest of nature, Their blood be upon us and
upon *our* children! This is the best account I can give
of the fundamental distinction which Mr. Malthus
makes between the impropriety and inhumanity of
destroying children by law, and the propriety and humanity of *starving* a family by law. But I shall recur
to the same subject presently, when I come to the
detail of his plan.

Mr. Malthus devotes the first and second chapters
of his fourth book to an inquiry into our obligations
to regulate the sexual passion by considerations of
prudence, &c. into the general capacity of human nature to act from rational motives, and the good effects
which would result from such a conduct. He begins
his third chapter in the following manner.

" He who publishes a moral code, or system of
" duties, however firmly he may be convinced of the
" strong obligation on each individual strictly to con-
" form to it, has never the folly to imagine that it
" will be universally or even generally practised.
" But this is no valid objection against the publication
" of the code. If it were, the same objection would
" always have applied; we should be totally without
" general rules; and to the vices of mankind arising
" from temptation, would be added a much longer

" list, than we have at present, of vices from igno
" rance." [This is well said, and 'tis a kind of good
deed to say well.] " Judging merely from the light
" of nature, if we feel convinced of the misery
" arising from a redundant population, on the one
" hand, and of the evils and unhappiness, particularly
" to the female sex, arising from promiscuous inter-
" course, on the other, I do not see how it is possi-
" ble for any person, who acknowledges the principle
" of utility as the great foundation of morals, to es-
" cape the conclusion that moral restraint, till we are
" in a condition to support a family, is the strict line
" of duty; and when revelation is taken into the
" question, this duty undoubtedly receives very pow-
" erful confirmation. At the same time, I believe
" that few of my readers can be less sanguine in their
" expectations of any great change in the general
" conduct of men on this subject than I am; and the
" chief reason, why, in the last chapter, I allowed
" myself to suppose the universal prevalence of this
" virtue, was, that I might endeavour to remove any
" imputation on the goodness of the Deity, by shew-
" ing that the evils arising from the principle of po-
" pulation were exactly of the same nature as the
" generality of other evils which excite fewer com-
" plaints, that they were increased by human igno-
" rance and indolence, and diminished by human
" knowledge and virtue; and on the supposition, that
" each individual strictly fulfilled his duty, would be
" almost totally removed; and this, without any ge-
" neral diminution of those sources of pleasure,
" arising from the regulated indulgence of the pas-

" sions, which have been justly considered as the
" principal ingredients of human happiness."

Mr. Malthus here appears in the double character
of a politician and divine. Sir Hugh Evans says, " I
" like not when a'omans has a great peard." I must
say, I do not like to see a philosopher in a cassock.
He has you at an unfair advantage, and it is a hundred
to one but he will make use of it. When he is pressed
hard, or sees his arguments in danger of being cut off,
he puts them into the false belly of theology. It is
like hunting an otter: you do not know where to
have him.—What our author says of moral systems is
certainly true: neither the preaching of St. Paul, nor
probably his own has been able to put an end to that
pious, courtly race of men, who strive equally to
serve God and mammon. Mr. Malthus in the last
chapter took an opportunity of paying his court to
the former: the leaf is no sooner turned, than he
begins to insinuate himself into the good graces of the
latter, by disclaiming the sincerity of his late profes-
sions. In the passage just quoted, Mr. Malthus not
only tells you that he had endeavoured to give a more
favourable account of the expectations of mankind
and their capacity for virtue and happiness than he
believes has any foundation in human nature; but he
at the same time lets you into his motive for so doing,
viz. his wish to remove any imputation on the divine
goodness, which purpose, it seems, would not have
been so well answered by the real statement of the
fact. Having thus decently paid his compliments to
his profession, and justified the goodness of God from

the ideal capacity of man for virtue he next proceeds
to prove the wisdom of human institutions by his *real
incapacity* for it. He was yesterday engaged to white-
wash Providence: to day he is retained on the other
side of the question, which he assures his clients
shall not suffer through any anxiety of his about consistency. This seems to be playing at fast and loose
both with religion and morality. Mr. Malthus has
indeed set apart the preceding chapter to shew that
" the evils arising from the principle of population
" are exactly of the same nature as the generality of
" other evils which excite fewer complaints, that they
" were increased by human ignorance and indolence,
" and diminished by human knowledge and virtue."
But I do not know what right he had to do this, seeing that it is the express object of his work to shew
that the evils of population are unlike all other evils,
neither generated by human folly, nor to be removed
or palliated by human wisdom, but by vice and misery alone: that they are *sui generis*, and not to be
reasoned upon, like any thing else. Neither do I understand how the evils of population can be said to excite
more complaints than other evils, when Mr. Malthus
tells us that till his time nobody had thought of tracing
them to their true source, but erroneously ascribed
them to human institutions, vice, folly, &c. Mr. Malthus himself was the first who proved them to be irremediable and inherent in the constitution of nature, and
thus brought an imputation upon Providence. To
remove this imputation he supposes them to admit of
a remedy: then again lest any one should take him
at his word and be for applying this remedy, he says

they admit of no such remedy; and that it was all an idle supposition of his own without any foundation, a harmless picture drawn to illustrate the *imaginary* goodness of Providence.

" If it will answer any purpose of illustration, I see " no harm in drawing the picture of a society in " which each individual is supposed strictly to fulfil " his duties: nor does a writer appear to be justly " liable to the imputation of being visionary, unless " he makes such universal or general obedience ne- " cessary to the practical utility of his system, and " to that degree of moderate and partial improve- " ment, which is all that can rationally be expected " from the most complete knowledge of our du- " ties."

" But in this respect, there is an essential diffe- " rence between that improved state of society which " I have supposed in the last chapter, and most of " the other speculations on this subject. The im- " provement there supposed, if we ever should make " approaches towards it, is to be effected in the way " in which we have been in the habit of seeing all " the greatest improvements effected, by a direct ap- " plication to the interest and happiness of each indi- " vidual. It is not required of us to act from mo- " tives, to which we are unaccustomed; to pursue " a general good, which we may not distinctly com- " prehend, or the effect of which may be weakened " by distance or diffusion."

Is there not such a virtue as patriotism? To what
class of motives would our author refer this feeling?
The way in which Mr. Malthus wishes to effect his
improvement in the virtue and happiness of mankind,
is one in which no such improvement has hitherto
been effected. But I see Mr. Malthus's object. He is
only anxious, lest any one should attempt to rear the
fabric of human excellence on any other basis than
that of vice and misery. So that we begin with this solid and necessary foundation, he does not care to what
height the building is carried. So that we set out on
our journey of reform through the gate at which Mr.
Malthus is sitting at the receipt of custom, (whether
it faces the road or not) it gives him little concern
what direction we take, or how far we go afterwards,
or whether we ever reach our promised destination.

" The duty of each individual is express and intel-
" ligible to the humblest capacity. It is merely that
" he is not to bring beings into the world for whom
" he cannot find the means of support. When once
" this subject is cleared from the obscurity thrown
" over it by parochial laws and *private benevolence,*
" every man must feel the strongest conviction of
" such an obligation. If he cannot support his
" children, they must *starve*; and if he marry in the
" face of a fair probability that he shall not be able
" to support his children, he is guilty of all the evils
" which he thus brings upon himself, his wife, and
" his offspring. It is clearly his interest, and will
" tend greatly to promote his happiness to defer
" marrying, till, by industry and economy, he is
" in a capacity to support the children, that he

" may reasonably expect from his marriage and
" as he cannot in the mean time, gratify his pas-
" sions, without violating *an express command of*
" *God,* and running a great risk of injuring himself,
" or some of his fellow creatures, considerations of
" his own interest and happiness will dictate to him
" the strongest obligation to moral restraint.

" However powerful may be the impulses of passion
" *they are generally in some degree modified by reason.*
" And it does not seem entirely visionary to suppose,
" that if the true and permanent cause of poverty
" were clearly explained," [This I take to be that the
rich have more than the poor] "and forc..ly brought
" home to each man's bosom, it would have some,
" and perhaps not an inconsiderable, influence on
" his conduct; at least, the experiment has never
" yet been fairly tried."

It is astonishing, what a propensity Mr. Malthus
has to try experiments, if there is any mischief to be
done by them. He has a perfect horror of experiments that are to be tried on the higher qualities of
our nature, from which any great, unmixed, and
general good is to be expected. But in proportion as
the end is low, and the means base, he acquires confidence, his tremours forsake him, and he approaches
boldly to the task with nerves of iron. His humanity
is of a singular cast. What is grand and elevated,
seems to be his aversion. Pure benefits are of too
cloying a quality to please his taste. He is willing to
improve the morals of the people by extirpating the

common feelings of mankind, and will submit to the introduction of a greater degree of plenty and comfort, provided it is prefaced by famine.

His ardour is kindled not so much in proportion to the difficulty, as to the disgusting nature of the task. He is a kind of sentimental nightman, an amateur chimney-sweeper, a patriotic Jack-ketch. The spirit of adventure is roused in him only by the prospect of dirty roads, and narrow, crooked paths. He never flinches where there is any evil to be done, that good may come of it! His present plan is an admirable one of the kind—*Omne tulit punctum*—it comprises both extremes of vice and misery. The poor are to make a formal surrender of their right to private charity or parish assistance, that the rich may be able to lay out all their money on their vices.

" Till these erroneous ideas have been corrected,
" and the language of *nature* and reason has been ge-
" nerally heard on the subject of population, instead
" of the language of error and prejudice, it cannot be
" said that any fair experiment has been made with
" the understandings of the common people; and
" we cannot justly accuse them of improvidence and
" want of industry, till they act as they do now,
" after it has been brought home to their comprehen-
" sions, that they are themselves the cause of their
" own poverty; that the means of redress are in their
" own hands, and *in the hands of no other per-*
" *sons whatever; that the society in which they live,*
" *and the government which presides over it, are totally*

345

" *without power in this respect* ; and however ardently
" they may desire to relieve them, and whatever at*
" tempts they may make to do so, they are really
" and truly unable to execute what they benevo-
" lently wish, but unjustly promise ; that when the
" wages of labour will not maintain a family, it is an
" incontrovertible sign that *their king and country do*
" *not want more subjects,* or at least *that they cannot*
" *support them* ; that if they marry in this case, so far
" from fulfilling a duty to society, they are throwing
" a useless burden on it, at the same time that they
" are plunging themselves into distress ; and that they
" are acting directly contrary to the will of God, and
" bringing down upon themselves various diseases,
" which might all, or in a great part, have been
" avoided, if they had attended to the repeated ad-
" monitions which he gives, by the general laws of
" nature, to every being capable of reason *.

* But a moment ago the subject was involved in the most
profound obscurity, and great advantages were expected from
the manner in which Mr. Malthus was to bring it home to each
man's comprehension. In the passage immediately following
the above, our author quotes Dr. Paley's Moral Philosophy, and
as he often refers to this work, I shall here take the liberty of
entering my protest against it. It is a school in which a man
learns to tamper with his own mind, and will become any thing
sooner than an honest man. It is a directory, shewing him how
to disguise and palliate his real motives (however unworthy) by
metaphysical subterfuges, and where to look for every infirmity
which can beset him, with its appropriate apology, taken from
the common topics of religion and morality. All that is good
in Paley is taken from Tucker; and even *his* morality is not the
most bracing that can be imagined.

The erroneous ideas of which Mr. Malthus here complains as prevailing in the minds of the common people, to the prejudice of the language of reason and nature, are, as he states just before, that their poverty and distress are *in part* owing to their not getting more for their labour, to the slowness with which the parish assist them, to the avarice of the rich, and to the institutions of society, or to fortune which has assigned them a place so beset with difficulties and dependence! No, poverty is owing to none of these causes, but it is owing entirely to *itself.* Mr. Burke has said, that people will not be argued into slavery. Our author attempts more than this. He tries to persuade them out of their senses, and to argue them into slavery and famine besides. There is a distinction which it is sometimes dangerous to insist on in common life; but which it is necessary to attend to in matters of reasoning, and that is the distinction between truth and falsehood. For instance, Mr. Malthus asserts, that the means of remedying their complaints are in the hands of the poor, and in the hands of no other persons whatever. Now this is not true. It is not true that the society in which they live and the government which presides over it are *totally* without power in this respect. It is not true that however ardently they may wish to relieve them, they are utterly unable to execute their benevolent intentions. It is not an incontrovertible sign that their king and country do not want more subjects, and that they cannot support them, when the common wages of labour will not maintain a family. As Mr. Malthus's positions exist no where but in the Essay of Population, they will hardly support those weighty practical conclusions which he wishes to build upon them. Some persons may perhaps be at a loss to understand what Mr. Malthus can mean by his assertions. The following may be some clue to what in itself has very much the appearance of irony.

" Among the other prejudices which have pre-
" vailed on the subject of population, it has been ge-
" nerally thought, that while there is either waste
" among the rich, or land remaining uncultivated in
" any country, the complaint for want of food cannot
" be justly founded, or, at least, that the pressure of
" distress upon the poor is to be attributed to the ill-
" conduct of the higher classes of society, and the
" bad management of the land. The real effect,
" however, of these two circumstances, is merely to
" narrow the limit of the actual population ; but they
" have little or no influence on what may be called
" the average pressure of distress on the poorer mem-
" bers of society. If our ancestors had been so frugal
" and industrious, and had transmitted such habits to
" their posterity, that nothing superfluous was now
" consumed by the higher classes, no horses were
" used for pleasure, and no land was left uncultivated,
" a striking difference would appear in the state of
" the actual population ; but probably none what-
" ever, in the state of the lower classes of people,
" with respect to the price of labour, and the facility
" of supporting a family. The waste among the
" rich and the horses kept for pleasure, have indeed a

" little the effect of the consumption of grain in dis-
" tilleries, noticed before with regard to China. On
" the supposition that the food consumed in this
" manner may be withdrawn on the occasion of a
" scarcity, and be applied to the relief of the poor,
" they operate, certainly, as far as they go, like gra-
" naries which are only opened at the time that they
" are most wanted, and must therefore tend rather
" to benefit than injure the lower classes of society.

" With regard to uncultivated land, it is evident, that
" its effect upon the poor is neither to injure, nor to
" benefit them. The sudden cultivation of it, will
" indeed tend to improve their condition for a time,
" and the neglect of lands before cultivated, will cer-
" tainly make their situation worse for a certain pe-
" riod; but when no changes of this kind are going
" forward, the effect of uncultivated land on the
" lower classes, operates merely like the possesion of
" a smaller territory.

After what has been said in various parts of these
observations, I might leave these passages to the contempt of the reader. But Mr. Malthus shall not
complain of my remissness. I will give him heaped
measure. I say then that the argument here employed leads to a direct absurdity: for it would justify
any degree of neglect, or waste, or wanton abuse that
can be imagined. If thirty-nine out of the forty
counties in England were laid waste to morrow, this
would be no evil, according to Mr. Malthus, because
it would not increase the average pressure of distress

in the remaining one. If half the corn that is grown
every year, besides what is already employed in supplying the waste of the rich, were regularly sent off
by waggon-loads, and thrown into the sea, there
would be still no harm done. A *striking* difference
would undoubtedly appear in the number of poor
people, but probably none whatever in the state of
those who had not been starved. If double the number of horses were kept for pleasure, and only half
the number of poor were kept alive, these latter
would have no reason to complain, because they
would be as well, or better off than ever; and if a
limited number are tolerably well provided for, this
is all that can ever be expected, because by the laws
of nature it is impossible to provide for an unlimited
number. To say nothing of those immense granaries
and boundless resources which are thus formed in the
uncultivated parts of the earth, or which might be
created at any time of extraordinary distress by employing in the service of man what had hitherto been
providently reserved for the beasts.

While there is waste among the rich, or neglect of
lands, or while the breed of horses is encouraged so
as to put a stop to the breed of men, I deny that the
distresses of the poor, or the restraints on population
are the necessary effects of the laws of nature, or of
the unavoidable disproportion between the increase of
mankind and the capacity of the earth to produce
food for a greater number. But Mr. Malthus has his
usual resource. Though the distresses of the poor
were actually relieved as they might be, and though
the unnecessary checks to population were taken off,

yet the time would come when these wants could no longer be supplied, and when the restraints on population would become necessary, from the inability of the earth to yield any more, and from the whole produce being applied to the best advantage. This is undoubtedly true: but I do not think it a reason that we are not to put off the evil as long as we can, or that we are not to attempt any improvement, because we cannot go on for ever improving. Death is certain, and " will come when it will come." Is that a reason why I should take poison? There is in all Mr. Malthus's arguments on this subject the same *twist* that there was in the Irish servant, who was told to call his master early, and waked him two hours before the time to tell him how much longer he had to sleep. Mr. Malthus would have insisted on his getting up and dressing himself in the middle of the night.

Mr. Malthus allows, that " the object of those " who really wish to better the condition of the poor " must be to raise the relative proportion between " the price of labour, and the price of provisions." Almost in the next paragraph, however, he adds, that if we are really serious in this object, " we must " explain to them the true nature of their situation, " and shew them that *the withholding the supplies of* " *labour is the only possible way of raising its real* " *price."* I cannot help thinking, to use his own words, that our author's " benevolence to the poor " must be either childish play, or hypocrisy : that it " must be either to amuse himself, or to pacify the " minds of the common people with a mere shew of

" attention to their wants." He proceeds to instruct the poor in their true situation in a chapter which requires a few comments.

" The pressure of distress on the lower classes of
" people, with the habit of attributing this distress
" to their rulers, appears to me to be the rock of de-
" fence, the castle, the guardian spirit, of despotism.
" It affords to the tyrant the fatal and unanswerable
" plea of *necessity*." [That is Mr. Malthus's plea.]
" While any dissatisfied man of talents has power to
" persuade the lower classes of people, that all their
" poverty and distress arise solely from the iniquity
" of the government, though perhaps the greatest
" part of what they suffer is totaly unconnected
" with this cause, it is evident that the seeds of fresh
" discontents, and fresh revolutions, are continually
" sowing."

That is, the way to prevent revolutions, and at the same time to produce lasting reforms is to persuade the people that all the evils which they suffer, or which the government may chuse to inflict upon them are their own fault. The way to put governments upon their good behaviour is to give them a licence to do as much mischief as they please, without being answerable for it.

" Of the tendency of mobs to produce tyranny, we
" may not be long without an example in this coun-
" try. *As a friend to freedom, and an enemy to large*
" *standing armies*, it is with extreme reluctance that

" I am compelled to acknowledge, that, had it not
" been for the organized force in the country, the
" distresses of the people during the late scarcities,
" encouraged by the extreme ignorance and folly of
" many among the higher classes, might have driven
" them to commit the most dreadful outrages, and
" ultimately to involve the country in all the horrors
" of famine."

Does Mr. Malthus think that this hint will dispose
the government to keep up their large standing armies,
or to mitigate the distresses of the people? I wonder,
if Blifil had happened to be an author, whether he
might not have written such a book as this.

" Should such periods often recur, a recurrence
" which we have too much reason to apprehend from
" the present state of the country, the prospect
" which opens to our view is melancholy in the ex-
" treme. The English constitution will be seen
" hastening with rapid strides to the *Euthanasia* fore-
" told by Hume; unless its progress be interrupted
" by some popular commotion; and this alternative
" presents a picture still more appalling to the ima-
" gination. If political discontents were blended
" with the cries of hunger, and a revolution were to
" take place by the instrumentality of a mob, cla-
" mouring for want of food, the consequences would
" be unceasing change, and unceasing carnage, the
" bloody career of which, nothing but the establish-
" ment of some complete despotism could arrest."

The gentleman seems greatly alarmed at his own predictions. He points out to government the dangers arising from mobs; and shews that these again arise from discontent, and repining against the good order of society. The way proposed to cure them of this discontent, and these false notions of society is to break asunder at once the link of humanity which binds the poor to the rich, to reduce them to extremity, to cut off all hope, all over-weening expectation, all mutual kindness and good offices, by exploding the very idea of the rights of the poor, or the duties of the rich, and thus to tame them so effectually and systematically, that we shall be in no danger from mobs, revolutions, or military despotism, but shall conclude with a happy Euthanasia!

" To say that our conduct is not to be regulated by " circumsances, is to betray an ignorance of the most " *solid* and incontrovertible principles of morality.' [An odd phrase. Solid seems to imply something fixed. We should hardly talk of a *solid* bridge of boats, though they might afford tolerably safe footing.] " Though the admission of this principle may some- " times afford a cloke to changes of opinion that do " not result from the purest motives; yet the admis- " sion of a contrary princ ple would be productive of " infinitely worse consequences. The phrase of ex- " isting circumstances has, I believe, not unfre- " quently created a smile in the English House of " Commons; but the smile should have been re- " served for the application of the phrase and not have been excited by the phrase itself." [He teaches

us to smile by the book.] " A very frequent re-
" petition of it, has indeed, of itself, rather a sus-
" picious air; and its application should always be
" watched with the most jealous and anxious atten-
" tion ; but no man ought to be judged *in limine* for
" saying, that existing circumstances had obliged him
" to alter his opinions and conduct. The country
" gentlemen were perhaps too easily convinced that
" existing circumstances called upon them to give up
" some of the most valuable privileges of English-
" men; but, as far as they were really convinced of
" this obligation, they acted consistently with the
" *clearest rule* of morality." [Begging the learned
writer's pardon, it is rather the exception than the
rule. Did Junius Brutus, when he killed his son, act
in conformity to the *clearest rule of morality ?* Mr.
Malthus has not quite got rid of the leaven of his old
philosophy.

" The degree of power to be given to the civil go-
" vernment, and the measure of our submission to it,
" must be determined by general expediency."

This is saying a good deal. The rule which Mr.
Malthus then lays down for " a rising of the people,"
seems to be that when they are enlightened and well
off, that is, when the government is a good one, they
may rebel against it : but when they are kept in a state
of ignorance and want, then they are to blame, if they
are at all refractory : they are to be considered as the
causes of that very oppression which they are endeavouring to resist, and as giving a farther handle to

that tyranny, which their superiors are thus forced
to exercise in self-defence, not from any innate love
of power, or predilection for violent measures.

" All improvements in government must necessa-
" rily originate with persons of some education, and
" these will of course be found among the people of
" property. Whatever may be said of a few, it is
" impossible that the great mass of the people of pro-
" perty should be really interested in the abuses of
" government. They merely submit to them, from
" the fear, that an endeavour to remove them, might
" be productive of greater evils. Could we but take
" away this fear, reform and improvement would
" proceed with as much facility, as the removal of nui-
" sances, or the paving and lighting the streets.
" Remove all apprehension from the tyranny or folly
" of the people, and the tyranny of government
" could not stand a moment. It would then appear
" in its proper deformity, without palliation, without
" pretext, without protector. Naturally feeble in it-
" self, when it was once stripped naked, and de-
" prived of the support of public opinion, and of the
" great *plea of necessity*, it would fall without a
" struggle."

This is a new view of the subject. What then, mankind are governed by the pure love of justice! The
people of property and education have no vices or
follies of their own, which blind their understandings,
no prejudices about royalty, or aristocracy, or church
or state, no attachment to party, no dependence on

great men, no hopes of preferment, no connections, no privileges, no interest in the abuses of government, no pride, none of the *esprit de corps*, to hinder them from pronouncing sentence on the laws, institutions, uses, and abuses of society with the same calmness, disinterestedness, and wisdom, as they would upon cleaning a sewer, or paving a street.

" The most succesful supporters of tyranny are
" without doubt those general declaimers, who attri-
" bute the distresses of the poor, and almost all the
" evils to which society is subject, to human insti-
" tutions and the iniquity of governments."

This is like those highwaymen, who attribute their ill treatment of their victims to the resistance they make.

" Whatever therefore may be the intention of
" those indiscriminate and wholesale accusations
" against governments, their real effect undoubtedly
" is, to add a weight of talents and principles to the
" prevailing power which it never would have re-
" ceived otherwise."

This is possible: but the effect of Mr. Malthus's method would be that they would not want the additional weight either of talents or principle, but would laugh in your face.

" The inference, therefore, which Mr. Paine and
" others have drawn against governments from the

" unhappiness of the people, is palpably unfair; **and**
" before we give a sanction to such accusations, it **is**
" a debt we owe to truth and justice, to ascertain **how**
" much of this unhappiness arises from the **principle**
" of population, and how much is fairly to be attri-
" buted to government. When this distinction **has**
" been properly made, and all the vague, indefinite,
" and false accusations removed, government would
" remain, as it ought to be, clearly responsible **for**
" the rest. A tenfold weight would be immediately
" given to the cause of the people, and every man **of**
" principle would join in asserting and enforcing, **if**
" necessary, their rights.

Timeo Danaos, et dona ferentes. Our author **here**
wishes to delay the question in order to give additional
weight to the cause of the people. This is something as if upon a stranger coming into a house almost
fainting with hunger and cold, we should advise him
not to go near the fire, nor take any thing to eat, for
that there is a great apothecary in the neighbourhood
who sometimes calls in about that time of the day,
who will be able to tell him exactly how much of his
illness proceeds from cold, and how much from hunger, whether he should eat, or warm himself first,
and how the one would assist the other. The man
might naturally answer, I know that I am very cold
and hungry: I will therefore first sit down by the fire,
and if, in the mean time, you can let me have any
thing to eat, I shall be heartily glad of it. Otherwise
the advice of the apothecary will come too late.

I cannot help thinking, therefore, that a know-
" ledge generally circulated, that the principal cause
" of want and unhappiness is unconnected with go-
" vernment, and totally beyond its power to remove
" would, instead of giving any advantage to govern-
" ments, give a great additional weight to the popular
" side of the question, by removing the dangers with
" which, from ignorance, it is at present accompanied ;
" and thus tend, in a very powerful manner, to pro-
" mote the cause of rational freedom."

The mode in which Mr. Malthus strengthens the
popular side is by disarming it of all power or pretence for resistance.   Undoubtedly that must be a
strange sort of strength which is founded on impotence.
The people are only secure against the encroachments of power from their inability to resist it.   This
is like clapping a man into a dungeon to save him
from the pursuit of his creditors.   Mr. Malthus pro-
motes the cause of rational freedom, as the husband
secured the virtue of his wife in the sign of the Good
Woman.

Mr. Malthus's plan for the abolition of the poor
laws is as follows :

" I should propose a regulation to be made, de-
" claring, that no child born from any marriage,
" taking place after the expiration of a year from
" the date of the law; and no illegitimate child
" born two years from the same date, should ever be
" entitled to parish assistance. And to give a more

" general knowledge of this law, and to enforce it
" more strongly on the minds of the lower classes of
" people, the clergyman of each parish should after
" the publication of banns, read a short address,
" stating the strong obligation on every man to sup-
" port his own children; the impropriety, and even
" immorality, of marrying without a fair prospect
" of being able to do this; the evils which had re-
" sulted to the poor themselves, from the attempt
" which had been made to assist by public institu-
" tions in a duty which ought to be exclusively ap-
" propriated to parents; and the absolute necessity
" which had at length appeared, of abandoning all
" such institutions, on account of their producing
" effects totally opposite to those which were in-
" tended.

" This would operate as a fair, distinct, and pre-
" cise notice, which no man could well mistake ; and
" without pressing hard on any particular individuals,
" would at once throw off the rising generation from
" that miserable and helpless dependence upon the
" government and the rich, the moral as well as
" physical consequencs of which are almost incalcu-
" lable.

" After the public notice which I have proposed
" had been given, and the system of poor laws had
" ceased with regard to the rising generation, if any
" man chose to marry, without a prospect of being
" able to support a family, he should have the most
" perfect liberty so to do. Though to marry, in this

" case, is in my opinion clearly an immoral act, yet
" it is not one which society can justly take upon
" itself to prevent or punish ; because the punishment
" provided for it by the laws of nature, falls directly,
" and most severely upon the individual who com-
" mits the act, and through him, only more remotely
" and feebly on the society. When nature will govern
" and punish for us, it is a very miserable ambition to
" wish to snatch the rod from her hands, and diaw
" upon ourselves the odium of executioner. To the
" punishment therefore of nature he should be left, the
" punishment of severe want. He has erred in the face
" of a most clear and precise warning, and can have
" no just reason to complain of any person but him-
" self, when he feels the consequences of his error. All
" parish assistance should be most rigidly denied him :
" and if the hand of private charity be stretched forth
" in his relief, the interests of humanity imperiously re-
" quire that it should be administered very sparingly.
" He should be taught to know that the laws of nature,
" which are the laws of God, had doomed him and
" his family to starve for disobeying their repeated
" admonitions ;" [nay his family had no hand in disobeying these admonitions]   " that he had no claim of
" *right* on society for the smallest portion of food,
" beyond that which his labour would fairly pur-
" chase; and that if he and his family were saved
" from suffering the extremities of hunger, he would
" owe it to the pity of some kind benefactor, to
" whom, therefore, he ought to be bound by the
" strongest ties of gratitude.

" If this system were pursued, we need be under
" no apprehensions that the number of persons in ex-
" treme want would be beyond the power and the
" will of the benevolent to supply. The sphere for
" the exercise of private charity would, I am confi-
" dent, be less than it is at present; and the only
" difficulty would be, to restrain the hand of benevo-
" lence from assisting those in distress in so indiscri-
" minate a manner as to encourage indolence and
" want of foresight in others."

I am not sorry that I am at length come to this passage. It will I hope decide the reader's opinion of
the benevolence, wisdom, piety, candour, and disinterested simplicity of Mr. Malthus's mind. Any
comments that I might make upon it to strengthen
this impression must be faint and feeble. I give up
the task of doing justice to the moral beauties that
pervade every line of it, in despair. There are some
instances of an heroical contempt for the narrow prejudices of the world, of a perfect refinement from the
vulgar feelings of human nature, that must only suffer
by a comparison with any thing else.

Mr. Malthus prefaces his plan by saying,

" I have reflected much onthe subject of the poor
" laws, and hope therefore that I shall be excused
" in venturing to suggest a mode of their gradual
" abolition, to which I confess that at present I can
" see no material objection. Of this indeed I feel
" nearly convinced, that should we ever become suf-
" ficiently sensible of the wide-spreading tyranny, de-

" pendence, indolence, and unhappiness, which they
" create, as seriously to make an effort to abolish
" them, we shall be compelled by a sense of justice
" to adopt the principle, if not the plan, which I
" shall mention. It seems impossible to get rid of so
" extensive a system of support, consistently with
" humanity, without applying ourselves directly to its
" vital principle, and endeavouring to counteract that
" deeply-seated cause, which occasions the rapid
" growth of all such establishments, and invariably
" renders them inadequate to their object. As a pre_
" vious step even to any considerable alteration in
" the present system, which would contract, or stop
" the increase of the relief to be given, it appears to
" me that we are bound in justice and honour for-
" mally to disclaim the *right* of the poor to sup-
" port."

Now I shall not myself be so uncandid as not to
confess, that I think the poor laws bad things; and
that it would be well, if they could be got rid of,
consistently with humanity and justice. This I do
not think they could in the present state of things
and other circumstances remaining as they are. The
reason why I object to Mr. Malthus's plan is that it
does not go to the root of the evil, or attack it in
its principle, but its effects. He confounds the cause
with the effect. The wide spreading tyranny, dependence, indolence, and unhappiness of which Mr.
Malthus is so sensible, are not occasioned by the increase of the poor-rates, but these are the natural
consequence of that increasing tyranny, dependence, indolence, and unhappiness occasioned by other causes.

Mr. Malthus desires his readers to look at the enormous proportion in which the poor-rates have increased within the last ten years. But have they increased in any greater proportion than the other
taxes, which rendered them necessary, and which I
think were employed for much more mischievous
purposes? I would ask, what have the poor got by
their encroachments for the last ten years? Do they
work less hard? Are they better fed? Do they marry
oftener, and with better prospects? Are they grown
pampered and insolent? Have they changed places with
the rich? Have they been cunning enough, by means of
the poor-laws, to draw off all their wealth and superfluities from the men of property? Have they got so
much as a quarter of an hour's leisure, a farthing
candle, or a cheese-paring more than they had? Has
not the price of provisions risen enormously? Has not
the price of labour almost stood still? Have not the
government and the rich had their way in every
thing? Have they not gratified their ambition, their
pride, their obstinacy, their ruinous extravagance?
Have they not squandered the resources of the country as they pleased? Have they not heaped up
wealth on themselves, and their dependents? Have
they not multiplied sine-cures, places, and pensions?
Have they not doubled the salaries of those that existed before? Has there been any want of new crea-
tions of peers, who would thus be impelled to beget
heirs to their titles and estates, and saddle the
younger branches of their rising families, by means of
their new influence, on the country at large? Has
there been any want of contracts, of loans, of monopolies of corn, of a good understanding between the

rich and the powerful to assist one another, and to
fleece the poor? Have the poor prospered? Have the
rich declined? What then have they to complain
of? What ground is there for the apprehension, that
wealth is secretly changing hands, and that the whole
property of the country will shortly be absorbed in
the poor's fund? Do not the poor create their own
fund? Is not the necessity for such a fund first occasioned by the unequal weight with which the rich
press upon the poor, and has not the increase of that
fund in the last ten years been occasioned by the additional exorbitant demands, which have been made
upon the poor and industrious, which without some
assistance from the public they could not possibly
have answered? Whatever is the increase in the nominal
amount of the poor's fund, will not the rich always
be able ultimately to throw the burthen of it on the
poor themselves? But Mr. Malthus is a man of general principles. He cares little about these circum-
stantial details, and petty objections. He takes higher
ground. He deduces all his conclusions, by an infal-
lible logic, from the laws of God and nature. When
our Essayist shall prove to me, that by these paper
bullets of the brain, by his ratios of the increase of
food and the increase of mankind, he has prevented
one additional tax, or taken off one oppressive duty,
that he has made a single rich man retrench one
article at his table, that he has made him keep a
dog or a horse the less, or part with a single vice,
arguing from a mathematical admeasurement of the
size of the earth, and the number of inhabitants
it can contain, he shall have my perfect leave
to disclaim the right of the poor to subsistence,

and to tie them down by severe penalties to their good behaviour on the same profound principles. But why does Mr. Malthus practise his demonstrations on the poor only? Why are they to have a perfect system of rights and duties prescribed to them? I do not see why they alone should be put to live on these *metaphysical* board-wages, why they should be forced to submit to a course of *abstraction*; or why it should be meat and drink to them, more than to others, to do the will of God. Mr. Malthus's gospel is preached only to the poor!—Even if I approved of our author's plan, I should object to the principle on which it is founded. The parson of the parish, when a poor man comes to be married—No, not so fast. The author does not say, whether the lecture he proposes is to be read to the poor only, or to all ranks of people. Would it not sound oddly, if when the squire, who is himself worth a hundred thousand pounds, is going to be married to the rector's daughter, who is to have fifty, the curate should read them a formal lecture on their obligation to maintain their own children, and not turn them on the parish? Would it be necessary to go through the form of the address, when an amorous couple of eighty presented themselves at the altar? If the admonition were left to the parson's own discretion, what affronts would he not subject himself to, from his neglect of old maids, and superannuated widows, and from his applying himself familiarly to the little shopkeeper, or thriving mechanic? Well then let us suppose that a very poor hardworking man comes to be married, and that the clergyman can take the liberty with him: he is to warn him first against fornication, and in the next place against matrimony. These are the two greatest sins which a poor man can commit, who can neither be supposed to keep his wife, nor his girl. Mr. Malthus, however, does not think them equal: for he objects strongly to a country fellow's marrying a girl whom he has debauched, or, as the phrase is, making an honest woman of her, as aggravating the crime, because by this means the parish will probably have three or four children to maintain instead of one. However, as it seems rather too late to recommend fornication or any thing else to a man who is actually come to be married (he must be a strange sawney who could turn back at the church-door after bringing a pretty rosy girl to hear a lecture on the principle of population) it is most natural to suppose that he would marry the young woman in spite of this principle. Here then he errs in the face of a precise warning, and should be left to the punishment of *nature*, the punishment of severe want. When he begins to feel the consequences of his error, all parish assistance is to be rigidly denied him, and the interests of humanity imperiously require that all other assistance should be withheld from him, or most sparingly administered. In the mean time to reconcile him to this treatment, and let him see that he has nobody to complain of but himself, the parson of the parish comes to him with the certificate of his marriage, and a copy of the warning he had given him at the time, by which he is taught to know that the laws of nature, which are the laws of God, had doomed him and his family to starve for disobeying their repeated admonitions; that he had no claim of right to the smallest portion of food beyond what his labour would actually purchase; and that he ought to kiss the feet and lick the dust off the shoes of him, who gave him a reprieve from the just sentence which the laws of God and nature had passed upon him. To make this clear to him, it would be necessary to put the Essay on Population into his hands, to instruct him in the nature of a geometrical and arithmetical series, in the necessary limits to population from the size of the earth, and here would come in Mr. Malthus's plan of education for the poor, writing, arithmetic, the use of the globes, &c. for the purpose of proving to them the necessity of their being starved. It cannot be supposed that the poor man (what with his poverty and what with being priest-ridden) should be able to resist this body of evidence, he would open his eyes to his error, and " would sub-" mit to the sufferings that were absolutely irreme-" diable with the fortitude of a man, and the resign-" ation of a Christian." He and his family might then be sent round the parish in a starving condition, accompanied by the constables and *quondam* overseers of the poor, to see that no person, blind to " the in-" terests of humanity," practised upon them the abominable deception of attempting to relieve their remediless sufferings, and by the parson of the parish to point out to the spectators the inevitable conse-quences of sinning against the laws of God and man. By celebrating a number of these *Auto da fes* yearly in every parish, the greatest publicity would be given to the principle of population, " the strict line of du-" ty would be pointed out to every man," enforced by the most powerful sanctions, justice and humanity would flourish, they would be understood to signify that the poor have no right to live by their labour, and that the feelings of compassion and benevolence are best shewn by denying them charity, the poor would no longer be dependent on the rich, the rich could no longer wish to reduce the poor into a more complete subjection to their will, all causes of contention, of jealousy, and of irritation would have ceased between them, the struggle would be over, each class would fulfil the task assigned by heaven, the rich would oppress the poor without remorse, the poor would submit to oppression with a pious gratitude and resignation, the greatest harmony would prevail between the government and the people, there would be no longer any seditions, tumults, complaints, petitions, partisans of liberty, or tools of power, no grumbling, no repining, no discontented men of talents proposing reforms, and frivolous remedies, but we should all have the same gaiety and lightness of heart, and the same happy spirit of resignation that a man feels when he is seized with the plague, who thinks no more of the physician, but knows that his disorder is without cure. The best laid schemes are subject, however, to unlucky reverses. Some such seem to lie in the way of that pleasing Euthanasia, and contented submission to the grinding law of necessity, projected by Mr. Malthus. We might never reach the philosophic temper of the inhabitants of modern Greece and Turkey in this respect. Many little things might happen to interrupt our progress, if we were put into ever so fair a train. For instance, the men might perhaps be talked over by the parson, and their understandings being convinced by the geometrical and arithmetical ratios, or at least so far puzzled, that they would have nothing to say for themselves, they might prepare to submit to their fate with a tolerable grace. But I am afraid that the women might prove refractory. They never will hearken to reason, and are much more governed by their feelings than by calculations. While the husband was instructing his wife in the principles of population, she might probably answer that she did not see why her children should starve when the squire's lady, or the parson's lady kept half a dozen lap-dogs, and that it was but the other day that being at the hall, or the parsonage house, she heard Miss declare that not one of the brood that were just littered should be drowned—It was *so inhuman* to kill the poor little things—Surely the children of the poor are as good as puppy-dogs! Was it not a week ago that the rector had a new pack of terriers sent down, and did I not hear the squire swear a tremendous oath, that he would have Mr. Such-a-one's fine hunter, if it cost him a hundred guineas? Half that sum would save us from ruin.—After this curtain-lecture, I conceive that the husband might begin to doubt the force of the demonstrations he had read and heard, and the next time his clerical monitor came, might pluck up courage to question the matter with him; and as we of the male sex, though dull of apprehension, are not slow at taking a hint, and can draw tough inferences from it, it is not impossible but the parson might be *gravelled*. In consequence of these accidents happening more than once, it would be buzzed about that the laws of God and nature, on which so many families had been doomed to starve, were not so clear as had been pretended.

This would soon get wind among the mob: and at
the next grand procession of the Penitents of famine, headed by Mr. Malthus in person, some discontented man of talents, who could not bear the
distresses *of others* with the fortitude of a man and
the resignation of a Christian, might undertake to
question Mr. Malthus, whether the laws of nature or
of God, to which he had piously sacrificed so many
victims, signified any thing more than the limited
extent of the earth, and the natural impossibility of
providing for more than a limited number of human
beings; and whether those laws could be justly put
in force, to the very letter, while the actual produce
of the earth, by being better husbanded, or more
equally distributed, or given to men and not to beasts,
might maintain in comfort double the number that
actually existed, and who, not daring to demand a
fair proportion of the produce of their labour, humbly
crave charity, and are refused out of regard to the
interests of justice and humanity. Our philosopher,
at this critical juncture not being able to bring into
the compass of a few words all the history, metaphy-
sics, morality and divinity, or all the intricacies, subtleties, and callous equivocations contained in his
quarto volume, might hesitate and be confounded—
his own feelings and prejudices might add to his perplexity—his interrogator might persist in his question
—the mob might become impatient for an answer,
and not finding one to their minds, might proceed to
extremities. Our unfortunate Essayist (who by that
time would have become a bishop) might be ordered
to the lamp-post, and his book committed to the
flames.—I tremble to think of what would follow:—

the poor laws would be again renewed, and the poor no longer doomed to starve by the laws of God and nature! Some such, I apprehend, might be the consequence of attempting to enforce the abolition of the poor-laws, the extinction of private charity, and of instructing the poor in their metaphysical rights. In a few years time it is probable, however, that no such consequences would follow. In that time, if Mr. Malthus's systematic ardour will let him wait so long, they may be gradually crushed low enough in the scale of existence to be ripe for the ironical benefits, and sarcastic instruction prepared for them. Mr. Malthus says,

" The scanty relief granted to persons in distress,
" the capricious and insulting manner in which it is
" sometimes distributed by the overseers, and the na-
" tural and becoming pride not yet quite extinct
" among the peasantry of England, have deterred the
" more thinking and virtuous part of them, from ven-
" turing on marriage, without some better prospect
" of maintaining their families, than mere parish as-
" sistance. The desire of bettering our condition
" and the fear of making it worse, like the *vis medi-*
" *catrix naturæ* in physics, is the *vis medicatrix reipu-*
" *blicæ* in politics, and is continually counteracting the
" disorders arising from narrow human institutions.
" In spite of the prejudices in favour of population,
" and the direct encouragements to marraige from
" the poor laws, it operates as a preventive check to
" increase; and happy for this country is it that it
" does so."

If then this natural repugnance in the poor to subject themselves to the necessity of parish relief has ceased to operate, must it not be owing to extreme distress, or to the degradation of character consequent upon it? How does Mr. Malthus propose to remedy this? By subjecting them to severer distress, and *teaching them patience under their sufferings*. But the rational desire of bettering our condition and the fear of making it worse is not increased by its being made worse. The standard of our notions of decency and comfort is not raised by a familiarity with unmitigated wretchedness, nor is the love of independence heightened by insults, and contempt, and by a formal mockery of the principles of justice and humanity. On the previous habits and character of the people, it is, however, that the degree of misery incurred always depends, as far as relates to themselves. The consequence of an effectual abolition of the poor laws would be all the immediate misery that would be produced, aggravated by the additional depression, and proneness to misery in the lower classes, and a beautiful petrefaction of all the common feelings of human nature in the higher ones. Finally, I agree with Mr. Malthus, that, " if, as in " Ireland and in Spain, and many of the southern " countries, the people be in so degraded a state, as " to propagate their species like brutes, it matters " little, whether they have poor laws or not. Misery " in all its various forms must be the predominant " check to their increase: and with, or without poor " laws, no stretch of human ingenuity and exertion " could rescue the people from the most extreme " poverty and wretchedness."

As to the metaphysical subtleties, by which **Mr.** Malthus endeavours to prove that we ought systematically to visit the sins of the father on the children, and keep up the stock of vice and misery in the family (from which it would follow, that the children of thieves and robbers ought either to be hanged outright, or at least brought up in such a manner as to ensure their following the fate of their parents) I feel and know my own superiority on that ground so well, that it would be ungenerous to push it farther. Mr. Malthus has a curious chapter on old maids. He might have written one on suicide, and another on prostitutes. As far as the question of population is concerned, they are certainly of more service to the community, because they tempt others to follow their example, whereas an old maid is a beacon to frighten others into matrimony. But this, says our author, is owing to unjust prejudice. I shall give the reader some of his arguments, as otherwise he might not guess at them.

" It is not enough to abolish all the positive insitu-
" tions which encourage population; but we must en-
" deavour, at the same time, to correct the prevailing
" opinions, which have the same, or perhaps even a
" more powerful, effect. The matron who has reared
" a family of ten or twelve children, and whose sons,
" perhaps, may be fighting the battles of their coun-
" try, is apt to think that society owes her much ;
" and this imaginary debt, society is, in general,
" fully inclined to acknowledge. But if the subject
" be fairly considered, and the respected matron
" weighed in the scales of justice against the neg-
" lected old maid, it is possible that the matron might

" kick the beam. She will appear rather in the cha-
" racter of a monopolist, than of a great benefactor
" to the state. If she had not married and had so
" many children, other members of the society might
" have enjoyed this satisfaction; and there is no par-
" ticular reason for supposing that her sons would
" fight better for their country than the sons of other
" women. She has therefore rather subtracted from,
" than added to, the happiness of the other part of
" society. The old maid, on the contrary, has ex-
" alted others by depressing herself. Her self-denial
" has made room for another marriage, without any
" additional distress; and she has not, like the gene-
" rality of men, in avoiding one error, fallen into its
" opposite. She has really and truly contributed
" more to the happiness of the rest of the society
" arising from the pleasures of marriage, than if she
" had entered into this union herself, and had besides
" portioned twenty maidens with a hundred pounds
" each; whose particular happiness would have been
" balanced, either by an increase in the general diffi-
" culties of rearing children and getting employ-
" ment, or by the necessity of celibacy in twenty
" other maidens somewhere else. Like the truly be-
" nevolent man in an irremediable scarcity, she has
" diminished her own consumption, instead of rais-
" ing up a few particular people, by pressing down
" the rest. On a fair comparison, therefore, she
" seems to have a better founded claim to the grati-
" tude of society than the matron. Whether we
" could always completely sympathize with the mo-
" tives of her conduct, has not much to do with the
" question. The particular motive which influenced

" the matron to marry, was certainly not the good of
" her country. To refuse a proper tribute of respect
" to the old maid, because she was not directly influ-
" enced in her conduct by the desire of conferring
" on society a certain benefit, which, though it must
" undoubtedly exist, must necessarily be so diffused
" as to be invisible to her, is in the highest degree
" impolitic and unjust. It is expecting a strain of
" virtue beyond humanity. If we never reward any
" persons with our approbation, but those who are
" exclusively influenced by motives of general bene-
" volence, this powerful encouragement to do good
" actions will not be very often called into ex-
" ercise."

Mr. Malthus would make an excellent superior of a
convent of nuns of the Order of Population.—The better to remove what he considers as an unjust stigma
on old maids; he has endeavoured to set one on married women. He would persuade every one to look
upon his mother as a person of bad character. He
would pass an act of bastardy on every mother's son
of us; and prove that we come into the world without a proper license (from him) merely to gratify the
coarse, selfish, immoral propensities of our parents.
Till however he can do away the filial relation, or the
respect attached to it, or so contrive it that all men
should be " born of a virgin" contrary to all our experience, it will I believe be impossible to get rid of
the unjust prejudice against old maids, or to place
them on a level with married women. Mr. Malthus
has gone the wrong way to ingratiate himself with
the mothers of families: but he has not taken his
measures ill. He knows that the partiality and fa-

vours of such persons are generally confined to run in their own low, narrow, domestic channels. But this is not the case with those reverend persons, to whom he pays his court. He knows that their bounty is not confined by any such selfish limits, it flows liberally to all, and they have the best chance of sharing in it, who endeavour to indemnify them for their personal sacrifices, or the ridicule of the world by a succession of little agreeable attentions, or by offering theoretical incense to their virtue and merit.

" It is perfectly absurd as well as unjust, that a " giddy girl of sixteen should, because she is married " be considered by the forms of society as the pro- " tector of women of thirty, should come first into " the room, should be assigned the highest place at " table, and be the prominent figure to whom the at- " tentions of the company are more particularly ad- " dressed."—Not more absurd than that a child or an ideot should be a king, or that a grave man of fifty should call a young coxcomb, My lord. Our sophist would overturn all the established order of society with his out-of-the-way principles.—Mr. Malthus has huddled into the same chapter his attack on the monopoly made by the married women of the men, and his defence of the monopoly of corn by farmers and others. It is the last passage I shall quote, though there are many others worthy of rebuke.

" In some conversations with labouring men during " the late scarcities, I confess that I was to the last " degree disheartened, at observing their inveterate " prejudices on the subject of grain : and I felt very " strongly the almost absolute incompatibility of a go- " vernment really free, with such a degree of igno-

" rance. The delusions are of such a nature, that, if
" acted upon, they must, at all events, be repressed
" by force; and it is extremely difficult to give such
" a power to the government as will be sufficient at
" all times for this purpose, without the risk of its
" being employed improperly, and endangering the
" liberty of the subject. And this reflection cannot
" but be disheartening to every friend to freedom.

" It is of the very utmost importance, that the gen-
" tlemen of the country, and particularly the clergy,
" should not, from ignorance, aggravate the evils of
" scarcity every time that it unfortunately occurs.
" During the late dearths, half of the gentlemen and
" clergymen in the kingdom richly deserved to have
" been prosecuted for sedition. After inflaming the
" minds of the common people against the farmers
" and corn-dealers, by the manner in which they
" talked of them, or preached about them, it was
" but a feeble antidote to the poison which they had
" infused, coldly to observe, that however the poor
" might be oppressed or cheated, it was their duty to
" keep the peace. It was little better than Anthony's
" repeated declaration, that the conspirators were
" all honourable men; which did not save either their
" houses or their persons from the attacks of the
" mob. Political economy is perhaps the only sci-
" ence of which it might be said, that the ignorance
" of it is not merely a deprivation of good, but pro-
" duces great positive evil."

I shall accompany this passage with an extract
from the Author's first edition, and leave it to the
reader to apply the hint of Antony's speech to whom
he thinks fit.

" It very rarely happens that the nominal price of
" labour universally falls; but we well know that it
" frequently remains the same, while the nominal
" price of provisions has been gradually increasing.
" This is, in effect, a real fall in the price of labour;
" and during this period, the condition of the lower
" orders of the community must gradually grow
" worse and worse. But the farmers and the capita-
" lists are growing rich from the real cheapness of
" labour. Their increased capitals enable them to
" employ a greater number of men. Work therefore
" may be plentiful; and the price of labour would
" consequently rise. But the want of freedom in the
" market of labour, which occurs more or less in all
" communities, either from parish laws, or the more
" general cause of the facility of combination among
" the rich, and its difficulty among the poor, ope-
" rates to prevent the price of labour from rising at
" the natural period, and keeps it down some time
" longer; perhaps, till a year of scarcity, when the
" clamour is too loud, and the necessity too apparent
" to be resisted.

" The true cause of the advance in the price of
" labour is thus concealed; and the rich affect to
" grant it as an act of compassion and favour to the
" poor, in consideration of a year of scarcity; and
" when plenty returns, indulge themselves in the
" most unreasonable of all complaints, that the price
" does not again fall; when a little reflection would
" shew them, that it must have risen long before,
" but from an unjust conspiracy of their own."

THE END.